T0285206

The Future of the Catholic Church in the American Political Order

The Future of the Catholic Church in the American Political Order

EDITED BY KENNETH L. GRASSO AND
THOMAS F. X. VARACALLI

FRANCISCAN UNIVERSITY PRESS

Franciscan University Press
1235 University Boulevard
Steubenville, OH 43952
740-283-3771
Distributed by:
The Catholic University of America Press
c/o HFS
P.O. Box 50370
Baltimore, MD 21211
800-537-5487

Library of Congress Cataloging-in-Publication Data available:
https://locexternal.servicenowservices.com/pub/?id=cip_data_block_viewer&lccn=2023013770

ISBN 978-1-7366561-7-4

Text and Cover Design: Kachergis Book Design
Cover Image: The *Annunciation,* Alessandro Vittoria, bronze, c. 1583; courtesy of the Edward E. Ayer Endowment in memory of Charles L. Hutchinson, the Art Institute of Chicago.
Printed in the United States of America.

The editors are grateful to Dr. Stephen Krason for permission to reprint essays originally published in the *Catholic Social Science Review.* The essays, which are greatly expanded in this volume, include the following.

Ryan J. Barilleaux, "Put Not Your Trust in Princes: Catholics in the American Administrative State," *Catholic Social Science Review* 22 (2017): 109–21.

Steven Brust, "Catholicism, American Culture, and Politics: Being Transformed or Transforming?," *Catholic Social Science Review* 22 (2017): 95–107.

Gary Glenn, "The Downside of Constitutional 'Protection' for Religious Liberty (or, How Can Religious Constitutional Protection for Religious Liberty Actually Undermine It?)," *Catholic Social Science Review* 23 (2018): 7–19.

Kenneth Grasso, "Whose Religious Liberty? Which Intellectual Horizon?," *Catholic Social Science Review* 23 (2018): 33–45.

Robert Hunt, "Liberal Individualist Monism and the Future of Religious Freedom," *Catholic Social Science Review* 23 (2018): 21–32.

The editors are also grateful to Fr. Anthony Giampietro for permission to reprint an essay originally published in *Fellowship of Catholic Scholars Quarterly.* This essay was slightly expanded and revised:

Gerard V. Bradley, "Catholic Higher Education in America in 2018 and Beyond," *Fellowship of Catholic Scholars Quarterly* 41, no. 2 (2018): 177–96.

CONTENTS

The Future of the Catholic Church in the American Political Order

INTRODUCTION

The Future of the Catholic Church in the American Public Order

KENNETH L. GRASSO AND
THOMAS F. X. VARACALLI

As anyone even slightly familiar with the history of American Catholicism knows, there is a long tradition of reflection among Catholics about the relationship of Catholicism to American democracy. Alexis de Tocqueville, Orestes Brownson, John Courtney Murray, and countless other thinkers—not to mention several popes and numerous bishops—have deliberated at length upon the compatibility of what Murray famously called "the American Proposition" with "the principles of Catholic faith and morality."[1]

Efforts to reflect on this topic have been complicated by ongoing disagreements about the nature of America's founding commitments. For example, some scholars maintain that the roots of the American founding are to be found in Christian revelation and in the tradition of natural law thought that found its classic expression in the thought of Thomas Aquinas, as both were mediated through the British heritage. So understood, the American democratic experiment must be seen, as Robert Reilly has written, as an attempted "reestablishment" of "the principles and practices" of medieval constitutionalism.[2] In contrast, others argue that the founding's intellectual roots are to be found in the rejection of classical and Christian thought by modern thinkers

1. John Courtney Murray, *We Hold These Truths: Catholic Reflections on the American Proposition* (New York: Sheed & Ward, 1960; reprint, Lanham, MD: Rowman & Littlefield, 2005), xi, xiii.

2. Robert R. Reilly, *America on Trial: A Defense of the Founding* (San Francisco: Ignatius Press, 2020), 107.

like Machiavelli, Hobbes, and Locke. The founding, in this view, was rooted in ideas "incompatible with Christian doctrine." While religion might be tolerated and even utilized for political purposes, the founding was rooted in the belief "that traditional Christian doctrine was false. It sought to subordinate Christianity (and any other allegedly "revealed" religion) to the needs of a political order predicated on a body of "'self-evident' philosophical truths respecting the natural freedom and equality of all men," on the "subordination" of religion to a secular "political" creed.[3]

Efforts to reflect on the relationship of Catholicism and "Americanism" have been further complicated by the fact that over the course of its history, America has undergone a series of far-reaching changes.[4] In fact, it has now become customary to divide America's history into a succession of eras, each constituting different regimes or republics. Michael Sandel, for example, divides American political history into three eras: the civic republic, which ends with the Civil War; the national republic, which extends until the 1930s and 1940s; and the procedural republic.[5] Likewise, in his widely praised study, Morton Keller distinguishes between a "Deferential and Republican" regime ending in the 1820s, a "Party and Democratic" regime running from the 1830s until the 1930s, and a "Populist and Bureaucratic" regime beginning in the 1930s.[6]

In recent decades, a new and very public order has been taking shape in America that differs in important respects from that which preceded it. Ryan Barilleaux's contribution to this volume captures the dramatic character of the change:

> At the opening of the century, federal and state laws protected the institution of marriage, religious institutions were able to conduct their affairs with a minimum of state interference, and no one seriously questioned which bathroom a male or a female should use. Since then, however, each of these facts had changed or were seriously challenged: following passage of the Affordable Care Act (ACA) in 2010, the Obama Administration mandated that

3. Walter Berns, *The First Amendment and the Future of American Democracy* (New York: Basic Books, 1976), 16, 19, 24, 26.

4. For an overview of these changes, see Stephen M. Krason, *The Transformation of the American Democratic Republic* (New Brunswick, NJ: Transaction, 1976).

5. Michael J. Sandel, "The Political Theory of the Procedural Republic," in *Constitutionalism and Rights* (Provo, UT: Brigham Young University Press, 1987), 141–53.

6. Morton Keller, *America's Three Regimes* (New York: Oxford University Press, 2007).

> all employers in the nation—secular or religious—provide free contraceptive and abortifacient drugs to their employees; in 2015 the U.S. Supreme Court discovered a right to same-sex marriage in the Constitution; and in 2016 the Obama Administration tried to require schools across the nation to allow transgender students to use the bathroom or locker-room that corresponds to each student's "gender identity." Along with these legal and regulatory changes, public opinion had changed: in 2001, fifty-seven percent of Americans opposed same-sex marriage; by 2016, fifty-five percent supported it.[7]

What only a decade or two ago had been the mainstream view, as Barilleaux notes, has now increasingly become a "fringe" position.[8] To this must be added the threats to religious liberty that loom so large on the contemporary American public scene; these threats were unimaginable only a few years ago.[9]

At the institutional level, this new order takes the form of a highly centralized state in which the powers of the national government are seen as essentially plenary in nature. Governmental power is likewise concentrated in an imperial executive and an even more imperial judiciary, as well as in administrative agencies that simultaneously exercise executive, legislative, and judicial power. In this new order, government by the people has been largely supplanted with government by technocrats—government by executive, administrative, and judicial fiat—and the reach of the centralized state has become all-encompassing. No area of human life lies beyond its jurisdiction. We have witnessed the rise of what Bertrand de Jouvenel memorably called "statolatry" in contemporary America, the absorption of more and more sectors of social life in the state, causing our gradual slide toward the soft despotism of the omnicompetent bureaucratic state whose rise Tocqueville feared.[10]

But the transformation we have experienced runs far deeper than a change in the structure of political and legal orders. It includes dramatic cultural changes driven by a far-reaching de-Christianization of American society. One of the first things that struck Alexis de Tocqueville when he visited America in the early 1830s was the fervent religiosity of the American people. "With

7. Ryan Barilleaux, "Put Not Your Trust in Princes: Catholics in the American Administrative State," *Catholic Social Science Review* 22 (2017): 109.

8. Barilleaux, "Put Not Your Trust in Princes."

9. On this point, see Mary Eberstadt, *It's Dangerous to Believe* (New York: Harper, 2016).

10. Alexis de Tocqueville, *Democracy in America*, ed. J. P. Mayer, trans. George Lawrence (New York: Harper & Row, 1969), vol. 2, part 4, chap. 6, 690–95.

America," he remarks, "it is not a question . . . of sterile beliefs bequeathed by the past and vegetating rather than living in the depths of the soul"; indeed, the United States is "the place where the Christian religion has kept the greatest power over men's souls." "Reigning by universal consent," in America, "Christianity is an established and irresistible fact" that had a far-reaching impact on American culture, on the character of Americans, both individually and collectively. While there were "an innumerable multitude of sects" in which this fervent religiosity of the American people found institutional expression, he also noted that these sects "all . . . belong to the great unity of Christendom" and professed a common Christian morality.[11] In fact, the pluralism of Tocqueville's America was largely an intra-Protestant affair; the America he visited was a demographically and culturally Protestant society. As James Davison Hunter reminds us, in early America "a common Protestantism" enjoyed a quasi-established status. It was "largely through the language and ideals of [this] common Protestantism that the legitimating myths of institutions and society were formed and articulated."[12]

When America's religious pluralism expanded beyond the borders of Protestantism during the nineteenth century and the first part of the twentieth century, it came to include large numbers of Catholics and Jews. This expansion was the occasion of considerable controversy, and Catholicism faced suspicion and cultural and political hostility. The rise of American Catholicism challenged the belief that America was a Protestant nation. A faithful Catholic, it was widely held, could not be a good American. Nevertheless, as Francis Canavan observed, until recently, our religious pluralism was a pluralism of "a multitude of religious branches that sprang from a common stem." Indeed, "all of the religions that had adherents numerous enough to matter shared a common Judeo-Christian tradition" and in most respects—particularly regarding "matters of public concern"—taught "the same biblical morality."[13] What Hunter calls "the suppositions of a biblical theism" played a critical role in American life and our self-understanding. Until recently, we remained "a deeply biblical, albeit no longer, Protestant, culture."[14]

11. Tocqueville, *Democracy in America*, vol. 1, part II, chap. 9, pp. 290–94.

12. James Davison Hunter, *Culture Wars: The Struggle to Define America* (New York: Basic Books, 1991), 69.

13. Francis Canavan, *The Pluralist Game: Pluralism, Liberalism, and the Moral Conscience* (Lanham, MD: Rowman & Littlefield, 1995), 63, 65, 110.

14. Hunter, *Culture Wars*, 71–72.

Today, however, this is no longer the case. What we have experienced over the past half century has been the slow—and today, not so slow—collapse of American Christendom. By Christendom, I mean a society whose culture is informed by the vision of God and man issuing from Christian revelation. At the societal level, Christianity has increasingly been privatized and excluded from our public culture. At the same time, during the twentieth century, for the bulk of our populace, Christianity was gradually transformed into a largely decorative phenomenon, a mere matter of routine, cultural conformity, and social utility. As Martin Marty noted, by the 1950s, the underlying beliefs of most Americans, even though they might be expressed in Christian terms, were essentially "secular and humanistic."[15] Today, the rise of the "nones" and a sharp decline in church affiliation is causing a "secular surge,"[16] providing further evidence that we are witnessing the collapse of this cultural Christianity.

For a long time, something like an adulterated version of biblical morality endured despite the gradual loss of belief in the Christian doctrine. Today, this is increasingly not the case. Although it took some time, the rejection of the Christian understanding of God, man, and the universe has been followed by the rejection of the morality that followed from it. The same process that occurred in Europe generations ago is now being repeated (with accidental variations) here: the gradual loss of the faith followed by the gradual—or not so gradual—repudiation of Christian morality.

The cultural revolution of the past fifty years has consisted in the gradual evacuation of the Christian substance of society and its replacement by a new ethic rooted in a different understanding of the nature and destiny of man. The United States may consist mostly of nominal Christians, but our public culture is no longer Christian. In fact, it is now clearly post-Christian and, in some important respects, anti-Christian.

At the mass level, this new ethic finds expression in the individualism,

15. Martin Marty, *The New Shape of American Religion* (New York: Harper & Row, 1959), 79.

16. On the "nones," see Ryan P. Burge, *The Nones: Where They Came From, Who They Are, and Where They Are Going* (Minneapolis: Fortress Press, 2021). On declining church membership, see Jeffrey M. Jones, "U.S. Church Membership Falls Below Majority for the First Time," Gallup, March 29, 2021, https://news.gallup.com/poll/341963/church-membership-falls-below-majority-first-time.aspx. On the increasing secularization of American politics and culture, see David E. Campbell, Geoffrey C. Layman, and John C. Green, *The Secular Surge: A New Faultline in American Politics* (New York: Cambridge University Press, 2021).

moral emotivism, non-judgmentalism, immediate gratification, and frenzied consumerism that pervade our popular culture. At the level of public philosophy, this order is rooted in a radically post-Christian understanding of man and society whose most striking features are its individualism, subjectivism, and secularism. In this view, as Sandel writes, human beings are by nature "free and independent," unbound by "ends we have not chosen—ends given by nature or God, for example, or by identities as members of families, peoples, cultures, or traditions."[17] In short, a human being is simply a sovereign will, an arbitrary center of volition, free to make of himself (or herself) and the world, whatever he (or she) chooses.

The public morality that flows from this vision is simple and straightforward. "Truth," as Canavan notes, becomes "only what the individual thinks is true," and "good" becomes "what the individual personally prefers."[18] What George Will terms the "moral equality of appetites"[19] becomes the organizing principle of law and public policy. Choice and self-creation are elevated to the status of the human good. Tolerance becomes the highest moral virtue. The job of government comes to be understood as the creation of a neutral framework of order, allowing individuals the greatest possible freedom to pursue their visions of the good life consistent with the exercise of that same freedom by others. Substantive conceptions of the human good, especially those rooted in what Steven D. Smith calls "strong religion" (i.e., the type of religion that insists that "some people's deeply held beliefs are true while others are false" and that "some ways of living are acceptable to God while others are abhorrent"[20]), must be systematically excluded from the public square.

We have spoken of the "de-Christianization" of American society rather than its "secularization" because, as Smith has recently argued, what we see culturally today is a struggle between two different types of religiosity: a religion of immanence and a religion of transcendence. The question that divides the two is the location of the sacred. A religion of immanence locates the sacred, the holy, within "this world and this life"; a religion of transcendence locates the sacred "outside the world—'beyond time and space.'" Whereas

17. Michael J. Sandel, *Democracy's Discontent: America in Search of a Public Philosophy* (Cambridge, MA: Belknap Press of Harvard University Press, 1996), 12.

18. Canavan, *Pluralist Game*, 133.

19. George Will, *Statecraft as Soulcraft* (New York: Simon & Schuster, 1983), 158.

20. Steven D. Smith, *The Rise and Decline of American Religious Freedom* (Cambridge, MA: Harvard University Press, 2014), 153.

Christianity locates the divine beyond the world, the newly ascendant religiosity locates the sacred within the universe, in man or certain human experiences (e.g., sex, love, beauty), values (e.g., human dignity, freedom, equality, autonomy), or institutions (e.g., the state, market).

The conflict between these two religiosities is not limited simply to matters of theology and worship but involve fundamentally different understandings of the human good, the world, human sexuality and the family, the nature of the political order, the proper structure of human social relations, and the organizing principles of a rightly ordered society. The nature of this clash between two religiosities is obscured by what Smith calls "the facade of secularism," whereby the religious commitments informing the enemies of transcendent religion are simply ignored, and today's culture war is presented as clash between a religious worldview and a neutral, secular one.[21]

In the newly emerging public order, moreover, this ultimately religious vision would be our "new national orthodoxy with features reminiscent of those that characterized state supported orthodoxies during the centuries of Christendom." Like those earlier state-supported orthodoxies, it "is not content [merely] to regulate outward conduct" but instead seeks "to penetrate into hearts and minds, to shape the beliefs and values" of its citizenry.[22]

To put it gently, this new public order poses serious challenges for Catholics. There can be no question that this new order is irreconcilable with these principles. It is at odds with the Catholic vision of man, society, and the state. It is also incompatible with both the Church's freedom to exercise her divinely ordained ministry and with the freedom of Catholics to live out their faith. While Americans continue to celebrate the ideal of religious liberty, our understanding of the scope of this liberty is becoming progressively narrower and less friendly to Catholics and Catholic institutions. We seem to be witnessing the fruition of what John Courtney Murray feared was in its early stages in his day, namely "the retheoretization of the American way of life"—and thus of our understanding of the legal and constitutional norms relating to religion—along lines that "resemble nineteenth-century Continental theories,"[23]

21. Steven D. Smith, *Pagans and Christians in the City: Culture Wars from the Tiber to the Potomac* (Grand Rapids, MI: Eerdmans, 2018), 44, 112, 218.

22. Smith, *Rise and Decline of American Religious Freedom,* 142, 154.

23. John Courtney Murray, "Leo XIII: Separation of Church and State," *Theological Studies* 14, no. 2 (June 1953): 151.

in which Catholicism was "relegated to the hushed confines of the sacristy"[24] and the public square monopolized by "a new religion, a new ultimate view of man, sovereignty, law and society."[25]

While tensions between Catholicism and what might be called "Americanism" are nothing new, these tensions have been greatly exacerbated by the nature of the emerging new order. Whatever challenges the original American order posed for Catholics and whatever reservations Catholic thinkers might have harbored concerning it, they pale before the challenges posed by this newly emergent regime.

While Catholics must try with every means at our disposal to turn back this new order, we must reckon with the very real possibility that we will fail with the very real possibility that its proponents will succeed in reconfiguring America along the lines that Murray feared. At a minimum, we face a period of protracted and brutal cultural conflict in which the commanding heights of government and culture are controlled by elites dedicated to the new regime and hostile to what Catholicism represents.

Thus today the American Catholic community confronts a fundamentally new situation. It is one thing to live as a Catholic minority in a Protestant Christendom whose commitment to limited government and religious freedom afforded Catholics the considerable space to live out their faith commitments, and whose Christian character assured the existence of substantial moral and religious commonality. It is an altogether different thing to live as a Catholic minority in a post-Christian society animated by an anthropology and public morality incompatible with Catholic truth and committed to the exclusion of Christianity from public life.

The rethinking that this new situation demands will not be easy. Catholics have a deep and long-standing psychological investment in being good Americans and have devoted much time and energy to insisting that Catholicism and Americanism were compatible. Culturally, however, America is not the same place it was in 1776, 1900, or even 1960. The America to which Catholics offered, in Murray's words, their "full and free, unreserved and unembarrassed" allegiance no longer exists. The principles that allowed Catholics to embrace the American experiment in self-government and ordered liberty no

24. John Courtney Murray, "Law or Prepossessions?," *Law and Contemporary Problems* 14, no. 1 (Winter 1949): 31.

25. Murray, "Leo XIII," 165.

longer govern our public life; the understandings that assured Catholics the freedom to profess and practice their faith in its full integrity are no longer operative.[26] Ironically, at almost the very moment Catholics were accepted as legitimate members of the club they had fought so hard to join, the club ceased to exist.

In the new cultural world we inhabit, Catholics will need to self-consciously distance themselves from both the American state and American culture. Given the direction of American culture, it might well be that a "good" Catholic can no longer be a "good" American. Catholics will need to recover the ancient Christian wisdom expressed in the *Epistle to Diognetus:*

> For the Christians are distinguished from other men neither by country, nor language, nor the customs which they observe. For they neither inhabit cities of their own, nor employ a peculiar form of speech, nor lead a life which is marked out by any singularity.... [I]nhabiting Greek as well as barbarian cities, according as the lot of each of them has determined, and following the customs of the natives in respect to clothing, food, and the rest of their ordinary conduct, they display to us their wonderful and confessedly striking method of life. They dwell in their own countries, but simply as sojourners. As citizens, they share in all things with others, and yet endure all things as if foreigners. Every foreign land is to them as their native country, and every land of their birth as a land of strangers.... They pass their days on earth, but they are citizens of heaven.[27]

In other words, we will have to realize that we have no lasting city here.

At the same time, if we must not uncritically embrace American culture, neither must we succumb to the temptations to seek to wholly withdraw from the contemporary American culture into some type of psychological and cultural enclave, to simply reject America and all things associated with it, or to wallow in the fantasy of recapturing the glories of the Age of Faith through the technocratic dictatorship of the administrative state.[28] (The latter two

26. On this point, see Russell Shaw, *American Church: The Remarkable Rise, Meteoric Fall, and Uncertain Future of Catholicism in America* (San Francisco: Ignatius Press. 2013). While proponents of the compatibility of Catholicism and American culture such as Cardinal Gibbons "may have been mostly right in their day," Shaw argues, "their prescriptions for Americanizing Catholics and their Church are resoundingly wrong in ours. American culture has changed" (58).

27. "The Epistle of Mathetes to Diognetus," Early Christian Writings, accessed June 21, 2022, http://www.earlychristianwritings.com/text/diognetus-roberts.html.

28. On this point, see John Zmirak's discussion of the rise of what he calls "Illiberal Catholicism"

temptations help explain the current resurgence of what is often called "integralism.")

Even leaving aside its practicality, embracing the first option—what one might be tempted to call the "Amish option" (to avoid identifying it with Rod Dreher's "Benedict Option"[29])—would involve a betrayal of the responsibility of American Catholics to engage and evangelize the world around them. As the *Epistle to Diognetus* reminds us, "what the soul is to the body, Christians are to the world," and it is the soul that "holds the body together."[30] Similarly, we must remember God's instruction to people of Israel at the time of the Babylonian captivity:

> Build houses and live in them; plant gardens and eat their produce. Take wives and have sons and daughters; take wives for your sons, and give your daughters in marriage, that they may bear sons and daughters; multiply there, and do not decrease. But seek the welfare of the city where I have sent you into exile, and pray to the Lord on its behalf, for in its welfare you will find your welfare.[31]

At the same time, the type of cultural Manicheanism represented by the rejection of America and all its works is, to put it gently, simplistic. Among other things, it involves a failure to make a whole series of important distinctions (e.g., between the "old" America and the "new" America, and between true and false understandings of things like freedom, rights, religious liberty, democracy); a profound distortion of both the Catholic intellectual tradition and the American democratic experiment; and perhaps even a flawed understanding of the relationship of nature and grace. Distancing oneself from contemporary American culture, in any case, is not the same thing as rejecting wholesale the principles that originally inspired the American democratic experiment, much less seeing America as unalloyed evil.

Likewise, the fantasy of re-creating a Catholic society under the aegis of the administrative state (or judicial fiat) is just that: a fantasy (albeit an understandable one, given the situation we confront today, and the deep sense of anger

in response to recent developments in American culture. John Zmirak, "Illiberal Catholicism," Aleteia, December 31, 2013, http://www.aleteia.org/en/politics/article/illiberal-catholicism-6333360653729792.

29. Rod Dreher, *The Benedict Option: A Strategy for Christians in a Post-Christian Nation* (New York: Sentinel, 2017).

30. "Epistle of Mathetes to Diognetus."

31. Jer 29:4–7.

and betrayal Catholics feel in light of their profound and long-standing investment in the American project). Given the state of contemporary American life, how could such a public order possibly emerge? And how could such a polity possibility secure the consent of the government? (Self-identified Catholics, after all, compose less than a quarter of the population, and if polls are to be believed, most of them do not profess the faith in its full integrity.) Although it is an understandable fantasy, it is nevertheless a dangerous one. It is dangerous because it will be seen as confirming the worst stereotypes about Catholic authoritarianism, and because it distracts us from the realities of the cultural and political world we inhabit and the courses of action available to us. A prudent politics needs to take its bearings from the real possibilities available to us.

It is also dangerous because it represents an impoverished understanding of the riches of the Catholic intellectual tradition. It fails to recognize how the Catholic tradition imparted to Western society its distinctive character and inspired the quest for freedom that looms so large in the modern world. One thinks in this context of that tradition's commitment to the distinction between Church and state and the freedom of Church vis-à-vis the state; to what might be called institutional or normative pluralism; to a vision of society as a *communitatis communitatum*; and to the idea that political life must be ordered in accordance with the demands of our nature and dignity as persons, as beings who possess intelligence and free will and hence are privileged to bear responsibility.

Over time, these principles laid the foundations for a new understanding of political order. This political order is one in which government is limited in its scope, subject in its operations to the rule of law, responsible to those it governs, and respectful of the demands of social pluralism (wherein man's nature as a social being finds expression not merely in the state but in a wide array of diverse institutions and communities). It should also be committed to what Canavan calls "the self-organization of society," to a political order in which "the energies of society" should flow "from below upwards, not from the top down,"[32] and the protection of the rights that flow from our nature and dignity as individual human persons as well as the communities and institutions in which our social nature finds expression.[33]

32. Francis Canavan, "The Popes and the Economy," *Notre Dame Journal of Law, Ethics, and Public Policy* 11, no. 2 (1997): 440.

33. For brief discussions of the impact of Christianity on Western politics, see Kenneth L. Grasso,

The top-down, paternalistic vision of society inherent in the vision of the proponents of a Catholic administrative state flies in the face of this vision and seeks to reverse the revolution in Western political life set in motion by Christianity. Whereas that revolution has sought to tame Leviathan, the proponents of modern integralism seem to want to unleash it—so long as it is under Catholic auspices.

Given our need for a new cultural orientation, it is not surprising that many alternatives have been proposed (e.g., the "Benedict" Option,[34] the "Dominic" Option,[35] the "Jeremiah" Option,[36] the "Creative Minority" Option,[37] the "Augustine" Option[38]). Nor is it surprising that there is little agreement on what each of these options means. Forging this new understanding will require a balanced grasp of the Catholic tradition in its full richness and diverse manifestations, and a keen grasp of the American experience both past and present. Successfully living it out, it might be added, will involve having the wisdom and courage necessary to navigate the tension inherent in our status as "alien citizens," as men and women who embrace their responsibilities as members of a particular earthly community, while recognizing that the true homeland lies elsewhere. We must, in other words, learn, in the time and place in which God has placed us, how to be in the world without being of the world.

The obvious question is, Where do we go from here? *Gaudium et Spes* reminds us that "in every age, the church has the duty of scrutinizing the signs of the times and of interpreting them in the light of the Gospel."[39] The essays in the volume are an attempt to help read these signs, to cast some light on

---

"Christianity, Enlightenment Liberalism and the Modern Quest for Freedom," *Modern Age* 48 (Fall 2006): 301–11; and "The Freedom of the Church and the Taming of Leviathan: The Christian Revolution, *Dignitatis Humanae*, and Western Liberty," *Catholic Social Science Review* 27 (2012): 221–40. For longer, recent treatments of this theme, see Larry Siedentop, *Inventing the Individual: The Origins of Western Liberalism* (Cambridge, MA: Harvard University Press, 2017), and Tom Holland, *Dominion: How the Christian Revolution Changed the World* (New York: Basic Books, 2021).

34. Dreher, *Benedict Option.*

35. C. C. Pecknold, "The Dominican Option," First Things, October 6, 2014, https://www.firstthings.com/web-exclusives/2014/10/the-dominican-option.

36. Samuel Goldman, "What Would Jeremiah Do?," American Conservative, August 13, 2014, https://www.theamericanconservative.com/articles/what-would-jeremiah-do/.

37. This option is sometimes associated with Benedict XVI / Joseph Ratzinger. See Joseph Ratzinger and Marcello Pera, *Without Roots: The West, Relativism, Christianity, Islam* (New York: Basic Books, 2007).

38. Joseph Duggan, "Answering Wokeness with an Augustine Option," American Greatness, August 8, 2021, https://amgreatness.com/2021/08/08/answering-wokeness-with-an-augustine-option/.

39. *Gaudium et Spes,* website of the Holy See, accessed June 29, 2022, https://www.vatican.va/archive/hist_councils/ii_vatican_council/documents/vat-ii_const_19651207_gaudium-et-spes_en.html.

the nature of the new public order that seems to be emerging, and to parse out its implications for the Church in America. It is our hope that it contributes in some small measure to a much-needed discussion among Catholics about their relationship to the new America that is rapidly emerging.

An Overview of the Volume

The first part of this book examines the enduring tensions faced continuously by Catholics in the public square. These problems include a latent suspicion or downright hostility to Catholicism, apathy and apostacy, embedded Protestant assumptions about religion, the Enlightenment's skepticism of revelation, the progressive push to separate church and state further (a view contrary to many of the founding fathers), divergent concepts of the scope of "religious liberty," the seduction for Catholics to "accommodate" to the times, the plausibility of the Benedict Option, and the temptation for Catholics to abandon American principles altogether by yearning for former European Catholic models of governance, like integralism. The five chapters that constitute the first part address several of these enduring tensions.

Steven J. Brust begins the volume with a sweeping examination of the cultural tensions between Catholicism and American political life. Brust emphasizes the prevalence of Protestant hostility to Catholicism throughout American history. In response to this animosity, certain notable Catholics attempted to assimilate to an American culture somewhat in tension with Catholic doctrine. Catholicism affirms objective truth, unchanging doctrine, magisterial teachings, and the role of tradition. American Protestantism, in contrast, emphasized subjectivity, individualism, and evolutionary change. Brust demonstrates how Catholic politicians such as Al Smith, John F. Kennedy, Mario Cuomo, and Joe Biden accepted certain American tendencies contrary to the Catholic faith. Smith attempted to minimalize the difference between Catholicism and Americanism, while Kennedy privatized his faith by creating a strict separation between Catholic adherence and American citizenship. This separation, Brust argues, paved the way for Catholic dissidents, such as Cuomo and Biden, to come to power. For Brust, then, there is no golden era of Catholic engagement in the public square, since Catholic politicians mostly gained prominence by either ignoring or abandoning pivotal Catholic teachings, such as the protection of the unborn or the defense of marriage.

In a somewhat different vein, Gary Glenn also suggests that there are certain problems baked into American politics. Glenn argues that the Religion Clauses in the First Amendment do not sufficiently protect religious liberty. In his examination of the congressional debates concerning the First Amendment, Glenn analyzes the arguments of certain conservative Anti-Federalists who worried that James Madison and the Federalists composed the Religion Clauses to mitigate religion's role in the public square. Many Anti-Federalists believed that religion was necessary to preserve republican government and American cohesion. Thus these Anti-Federalists feared the ambiguity of the word "establishment" in the Establishment Clause. Glenn notes that there were at least five different ways in which the term establishment was employed during the founding. The ambiguity of the term therefore provided a pathway to the disastrous jurisprudence of the Warren Court, which radically and undemocratically secularized public school and government institutions. Likewise, the Free Exercise Clause does not necessarily provide complete liberty to religious denominations; its vague language was forged through an unwillingness to codify reasonable religious exemptions to pacifist Quakers. Glenn ends the essay by leaving open the question whether certain founders believed religion itself to be a political nuisance.

While Glenn scopes the debates of the First Congress to identify the potential limitations of the Religion Clauses, Kenneth L. Grasso argues that part of the tension between American government and established religion rests in the ambiguity of the concept "religious liberty." Grasso identifies several competing definitions of religious liberty and draws out their different implications. The founding era's thinking on religious liberty was shaped both by the Enlightenment and Christianity. As the Enlightenment evolved into a more progressive, evolutionary, and secular body of thought, however, its defense of religious liberty narrowed, over time, to a mere defense of worship. As a consequence, the secular defenses of religious liberty do not provide robust legal protection for Christian institutions (like schools or hospitals). The bifurcation of the Enlightenment and Christian origins of religious liberty explains how Christians and secularists understand the term so differently. More importantly, the divergence between Christians and secularists highlights the ideological and linguistic differences between conservatives and liberals that make consensus on religious claims harder to achieve.

Robert P. Hunt similarly identifies hostility to religion through our contemporary culture's embrace of liberal individualist monism. Liberal individualists, Hunt begins, often attempt to frame their positions as neutral. They portray secularism as neutral; religion (especially Catholicism) is the antithesis of neutrality. Thus individualist monism questions the extent to which Catholicism can influence the public square. Hunt retorts, however, that no position is neutral; every argument makes some sort of moral claim. Under the guise of neutrality, liberals have pushed their ideologies stealthily into the mainstream through judicial, executive, and administrative fiat. Hunt concludes by challenging Catholics to embrace their intellectual heritage and defend both religious liberty and the goodness of politics upon its traditional teleological and personalist foundations.

The problems with liberal individualist monism have inspired, over the past ten years, a renaissance of integralist and neo-integralist literature. James R. Stoner Jr. is critical of the integralist movement, arguing that many of its political assumptions rest upon the centralized and unitary political structures of monarchical Europe. Stoner finds an alternative to monarchical integralism in republicanism (which also has a strong Catholic political tradition). Stoner draws attention to the fact that, in republican government, prudent Catholics can serve as faithful Catholics while serving in political office. He provides the examples of Chief Justice Edward Douglass White, Governor Al Smith, and Speaker of the House John W. McCormack—one for each branch of government. Yet Stoner is also aware of the limitations of republicanism. The goodness of the regime rests upon the people and culture of the regime. Thus Stoner provides two counterexamples—President John F. Kennedy and Governor Mario Cuomo—who failed to integrate their office with the teachings of Catholic social thought. Stoner concludes his remarks by arguing that White, Smith, and McCormack had the support of a strong and active Church, energetic Catholic institutions, and courageous bishops. The weakening of a uniform Catholic culture allowed Kennedy and especially Cuomo to go rouge. Stoner emphasizes that without a vibrant and healthy culture, there is unlikely to be a sufficient political solution.

While the first part of the volume outlines the enduring tensions in the Catholic political order, the second part addresses how Catholics can address these contemporary problems through political institutions, religious organizations, and various creative minorities. The last six essays therefore propose various political and social ways in which to respond to an increasingly hostile political and cultural environment. Moreover, it outlines several snares that Catholics should avoid.

Thomas F. X. Varacalli examines the complicated and somewhat disappointing history of the Catholic vote since the nineteenth century. Catholics were instrumental in developing the Democratic Party to protect Catholic interests, ensure political advancement, and implement certain core components of Catholic social thought, such as the preferential treatment for the poor, solidarity, and social conservatism. Yet the Democratic Party betrayed Catholics with its embrace of the New Left in the 1960s. The leading pro-life party in the 1960s became the leading pro-choice party in the 1980s. Catholics faithful to the teachings of the Magisterium began to gravitate to the Republican Party for its defense of the pro-life cause, religious liberty, school choice, and law and order, among several other issues. Varacalli ultimately defends Catholic migration to the Republican Party, but he warns that the Republicans are imperfect allies. He also fears that the Republican Party may be weakening its commitment to several important causes. Younger Republicans are less religious and more socially progressive on pertinent issues, like gay "rights." Although the Republicans are to be preferred to the Democrats, Catholics must continuously lobby Republicans to defend their religious liberty claims.

Ryan J. Barilleaux has an even more sobering view of the administrative state. Barilleaux uses Barack Obama's Health and Human Services mandate as an example of how Democrats can use the administrative state for purposes contrary to the teachings of the Catholic Church, such as requiring mandatory contraceptive coverage, expanding abortion access, and regulating the speech and activities of Catholic institutions. The administrative state has also attempted to expand its power over individuals and businesses to push progressive policies, such as those related to gender identity, through anti-discrimination legislation. Barilleaux is concerned that several of these policies have not sufficiently been challenged by the Catholic laity and clergy, owing to either accommodation, malaise, apathy, private disagreement with the Church, or a combination of these factors. Thus, like Varacalli, Barilleaux is openly concerned about the possibility of further cultural and political degeneration.

While the administrative state was in tension (to varying degrees) with Catholic social thought since its inception, the Catholic university system was once a relatively faithful institution. Gerard V. Bradley outlines the decline and deterioration of Catholic higher education. He begins by noting that the bishops, either out of cowardice, incompetence, or the unwillingness to challenge lay college administrators, have failed in implementing *Ex Corde Ecclesiae*. He acknowledges that there are several small faithful Catholic colleges, such as Franciscan University, Christendom College, and the approximately twenty schools listed in the Cardinal Newman Guide.[40] Yet the enrollments of all the Cardinal Newman colleges do not equal the number of students enrolled at either St. Leo's in Florida or DePaul University in Chicago—schools not known for providing a robust or thriving Catholic identity and atmosphere. In response to the dismal state of Catholic higher education, Bradley calls for a renewal of Catholic curricula faithful to the teachings of the Second Vatican Council and *Ex Corde Ecclesiae*. He provides several steps that universities can take to revamp their Catholic culture.

The decline of Catholic universities overlaps with the decline of white Catholics identifying as Catholic adherents. Ashleen Menchaca-Bagnulo draws attention to the one ethnic group responsible for Catholic growth: Hispanics. Menchaca-Bagnulo argues that the historical importance and contemporary relevance of Hispanics are often sidelined or outrightly ignored by the laity, clergy, and Catholic scholars. Menchaca-Bagnulo provides an alternative narrative that emphasizes the "mixed" character of Catholic Americans—a fusion of European and Latin American culture. For inspiration, Menchaca-Bagnulo draws upon Our Lady of Guadalupe, who visits St. Juan Diego not as a European but as a Native woman. In Our Lady of Guadalupe, the Church has a model for this fusion of European and Latin American culture.

Marjorie Jeffrey also turns our attention to the Virgin Mary, but for the purpose of providing a powerful testament to the importance of femininity. Jeffrey provides a comprehensive defense of the natural differences between masculinity (with its emphasis on rationality and assertion) and femininity (with its emphasis on intuition and love of poetry). Jeffrey affirms that the Church, in order to affirm her mission, must provide clear examples of authentic masculinity and femininity. She criticizes second- and third-wave feminism for attempting to blur sex distinctions. These feminists do not empower women; instead, they make women more mannish. Jeffrey notices that this

40. "Recommended U.S. Residential Colleges," Cardinal Newman Society, accessed June 21, 2022, https://newmansociety.org/college/.

defeminization overlaps with some of the liberal misinterpretations of the Second Vatican Council. Jeffrey rejects the notion that the Church has become more "feminine." Instead, she flips the script and argues that the Church—following the trend of defeminization—has become too masculine, unpoetic, brutal, rational, minimalistic, and unintuitive. This trend is particularly indicative in the heretical push among some feminists for female priests and the destruction of gender roles. Instead, the Church must embrace a genuine understanding of femininity to have strong families, heroic priests, inspired liturgy, and a renewal of mysticism.

Our last essay centers on one of the most important debates in Catholic and Christian circles over the past five years: the prospect of a Benedict Option. The term was coined by Rod Dreher, a former Catholic who converted to Orthodoxy. James Kalb embraces certain aspects of the Benedict Option but distances himself from Dreher's interpretation. Kalb addresses a variety of problems embedded in modern liberalism—radical individualism, crass materialism, commercialism, hedonism, voluntarism, and solipsism, among a variety of other ills. Modern liberalism pays lip service to toleration, but it is staunchly intolerant of any creed, like Catholicism, that does not adhere to its tenets. Kalb notes that liberalism has attempted (and will continue) to remove Catholicism from the public square, political institutions, public organizations, and contemporary culture. In the face of this hostility, Catholics must come together to build (or rebuild) their own networks, groups, institutions, and parishes to preserve, protect, defend, and bequeath authentic Catholicism for future generations. In this way, Kalb points us to St. Benedict, whose monks for centuries preserved high culture during tumultuous times. Kalb does not envision a "retreat to the hills," but he does emphasize that Catholics must prioritize their own communities and institutions.

All eleven contributors recognize that the Catholic Church faces several threats from secular liberalism (the winnowing of religious liberty, an overly stringent interpretation of the separation of church and state), government institutions (political parties, the administrative state), and contemporary culture (gay "rights," transgenderism). The tone of these essays is sober; there is hardly any levity in this volume. Yet the views of the scholars in this book are not strictly uniform. Some see an immediate impending threat, while others are more concerned with a slower generational decline. Some view the administration of Donald Trump in relatively positive terms, while others see deep problems. Some argue that liberalism (if guided by Catholic principles) can be reformed, while others suggest that liberalism is doomed to fail. Still, regardless of the differences, the eleven authors are united by their adherence to the Catholic Church, their loyalty to the United States, and their deep hope that the Catholic Church can have a significant role in the public square.

PART I

The Enduring Tensions

CHAPTER 1

Catholicism and the Culture and Politics of America

The Enduring Tensions

STEVEN J. BRUST

And do not be conformed to this world, but be transformed by the renewing of your mind, so that you may prove what the will of God is, that which is good and acceptable and perfect.

—Romans 12:2

Many of his disciples, when they heard it, said, "This is a hard saying; who can listen to it?" . . . After this, many of his disciples drew back and no longer went about with him.

—John 6:60, 6:66

We must obey God rather than men.

—Acts 5:29

If Catholicism could ultimately escape from the political animosities to which it has given rise, I am almost certain that same spirit of the age which now seems to be so contrary to it would turn into a powerful ally and that it would suddenly make great conquests.

—Alexis de Tocqueville, *Democracy in America*

The question is sometimes raised, whether Catholicism is compatible with American democracy. The question is invalid as well as impertinent; for the manner of its position inverts the order of values. It must, of course, be turned round to read, whether American democracy is compatible with Catholicism.

—John Courtney Murray, SJ, *We Hold These Truths*

The above passages from the Bible, Alexis de Tocqueville, and Father John Courtney Murray, SJ, serve as a background for this chapter, which explores the relationship between Catholicism and American culture and politics. At the foundation of this relationship is whether one is an American Catholic or a Catholic American. Is one first a Catholic who takes on the accidental features of whatever it means to be American, or is one first an American who accepts only those Catholic features that fit with this American identity?[1] This question arises out of the two-thousand-year challenge Christians and the Church confront in relation to any political order and culture. The challenge is to prioritize an allegiance to the Church over America. Therefore, before exploring Catholicism and American politics and culture, I briefly look at this underlying challenge. I then provide a brief summary of the history of Catholics at the time of the American founding to show the deep-seated anti-Catholic milieu, which was a reaction against Catholics' allegiance to God and his Church before their allegiance to the state. The tension has been ever-present in the American political order and culture, continually affecting Catholics' relationship to it. I then turn to one aspect of the phenomenon known as Americanism. I primarily but not exclusively focus on how this Americanism manifests itself in the lives of Catholic politicians at the national level, as well as in in the lives of Catholics in general. I then offer some thoughts on the future of Catholicism and America by revisiting Murray's concern about the American rejection of the Church's "two powers" doctrine, which prioritizes allegiance to the Church over the state.

The Church and Culture

Established by Jesus Christ as his means of eternal salvation, the Catholic Church—which is in this world but not of it—always exists in tension with the world as found in the different regimes in which she advances her mission. The perennial question has been how should the Church fulfill her God-given mission: "Go, therefore, and make disciples of all nations, baptizing them in the name of the Father, and of the Son, and of the Holy Spirit" (Mt 28:19).[2]

1. Glenn Olsen, *On the Road to Emmaus: The Catholic Dialogue with Modernity and America* (Washington, DC: Catholic University of America Press, 2012), 125, 157. This is not to be confused with one who self-identifies as an American Catholic but nonetheless puts the American identity first.

2. All translations are from the *New American Bible,* rev. ed.

In other words, how should the Church as a whole, and through her individual members, advance the Gospel when accounting for the cultural condition of particular peoples—their geographical location, customs, ways of life, tendencies, symbols, governing structures and institutions, and laws? The challenge for Catholics has always been to discern which aspects of culture can be accepted, which must be rejected, and which can and should be purified, adapted, and "baptized." Some have used the term "inculturation" to describe this process of discernment and interaction with a people's culture.[3] Related to this is the process of assimilation, which is, from the culture's perspective, the process by which new members adopt certain essential components of the culture in order to become part of it.

At the root of every culture is the way in which human persons think about God and their relationship with him and the rest of creation, particularly other human persons.[4] This way of thinking manifests itself in practice in the customs, ways of life, mores, economics, art, architecture, and laws of a particular culture. Catholics, aided by Scripture, Tradition, the Magisterium, and the natural moral law, have the means by which to judge the cultures of the world. They can discern what a culture lacks and how it opposes the Gospel, thereby determining how best to enculturate the Gospel among a certain people. In the process, Catholics can also adopt or assimilate the good aspects of a culture without endangering the Christian way of life.

For this to bear fruit, Catholics within a culture must be properly formed in their faith. Even so, there are temptations of the world, the flesh, and the devil that constitute hindrances in this discernment and inculturation process. As a result, there exists the real possibility that Catholics could assimilate too much. They can excessively adopt a culture's traditions, customs, principles, and tendencies that impair their understanding of the Faith. The fundamental question is: Are the Church and its members going to transform the culture

3. See Matthew Lamb, "Inculturation in Western Culture: The Dialogical Experience between the Gospel and Culture," in *Eternity, Time, and The Life of Wisdom* (Ave Maria, FL: Sapientia Press, 2007), 105–24, esp. 105–7; Francis Cardinal George, OMI, "Continuity in Change: Catholicism and American Culture," in *Catholicism and America* (Ave Maria, FL: Sapientia Press, 2012), 5–6. Also, following Lamb, see Olsen, *On the Road to Emmaus*, 19–50, esp. 25–29. Some have referenced the famous *Letter of Diognetus* as a paradigm for the way in which a Christian should approach the world. See Archbishop Charles J. Chaput, *Strangers in a Strange Land: Living the Catholic Faith in a Post-Christian World* (New York: Henry Holt, 2017), 205–8.

4. Christopher Dawson's book *Religion and Culture* (Washington, DC: Catholic University of America Press, 2013) demonstrates this historical fact.

and society for the better, or will they be transformed by it for the worse? With respect to America and Catholicism, John Courtney Murray remarks, "The question is sometimes raised, whether Catholicism is compatible with American democracy. The question is invalid as well as impertinent; for the manner of its position inverts the order of values. It must, of course, be turned round to read, whether American democracy is compatible with Catholicism."[5] The question centers on how much of American democracy (and I will use this term more broadly than Murray, to mean the political order and culture in general) is in accordance with Catholicism. Or, in Tocquevillian terms, which aspects of the "spirit of the age" (*zeitgeist*) are compatible with Catholicism and which are not? The answers to these questions will help determine who transforms whom.

Historical Relationship of Catholicism and American Culture and Politics

Catholicism in the United States begins in colonial America.[6] The Catholic Cecilius Calvert established the Act Concerning Religion of 1649 in Maryland, which, contrary to the Catholic penal laws in England, allowed Catholics freedom to worship and to practice their faith and to enjoy all the civil liberties of a typical non-Catholic Englishman.[7] After the so-called Glorious Revolution in 1688, Maryland outlawed Catholicism. Laws were enacted that, among other things, excluded Catholics from voting, fined them for educating their children in the Faith, and restricted public worship to the point of imprisoning priests up to life for celebrating Mass.[8] The early years of religious freedom experienced by Catholics in Maryland were the exception,

5. John Courtney Murray, *We Hold These Truths: Catholic Reflections on the American Proposition* (New York: Sheed and Ward: 1960), ix–x.

6. I exclude Catholic missionaries to other parts of North America, including Florida, California, Canada, and other areas.

7. Maura Jane Farrelly, *Anti-Catholicism in America, 1620–1860* (New York: Cambridge University Press, 2018), 59. For a full history of the Catholic settlement in Maryland up to the War of Independence, see Maura Jane Farrelly, *Papist Patriots: The Making of an American Catholic Identity* (Oxford: Oxford University Press, 2012), esp. 48–135.

8. Farrelly, *Papist Patriots*, 194–97; George Marlin, *The American Catholic Voter: 200 Hundred Years of Political Impact* (Notre Dame, IN: St. Augustine's Press, 2004), 6; Michael Schwartz, *The Persistent Prejudice: Anti-Catholicism in America* (Huntington, IN: Our Sunday Visitor, 1984), 25–28.

as many colonies had enacted anti-Catholic laws amidst the predominant anti-Catholicism in American culture.[9]

There were many contributing factors related to the cultural and legal hostilities toward Catholicism, but a primary one was that Catholics owed allegiance to a foreign power. This hostility has deep roots in British history dating back to King Henry VIII's takeover of the Catholic Church in England in 1534. Henry established the Anglican Church and required Catholics to take an oath of allegiance to the king as both political and spiritual leader. This transformation resulted in the persecution of Catholics in England over the following 240 years.[10] Since Catholics resisted in the name of God, his Catholic Church, and the pope, they were seen as treasonous because being English meant being Anglican (Protestant). Catholics were not trusted as loyal citizens to the Crown, the colonies, the states, and the United States in general.[11] To a more or less degree, this hostility has continued in US culture ever since, and it has had a profound impact on how Catholics are treated and on how Catholics have responded and reacted to this treatment.[12]

Despite these anti-Catholic views and laws at the time of the War of In-

9. Francis Curran, SJ, *Catholics in Colonial Law* (Chicago: Loyola University Press, 1963), 54, cited by Marian Horvat, "The Catholic Church in Colonial America," Tradition in Action, accessed August 19, 2022, http://www.traditioninaction.org/History/B_001_Colonies.html. See also Farrelly, *Anti-Catholicism*, 36–104; Marlin, *American Catholic Voter*, 3, 6–8. An example of the cultural manifestation is the celebration of Guy Fawkes Day, or Pope Day, which commemorated the arrest of Guy Fawkes, a Catholic involved in the attempt to blow up King James I and Parliament (the Gunpowder Plot) in retaliation for King James I's requirement that Catholics disavow a purported tenant of their faith. See Marlin, *American Catholic Voter*, 10, 16–17, and Farrelly, *Anti-Catholicism*, 47–49. For detailed accounts of anti-Catholicism throughout the history of America, see Mark S. Massa, SJ, *Anti-Catholicism in America: The Last Acceptable Prejudice* (New York: Crossroad, 2003); Schwartz, *Persistent Prejudice*; Philip Jenkins, *The New Anti-Catholicism: The Last Acceptable Prejudice* (Oxford: Oxford University Press, 2003); John Lockwood, ed., *Anti-Catholicism in American Culture* (Huntington, IN: Our Sunday Visitor, 2000); and especially with respect to Church-state relations, Philip Hamburger, *Separation of Church and State* (Cambridge, MA: Harvard University Press, 2002). Importantly, the labeling something as "anti-Catholic" should not necessarily have a pejorative meaning in that there might be some truth to some accusations against Catholics, as I will touch on in my conclusion.

10. Except the time under Queen Mary.

11. Farrelly, *Anti-Catholicism*, 1–103, provides many examples of anti-Catholic stances in England up through the War of Independence. Also see Schwartz, *Persistent Prejudice*, 25: New York's constitution stipulated that "all members of the legislature had to swear an oath renouncing 'all allegiance and subjection to all and every foreign king and state, in all matters ecclesiastical and civil'" (36).

12. The purveyors of Enlightenment thought were also hostile to Catholicism and the Church, both explicitly and implicitly with respect to their rejection of revealed truth and the authority of the Church. See Massa, *Anti-Catholicism in America*, 12.

dependence, many Catholics took the side of the colonists.[13] The most prominent of these were Charles Carroll of Carrollton, the only Catholic signer of the Declaration of Independence, and his cousin, Fr. John Carroll, who would become the first bishop in the United States. They also thought their political support would help the cause of religious freedom and republicanism in general, which they believed were compatible with the Catholic tradition. They hoped that their bravery and conviction would help remedy the discriminatory laws and lead to the flourishing of the Church in America.[14] Bishop Carroll was especially sensitive to the accusation that Catholics would be more loyal to the pope than to their government. He exhorted Catholics to participate in American society "by demeaning ourselves on all occasions as subjects to be zealously attached to our government & avoiding to give any jealousies on account of any dependence on foreign jurisdictions."[15] The Catholic penal laws aside, this call to allegiance was unproblematic for Catholics at the time because of the Christian and natural law milieu of the general culture.[16]

The Catholic Church and the State

In order to properly understand the priority of one's loyalties with respect to the Church and state, Catholics look to the words of Jesus: "Repay to Caesar what belongs to Caesar and to God what belongs to God" (Mk 12:17).[17] This shows the legitimacy of the state and its power, and the need for citizens to obey it. It also shows that a person has obligations to God. Christ relativizes the power of the state by proclaiming an entirely different type of community, the kingdom of God, which is not of this world (Jn 18:36) and above the state. The Church, where the kingdom of God is present in some mysterious way on earth, has the eternal salvation of all as its ultimate end. This purpose

13. Schwartz, *Persistent Prejudice*, 34.

14. See Matthew Spalding, "Faith of Our Fathers," Mary Foundation, September 3, 2009, http://www.catholicity.com/commentary/spalding/06808.html; Marlin, *American Catholic Voter*, 13–15; Farrelly, *Anti-Catholicism*, 120–23; Bradley J. Birzer, *American Cicero: The Life of Charles Carroll* (Wilmington, DE: Intercollegiate Studies Institute, 2010), ix–xvii.

15. Quoted in Spalding, "Faith of Our Fathers." Bishop Carroll states that the accusation that Catholics cannot be loyal to the Church and government is false.

16. I do not address American Catholics and slavery owing to its complexity. See John T. McGreevy, *Catholicism and American Freedom: A History* (New York: W. W. Norton, 2003), 43–67.

17. In Rom 13:1–7, St. Paul also shows that political power is ultimately given by God and therefore typically should be obeyed.

supersedes the state's end and purpose, which is simply the temporal happiness of all in the political community. Put another way, man's temporal life ultimately should be directed toward his eternal life. This distinction between the things of God and the things of Caesar is expressed through the notion of the two powers—the spiritual power of the Church as exercised through the Magisterium (the pope and the bishops in union with him) and the temporal political power of the state.[18] These two powers are intended by God to have a cooperative and harmonious relationship, as an individual person is ruled and guided by both powers in relation to their respective ends.[19] When there is a conflict between what the state commands and God's commandments, however, "We ought to obey God rather than men," as St. Peter and his apostolic confreres proclaim (Acts 5:29). Hence, with such a conflict, Catholics must obey God and what he definitively teaches through his Church, specifically the Magisterium. The taking of God's things by Caesar has manifested itself in a number of ways in American history, but an important way was the enactment of laws that commanded things contrary to God's divine positive and natural moral law. When a civil law or policy conflicts with the natural moral law, however, it is unjust and therefore no law at all; it is not to be obeyed.[20]

Recall that the primary accusation by English Protestants historically has been that the pope is looking to take control of America. Consequently, they believed Catholics could not be trusted as loyal and patriotic citizens because they would seek to restrict religious freedom and other civil liberties as papal surrogates.[21] This has been a constant accusation in some form or another throughout American history, from Protestants like Samuel Adams during the

18. Letter of Pope Gelasius I to Emperor Anastasius, "Two There Are (494 AD)," in Brian Tierney, *The Crisis of Church and State, 1050–1300* (Toronto: University of Toronto Press, 1996), 13–14: "Two there are, august emperor, by which this world is chiefly ruled, namely, the sacred authority of the priesthood and the royal power." See Joseph Lecler, SJ, *The Two Sovereignties: The Relationship between Church and State* (New York: Philosophical Library, 1952) for an overview.

19. Lecler, *Two Sovereignties*, 15–31. This ordering of ends and powers and the relationship between them is not to be confused with an "establishment of religion."

20. St. Thomas Aquinas, *Summa Theologiae* (*ST*) I–II, q. 96, a. 4, c.; St. John Paul II, *Evangelium Vitae*, no. 72, website of the Holy See, March 25, 1995, http://w2.vatican.va/content/john-paul-ii/en/encyclicals/documents/hf_jp-ii_enc_25031995_evangelium-vitae.html. Rights language could be used to express this, such as the law violates the right to religious freedom.

21. The irony, of course, is that Anglo-American Protestants were doing to the Catholics from the time of King Henry VIII—and thus the advent of the Church of England—exactly what they feared Catholics would do to them; namely, restrict religious and civil liberties.

founding, to secularists like Paul Blanshard 170 years later, and to present-day US senators.[22] But what this accusation boils down to is that Catholics would obey God and the Church's Magisterium over and against the immoral commands of the state, or the immoral opinions within the culture. Obeying the Church and her teachings (an external authority) has historically been thought by non-Catholics to be a slavish hindrance to one's freedom, and hence un-American.[23] This form of anti-Catholicism existed in the early Protestant American culture, well before condemnations of modern liberalism and liberty by Pius IX in his *Syllabus of Errors* and Pope Leo XIII's teaching on human liberty and Church-state relations.[24] This same anti-Catholicism in various forms subsequently existed throughout the twentieth century, emanating from both Protestants and secularists. As a result, many Catholics worked to demonstrate their acceptance of and loyalty to American republicanism, civil liberties, and American culture in general. They fully assimilated while simultaneously expressing their desire to build up the Catholic Faith in America.

22. See Farrelly, *Anti-Catholicism*, 77, for reference to Sam Adams' *Imperium in imperio* (the Church makes itself a state within a state). See Schwartz, *Persistent Prejudice*, 15–23. See also Hamburger, *Separation of Church and State*, 205, 234–35, 246–51. Paul Blanshard makes this exact same accusation approximately 150 years later. See Massa, *Anti-Catholicism in America*, 62, although Massa argues that Blanshard's views are rooted in a particular Protestant view of a church and its relation to the state (66–67; see also 24–25). For other examples of these types of claims, see McGreevy, *Catholicism and American Freedom*, 11, 13, 34, 36–37, 113–14.

23. For specific historical examples, see Farrelly, *Anti-Catholicism*, 17–19, 76, 82, 177, 179. But her entire narrative about freedom in America and Catholic understanding of freedom is not fully accurate, as her assessment that the contemporary understanding of freedom in America is more like Catholic freedom, shows. For other examples of these types of accusations, see Hamburger, *Separation of Church and State*, 192–94, 202, 218; Massa, *Anti-Catholicism in America*, 59–60, citing Paul Blanshard's same fear, and 79, citing Norman Vincent Peale's fears; and Jenkins, *New Anti-Catholicism*, 28, describing Thomas Nast's cartoon showing the papal flag flying over the Capitol. Senator Dianne Feinstein expressed concerns about whether a Catholic judge will be hostile to the law in upholding certain "rights" (primarily meaning legalized abortion). Alexandra DeSanctis, "Dianne Feinstein Attacks Judicial Nominee's Catholic Faith," *National Review*, September 6, 2017, https://www.nationalreview.com/corner/dianne-feinstein-amy-coney-barrett-senator-attacks-catholic-judicial-nominee/. I do note that the Catholic judge who was nominated actually rejects any influence of Church teaching on her judicial decision making, which is precisely the problem regarding Catholics in America that I am addressing in this chapter.

24. Pope Pius IX, *Syllabus of Errors*, Papal Encyclicals Online, 1864, http://www.papalencyclicals.net/Pius09/p9syll.htm; Pope Leo XIII, *On the Nature of Human Liberty*, website of The Holy See, 1888, http://w2.vatican.va/content/leo-xiii/en/encyclicals/documents/hf_l-xiii_enc_20061888_libertas.html.

Americanism

The Catholic population increased significantly beginning in the 1820s owing to the mass and legal migration of European Catholics.[25] Finding America different from their native countries and cultures, they had to discern how to adjust to the newness of their surroundings. This led to disagreements among Catholics—especially among German and Irish-Catholic immigrants, and American-born Catholics—about if and how they should adapt and assimilate to American culture.[26] Some Catholics saw in their religious confreres a dangerous tendency to adopt certain aspects of the American way of life and principles, exalting them as better than what the Church taught and what the faithful had traditionally practiced. Furthermore, they expressed concerns that Catholics who did this were weakening the Faith by omitting or downplaying certain aspects of it. These dangerous tendencies were subsumed under the term "Americanism."[27] For better or worse, Americanism was closely associated with the life and writings of Fr. Isaac Hecker, CSP, a convert to the Catholic Faith and founder of the Paulist Fathers religious order.[28] It is not my purpose herein to rehearse the controversy surrounding the different interpretations of Hecker's role in spreading Americanism, nor to address what constituted "Americanism." To this day, there is disagreement about both the specific content of Americanism and the extent to which it even existed among Catholics in the United

25. Schwartz, *Persistent Prejudice*, 39; McGreevy, *Catholicism and American Freedom*, 11.

26. A contrast among the two prelates on opposite sides is seen here: Archbishop John Ireland stated, "between Church and Country . . . one is not to be put before the other," whereas Bishop Bernard McQuaid stated that "after my God and my religion, my country is the dearest object of my life." Quoted in Glen Janus, "Bishop Bernard McQuaid: On 'True' and 'False' Americanism," *U.S. Catholic Historian*, 11, no. 3 (Summer 1993): 59. But they both accepted republicanism and its institutions.

27. Some of the many authors who have addressed Americanism: Thomas T. McAvoy, *The Great Crisis in American Catholic History, 1895–1900* (Chicago: Henry Regnery, 1957), and *The Americanist Heresy in Roman Catholicism* (Notre Dame, IN: Notre Dame University Press, 1963); William Portier, "Isaac Hecker and Testem Benevolentiae," in *Hecker Studies: Essays on the Thought of Isaac Hecker*, ed. John Farina (Paulist Press: 1983); James Gillis, "Americanism: 50 Years After," *Catholic World* 169 (July 1949): 248–253; John Tracy Ellis, *American Catholicism* (Chicago: University of Chicago Press: 1956); Gerald P. Fogerty, SJ, *The Vatican and the Americanist Crisis: Denis J. O'Connell, American Agent in Rome, 1885–1903* (Rome: Universita Gregorian Editrice, 1974); John C. Rao, *Americanism and the Collapse of the Church in the United States* (Charlotte, NC: Tan Books, 1994); Rev. William Barry, DD, "'Americanism,' True and False," *North America Review* 169 (July 1, 1899): 33–49.

28. Isaac Hecker's primary work on the Church in America is *The Church and the Age* (New York: H. J. Hewitt, 1887). For other articles on Hecker's thought, see John Farina, ed., *Hecker Studies: Essays on the Thought of Isaac Hecker* (New York: Paulist Press, 1983).

States.[29] Rather, I want to underscore the very real possibility and danger of being transformed by the prevailing culture. Bishops and priests disagreed with each other on the Americanist controversy. Some claimed that Americanism was not a problem for the Church, while others saw it as a real danger that had infiltrated the Church, influencing bishops, priests, and laymen alike.[30]

Regardless of whether anyone ever formally adhered to specific heretical ideas or acted on them, opposition to these specific Americanist ideas existed. One erroneous principle consisted in viewing the Church in America as the new model of the Church for the rest of the world, especially Europe. Influenced by American civil freedoms, it was thought that individual Catholics should have increased freedoms and paid attention to the internal workings of the Holy Spirit, with less external guidance and less consideration (and even changing) of the Church's teachings found in Scripture and Tradition, and as taught by the Church's Magisterium.[31] In his 1899 apostolic letter to Cardinal James Gibbons, *Testem Benevolentiae*, Pope Leo XIII addresses this problematic idea of a self-reliant individualism coupled with a distrust of religious authority that predominated in Protestantism, as manifested in individual private interpretation of Scripture.[32] Leo addressed those who would adopt this vein of thought:

> Moreover, as experience shows, these monitions and impulses of the Holy Spirit are for the most part felt through the medium of the aid and light of an external teaching authority [of the Church]. . . . Nor can we leave out of consideration the truth that those who are striving after perfection, since by that fact they walk in no beaten or well-known path, are the most liable to stray, and hence have greater need than others of a *teacher and guide*. Such guidance has ever obtained in the Church; it has been the universal teaching of those who throughout the ages have been eminent for wisdom and sanctity—and hence to reject it would be to commit one's self to a belief at once rash and dangerous.[33]

29. See Janus, "Bishop Bernard McQuaid," 75–76; McAvoy, *Great Crisis*, 260. The participants in this debate both accept the republican form of government.

30. See Janus, "Bishop Bernard McQuaid," 58; McAvoy, *Great Crisis*, 217–30, for parties to the whole phenomenon trying to clarify what the actual content of Americanism was. The question of supporting public schools or supporting a Catholic school system was part of the tension among the participants. See McGreevy, *Catholicism and American Freedom*, 112–26.

31. McAvoy, *Great Crisis*, 217–58, esp. 219, 223–34.

32. Janus, "Bishop Bernard McQuaid," 57.

33. Pope Leo XIII, *Testem Benevolentiae* (my emphasis). I note that everyone at the time adamantly

This disposition toward "less guidance" by the Church goes hand in hand with the desire to adhere to the spirit of the age. Leo anticipates these errant tendencies which could (and would) later come to bad fruition in the lives of many Catholics in America:

> The underlying principle of these new opinions is that, in order to more easily attract those who differ from her, the Church should shape her teachings more in accord with the spirit of the age and relax some of her ancient severity and make some concessions to new opinions. Many think that these concessions should be made not only in regard to ways of living, but even in regard to doctrines which belong to the deposit of the faith. They contend that it would be opportune, in order to gain those who differ from us, to omit certain points of her teaching which are of lesser importance, and to tone down the meaning which the Church has always attached to them.[34]

One point to note here is that the omission and/or toning down with respect to doctrine is done in order to gain adherents to the Faith. But many Catholics also wanted to assimilate to American culture so as to "fit in" to or be "accepted" by American culture by diminishing their own adherence to the Faith.[35] As the generation passed, many Catholics would take up these two desires, including Catholic politicians and jurists at the national level.

Catholic Politicians and the Americanist Temptation

The Catholic clerics promoting Catholic assimilation to the American *zeitgeist* wanted to overcome the perception that Catholics were not loyal to America. They were eager to demonstrate their allegiance to America. This question of loyalty persisted and came to the fore nationally in 1928, when Al Smith, a Catholic, was the Democratic presidential candidate.[36] In 1927, as

professed complete obedience to the Church and her teachings. See McAvoy, *Great Crisis*, 238–41, 247–49.

34. Leo XIII, *Testem Benevolentiae*, Papal Encyclicals Online, January 22, 1899, http://www.papalencyclicals.net/Leo13/l13teste.htm

35. McAvoy, *Great Crisis*, 1–50.

36. US Senator Thomas Heflin (D-Alabama) made the typical accusations against Catholics with respect to Al Smith. See "Warning against the 'Roman Catholic Party': Catholicism and the Election of 1928," History Matters, accessed March 27, 2023, http://historymatters.gmu.edu/d/5073/. Ironically, what brought on this specific criticism was Al Smith's (correct) opposition to the Ku Klux Klan (which was anti-Catholic as well), and his desire to have the Democratic Party denounce it. Also see Schwartz, *Persistent Prejudice*, 91–101.

the governor of New York, Al Smith kissed the ring of the papal legate, the symbolism of which reinforced the allegiance concerns of many Americans.[37] These concerns were articulated by a New York lawyer, Charles Marshall, who wrote an open letter to Smith in the influential *Atlantic Monthly*.[38] In it, he challenged Smith's ability to be loyal to the American Constitution, civil liberties, laws, and policies because of his loyalty to the pope, who claims for himself a superior sovereignty over the state. Marshall ultimately roots his accusations against Smith in what he labels the "dangerous two powers doctrine."[39]

In Al Smith's response in the *Atlantic Monthly*, we see the beginning of a disregard for Church teaching, or at least the downplaying of Catholic doctrine's authoritative and obligatory character. As he wrote, "As you will find in the *Catholic Encyclopedia* (Vol. V, p. 414), these encyclicals [which include the Church's teachings on social and political principles] are not articles of our faith."[40] But the encyclopedia entry states something slightly but noticeably different: "As for the binding force of these documents [encyclicals] it is generally admitted that the mere fact that the pope should have given to any of his utterances the form of an encyclical does not necessarily constitute it an *ex cathedra* pronouncement and invest it with the infallible authority. The degree to which the infallible magisterium of the Holy See is committed must be judged from the circumstances, and from the language used in the particular case."[41] This argument leaves open the possibility that teachings in encyclicals reaffirm definitive infallible doctrine, even though they are not pronounced in an *ex cathedra* manner.[42] In trying to overcome hostility toward his candidacy

37. See James H. Smylie, "The Roman Catholic Church, the State and Al Smith," in *Church History* 29, no. 3 (September 1960): 321–43, 336.

38. Charles Marshall, "An Open Letter to the Honorable Alfred E. Smith," *Atlantic Monthly* (April 1927): section III, V, https://www.theatlantic.com/magazine/archive/1927/04/an-open-letter-to-the-honorable-alfred-e-smith/306523/.

39. Marshall, "An Open Letter."

40. Al Smith, "Catholic and Patriot," *Atlantic Monthly* (May 1927): http://www.theatlantic.com/magazine/archive/1927/05/catholic-and-patriot/6522/.

41. H. Thurston, "Encyclical," in *Catholic Encyclopedia* (New York: Robert Appletown, 1909), http://www.newadvent.org/cathen/05413a.htm.

42. This manner of teaching is done by the universal ordinary magisterium. See Congregation for the Doctrine of the Faith, *Donum Veritatis*, 1990, nos. 23–31, website of the Holy See, http://www.vatican.va/roman_curia/congregations/cfaith/documents/rc_con_cfaith_doc_19900524_theologian-vocation_en.html. In addition, roughly forty years after the *Catholic Encyclopedia* was written, Vatican II's *Lumen Gentium* (Dogmatic Constitution on the Church), #22, 25, and later the *1983 Code of Canon Law*, canons 747–55, addresses the different levels of authority regarding Church doctrine. It suffices to say that even the teachings that are not proclaimed *ex cathedra* or otherwise taught definitively still command an obedience

by dispelling fears that Catholics would be more loyal to Church teaching, Smith included some unnecessary and misleading statements regarding what the Faith encompassed and the influence it should have on his duties as a politician.[43]

Furthermore, Smith added other ambiguous statements that lend themselves to incorrect understandings of the Church's teaching and laymen's responsibility toward them. These came in response to his allegiance if faced with a conflict between his Catholic beliefs and the civil law:

> What is this conflict about which you talk? It may exist in some lands which do not guarantee religious freedom. But in the wildest dreams of your imagination you cannot conjure up a possible conflict between religious principle and political duty in the United States, except on the unthinkable hypothesis, that some law were to be passed which violated the common morality of all God-fearing men. And if you can conjure up such a conflict, how would a Protestant resolve it? Obviously by the dictates of his conscience. That is exactly what a Catholic would do.[44]

Smith was so certain that American culture and laws were steeped in the common morality and natural moral law that he did not see the possibility of a civil law violating it. It is safe to conclude that "common morality" means the natural moral law, as expressed in the Ten Commandments.[45] Smith recognized, implicitly, the possibility of what the Tradition calls an unjust law. An unjust law puts someone, including the one responsible for executing the law, in a position to decide whether he will "obey God rather than man." His positive assessment about the moral health of American culture and laws helped him downplay any conflict between his Catholic Faith and his loyalty to the US Constitution and American laws as the country's prospective president.

---

of religious submission of mind and will. Smith's article also gives the impression that the non-definitive teachings can be summarily dismissed. Another important topic that could be addressed which goes beyond the scope of this limited chapter is the consistency in the Church's expression of her teachings and their development.

43. Congregation for the Doctrine of the Faith, *Donum Veritatis*. Smith also claims (echoed by John F. Kennedy thirty years later) that he believes "in the absolute separation of Church and State," which is a misunderstanding of the relationship at the founding. Hamburger, *Separation of Church and State*, 182–87, shows how this idea of separation is associated with a history of anti-Catholicism.

44. Smith, "Catholic and Patriot."

45. Smith, "Catholic and Patriot." Earlier, Smith states, "The essence of my faith is built upon the Commandments of God. The law of the land is built upon the Commandments of God."

Nevertheless, he does recognize the possibility of a conflict and makes an immediate appeal to the Protestant way of resolving it through appeals to individual conscience. Now, in one sense, it is true that Catholics must follow the *certain* judgment of his conscience (as Protestants and everyone else must do). But Catholics are also obligated to properly form his conscience by means of reason, Scripture, Tradition, and the related teachings of the Church's Magisterium, and *then* act accordingly. In other words, an outside authority (the dreaded foreign power) comes into play. This is something Smith immediately dismissed: "There is no ecclesiastical tribunal which would have the slightest claim upon the obedience of Catholic communicants in the resolution of such a conflict."[46] If he meant to include the Church's Magisterium in general or the pope in particular in the term "ecclesiastical tribunal," then he was wrong in this judgment.[47] If he did not mean to include it, "ecclesiastical tribunal" nonetheless gives the impression that no Church authority has a claim on his conscience, especially in his political life. In other words, he appears to adopt the attitude of the disciples who could not accept the "hard sayings" and left (Jn 6:60, 6:66). Catholics are bound in conscience by definitive teachings about moral principles and the nature of the human person. Consequently, if political issues implicate some basic principles of the natural law, then the Church's judgments (teachings) can obligate. On other matters pertaining to prudential judgments, however—that is, cases that admit of various legitimate courses of action—one is not definitely obligated, provided the aforementioned moral principles are upheld.[48]

When a conflict does exist between obeying God or the state, Catholics receive guidance from the Magisterium to know which of God's laws (divine positive and natural moral law) are being violated. In contrast, it appears Smith set a precedent for navigating possible conflicts by appealing to a Protestant understanding, that is, one of private interpretation of God's law and a private

46. Smith, "Catholic and Patriot."

47. Smith might have been trying here and throughout the article with his ambiguity to cleverly nuance his words, knowing it would not be a tribunal per se that would be brought to bear on him, but rather the quiet counsel of the pope through an informal discussion with a leading US prelate. Still, it laid the groundwork of a bad precedent for future politicians.

48. Congregation for the Doctrine of Faith, *Doctrinal Note on Some Questions Regarding the Participation of Catholics in Political Life*, 2004, nos. 3, 4, website of the Holy See, http://www.vatican.va/roman_curia/congregations/cfaith/documents/rc_con_cfaith_doc_20021124_politica_en.html. E.g., legal protection of the unborn pertains to principle and immigration policy primarily to prudential judgment.

judgment of conscience without guidance, the very "Americanist" problem that Leo XIII warned against in *Testem Benevolentiae.* In time, this precedent to downplay key Church teachings became the norm for many Catholics politicians. Smith did not succeed in his bid for the presidency, and it would take another thirty-two years before a Catholic would be elected president. That honor fell to John F. Kennedy, who followed in Smith's footsteps and helped solidify this problematic precedent as a model for Catholic politicians.

From the beginning of the twentieth century, the Catholic population grew amidst the American culture and established a vibrant Catholic (at least outwardly) culture sustained by an extensive array of social institutions.[49] Despite this apparent strength of Catholicism, the need to be fully accepted in American culture was still a strong desire among many Catholics. For many, John F. Kennedy, the Irish Catholic Democratic nominee in the 1960 presidential election, symbolized the extent to which Catholics had risen and become accepted in America. It was hoped that his victory in the general election would end anti-Catholicism in America. Kennedy still had to overcome the usual Protestant suspicions about his faith and its compatibility with being a loyal American. These suspicions were pushed to the forefront by the Peale Group, headed by the prominent Rev. Norman Vincent Peale.[50] Protestants cited the "separation of church and state" to imply that Catholics would try to establish Catholicism as the official state religion in America. They were particularly concerned about Catholic adherence to an external religious authority.[51] Kennedy sought to counteract these concerns by giving a well-publicized speech in September 1960 to the Greater Houston Ministerial Association.[52] In it, Kennedy presented his perspective on his Catholic faith and the First Amendment, and how the former would not interfere with the latter in carrying out his presidential duties to defend the Constitution in executing US laws.

In the speech, Kennedy went further than had Smith. First, he stated that he believed "in a President whose views on religion are his own private affair"

49. One scholar rightly calls it the Catholic "plausibility structure." See Joseph Varacalli, *Bright Promise, Failed Community: Catholics and the Failed Public Order* (Lanham, MD: Lexington Books, 2000), 61–74.

50. See Massa, *Anti-Catholicism in America*, 77–79.

51. Massa, *Anti-Catholicism in America*, 77–79.

52. John F. Kennedy, "Address to the Greater Houston Ministerial Association," American Rhetoric, September 12, 1960, http://www.americanrhetoric.com/speeches/jfkhoustonministers.html.

and "whose fulfillment of his Presidential office is not limited or conditioned by any religious oath, ritual, or obligation." Furthermore, he exclaimed: "Whatever issue may come before me as President—on birth control, divorce, censorship, gambling or any other subject—I will make my decision in accordance with these views, in accordance with what my conscience tells me to be the national interest, and without regard to outside religious pressure or dictates." He added, "No power or threat of punishment could cause me to decide otherwise."[53] To further allay concerns, Kennedy said he would resign if a conflict were to arise between his faith and his duties under the Constitution and laws. Nonetheless, the speech's overall message was a capitulation to Protestant pressures, rejecting the principle that Catholics must always be guided by the teaching authority of the Church, including by moral principles which relate to politics. In short, for Kennedy, there would be no allegiance to a foreign power.

To gain the presidency, Kennedy did not "renounce" his Catholic Faith per se, but he did neuter its effect in his political life by "privatizing" it and disavowing the Church's influence on his decision making. To understand how momentous Kennedy's concession was, recall that Protestants used *penal laws* to prevent Catholics in Ireland, Britain, Scotland, and the American Colonies from even participating in politics and other professions.[54] In contrast, Kennedy's political-religious concession was not legally required for him be elected president. To get ahead in the perceptibly oppressive anti-Catholic culture of his time, which was also nurtured by secularists, Kennedy abandoned core Church teachings *voluntarily*, and he most likely would not have won the election if he had not checked his faith at the political door.

Some have pointed to Kennedy's election as the moment that Catholics, at last, were accepted in America, overcoming the prejudice and anti-Catholicism of the past. This might be true so long as one understands that acceptance came precisely at the expense of the Faith itself. Catholics needed to conform to the culture and "privatize" their faith, rejecting the Church's influence—via her authoritative teachings—on one's public political duties, thus essentially rendering the Faith moot in one's political life and consequently the life of the nation.

53. Kennedy, "Address."

54. See Edwin Burton, Edward D'Alton, and Jarvis Kelley, "Penal Laws," in *The Catholic Encyclopedia* (New York: Robert Appleton, 1911), http://www.newadvent.org/cathen/11611c.htm.

The Kennedy Legacy and the Cultural Capitulation

Cultural acceptance developed as the fear that Catholics' allegiance to a foreign power began to dissipate. Perhaps one other important reason for this change was the writings of Fr. John Courtney Murray. In his 1960 book *We Hold These Truths: Catholic Reflections on the American Proposition*, Murray argued that the American principles expressed in the Declaration of Independence and Constitution, especially regarding the First Amendment's religion clauses, could be interpreted as compatible with the Church's social teachings, particularly those regarding Church-state relations and religious freedom.[55] Then, in 1965, at the Second Vatican Council, in the *Declaration on Religious Freedom*, the Church affirmed a right to religious freedom (not to be coerced in matters of religion) for everyone.[56]

But while fear dissipated that Catholics would engage in a hostile takeover of the US government, and all that negatively implied for religious freedom in America, the erosion of the moral order in US culture was advancing. In short, there was a turning away from the natural moral law that Smith had taken for granted and a turn toward a developing culture of moral utilitarianism and moral permissiveness, which had begun to affect many institutions and individuals in the United States.[57] This shift included the sexual revolution, which affected human sexuality, marriage, and family. General accusations now became more specific, with Catholics pitted against the perceived "rights" to contraception, abortion, and most recently same-sex "marriage." Both the Church and Catholic politicians were increasingly told to not im-

55. Murray, *We Hold These Truths*, 3–123. See McGreevey, *Catholicism and American Freedom*, 191*ff.*, where he also shows other Catholic intellectuals doing the same, and even arguing (pp. 192–93) that Catholicism is more in agreement with American principles and democracy than the secular liberals are.

56. Vatican Council II, *Dignitatis Humanae* (Declaration on Religious Freedom), 1965, website of the Holy See, http://www.vatican.va/archive/hist_councils/ii_vatican_council/documents/vat-ii_decl_19651207_dignitatis-humanae_en.html. In this document, the Church recognized religious freedom while upholding its "traditional teaching on the duties of individuals and societies to the one true Church" (no. 1). Whether the Church's understanding of religious liberty is the same as the American understanding of religious liberty is much debated, although the United States does not fully recognize the freedom of the Church. See David Schindler, *Heart of the World, Center of the Church* (Grand Rapids, MI: Eerdmans, 1997), 43–88, for a disagreement with Murray on attempting to reconcile *Dignitatis Humanae* and the First Amendment.

57. See Alan Petigny, *The Permissive Society: America, 1941–1965* (New York: Cambridge University Press, 2009).

pose its morality on the general US populace out of a concern for separation of church and state. Some claimed it was undemocratic[58] and an undue interference by the Church in American politics. This social erosion contributed to Kennedy's assertion that divorce and birth control are issues on which he would follow his conscience (and not the Church's teaching) in deciding the nation's best interest.

Unfortunately, many Catholics subsequently followed Kennedy's disposition, both publicly and privately. Instead of resisting the cultural changes, they were transformed by them, including from deleterious forces within the Church.[59] Nothing more demonstrates the influence of US culture on—and subsequently within—the Church than two episodes separated by a mere fifty years. The first concerns Msgr. John Ryan, who in a 1919 pastoral letter for the National Catholic Conference defended the Church's teachings on human sexuality against Margaret Sanger and her American Birth Control League (later renamed Planned Parenthood). Ryan countered Sanger's advocacy for artificial birth control, as well as her attacks against the Church as a "dictatorship" that sought "interference" in American democracy to impose Catholic morality.[60]

The second episode involves Fr. Charles Curran and more than five hundred Catholic theologians and professors who forcefully and publicly rejected Church teaching on marriage and human sexuality when Pope Paul VI issued his 1968 encyclical *Humanae Vitae*.[61] Although Curran and his academic colleagues did not speak officially in the name of the Church, as Ryan did via his 1919 letter, their widespread opposition—and the Church's ineffective

58. Massa, *Anti-Catholicism in America*, 65 shows Paul Blanshard's discovery of the Catholic teaching on sexuality led him to crusade to confront the Church as un-American.

59. See E. Michael Jones, *Libido Dominandi, Sexual Liberation as Political Control* (South Bend, IN: St. Augustine's Press, 2000), 278–384, 300, 403–17, 433–53, and *Cardinal Krol and the Cultural Revolution* (South Bend, IN: St. Augustine's Press, 1996), 227–300, 377–428, for an excellent presentation of the sad history of some Catholics' capitulation to the sexual morals of American culture. See also Will Herberg, *Protestant, Catholic, Jew* (New York: Anchor Books, 1970), who argues that there was a more general gradual weakening of faith (among these groups) in successive generations as they increasingly accepted the tenets of the American civil/secular religion.

60. Alan Carlson, "Sanger's Victory: How Planned Parenthood's Founder Played the Christians-and Won," *Touchstone Magazine* (2008): https://www.touchstonemag.com/archives/article.php?id=24-01-039-f. See also Jones, *Libido Dominandi*, 278–84.

61. Interview with Fr. Peter Mitchell, "1968: The Year of Revolution in American Catholic Education," *Catholic World Report*, May 11, 2015, https://www.catholicworldreport.com/2015/05/11/1968-the-year-of-revolution-in-american-catholic-education/. See Jones, *Libido Dominandi*, 377–428, for the complete background. Paul VI, *Humanae Vitae*, 1968, website of the Holy See, http://w2.vatican.va/content/paul-vi/en/encyclicals/documents/hf_p-vi_enc_25071968_humanae-vitae.html.

response—helped to legitimize the "freedom" of Catholics to reject Church teachings, particularly regarding sexual morality. If priests and theologians, who by their very ecclesiastical office were expected to uphold Church teachings could reject them, then so too could the laity, with "moral permission slips" of the former.

Ultimately, Curran had "sought to harmonize 'American and Catholic' by striving to eliminate from the Catholic understanding of authority the elements that he thought violated human rights and individual liberty. He believed that The Catholic University of America would gain prestige among American institutions of higher learning by throwing off its vestigial attachment to the juridical authority of the hierarchical Magisterium."[62] In addition, Curran and his academic confreres were now making the anti-Catholic claims in their embrace of the "sexual spirit of the age" and concomitant dismissal of the Magisterium's teaching authority. This is a clear example of obeying man rather than God, epitomizing a clear affirmation of the Americanist tendency against which Leo XIII had warned.[63]

Political opposition to Catholic (natural) moral law positions, especially in areas of human sexuality, increased among Catholic politicians, with many justifying their stance with a "personally opposed but" approach. Mario Cuomo, the Catholic governor of New York, advanced this position in his 1984 speech at the University of Notre Dame, arguing that in a pluralistic America, Catholics could not impose their personal moral views on others, but rather had to publicly endorse and legally enforce what the majority consensus wanted.[64] Of course, these Catholics failed to realize that others were imposing their morality on them, and so they, as politicians, were imposing some moral viewpoint on others. This important fact gets to the heart of inculturation regarding politics. Inevitably, the political community's laws spring from some anthropological and moral view; law is not morally neutral. The truths about the human person, liberty, and morality taught by the Church and affirmed by the natural moral law should be seen as one of various competing anthro-

62. Interview with Fr. Peter Mitchell.

63. Jennifer Roback Morse, *The Sexual State: How Elite Ideologies Are Destroying Lives and Why the Church Was Right All Along* (Charlotte, NC: Tan Books, 2018), details how secular elites used the government, especially the judiciary, to force their ideologies of contraception, divorce, human sexuality, and gender into US laws and culture in general.

64. Again, the same anti-Catholic arguments made by others. It is as if Governor Cuomo read Margaret Sanger's words. See Carlson, "Sanger's Victory."

pological views in society. One view *will* prevail in politics.[65] The view that does prevail should be determined by objectively discernible truth regarding the human person.

Unfortunately, the "personally opposed but" approach evolved further, to the point where some self-identified Catholic politicians became the most active, prominent, and leading advocates of these "changed" views regarding contraception, abortion, same-sex relationships, assisted suicide, and more, in contradiction to the Church's teachings, the natural moral law, and facts attained by the scientific method itself.[66] Thus, instead of opposing laws contrary to the natural moral law, they were and still are championing them. The most recent example from a long list is President Joe Biden, who identifies himself as a devout Catholic yet has done much to promote grave injustices that are contrary to the fundamental moral teachings of the Church.[67]

This is undoubtedly something far beyond what Smith and Kennedy might have done. Still, this stance is clearly a logical outgrowth of their posture toward the Church's teachings with respect to their political lives. The Americanist tendency diminishes the role of the Church's teachings in one's life, as Leo XIII recognized. In many cases over time, both lay Catholics and Catholic politicians have conformed to the "evolving" societal morality and subsequent political morality of the American culture. They have accepted the underlying predominant ideas of American culture: an understanding of the autonomous individual, moral relativism, freedom as license, and a voluntaristic conception of reality and the Church. It is thought that the individual decides for himself what reality is, what it means to be Catholic, and what it means to be a member of the Church. The individual is not conforming his desires to the truths of the Faith or reason but is creating the "truth" to fit his desires. At bottom is the cultural phenomenon of the triumph of the will: that reality can be constructed by willing it into being as opposed to coming to discover the nature of reality, and then acting in accord with the truth of

65. Olsen, *On the Road to Emmaus*, 162–63.

66. An example: Senator Ted Kennedy (brother of JFK). WND Staff, "Pro-Choice Kennedy Was Pro-Life in 1971," World Net Daily, August 3, 2005, http://www.wnd.com/2005/08/31615/.

67. Thomas D. Williams, "Catholic League Identifies 32 Times Biden Has Opposed Catholic Teaching," Breitbart News, June 8, 2021, https://www.breitbart.com/politics/2021/06/08/catholic-league-identifies-32-times-biden-has-opposed-catholic-teaching/. For the Catholic League's report, see "President Biden's Policies: Departures from Catholic Teachings," July 7, 2021, https://www.catholicleague.org/wp-content/uploads/2021/06/PRESIDENT-BIDENS-POLICIES-DEPARTURES-FROM-CATHOLIC-TEACHINGS-cover-page-final.pdf.

that reality. This is a profound metaphysical crisis, as it marks the rejection of a permanent human nature with its inherent moral laws and telos. This manifests itself with those who claim that some moral and political evils are good, and that some moral and political goods are evil—most notably in the areas of marriage, family, human sexuality, human life, and religious freedom. This has been detrimental not only to the lives of Catholics who conform to this way of thinking and living, but also to many other Americans and the culture in general.[68]

In summary, many Catholic politicians are using political power to promote the very injustices they should be resisting. They not only reverse the order of their allegiance, putting the state first, but they also are responsible for putting Catholics who adhere to the teachings in the position of having to choose between allegiance to the Church or the state. Instead, Catholic politicians should be fostering a harmonious cooperation between Church and state in accordance with the truth of the human person and the moral law.[69]

Into the Future: A Return to John Courtney Murray's Perspective on the Two Powers

Ultimately, the future of Catholicism in the American political order and culture will require a reordering of the relationship between the Church and the state. This necessarily includes a restoration of an authentic understanding of liberty. In the first four chapters of his book *We Hold These Truths: Catholic Reflections on the American Proposition*, Murray argues that the principles of the American political order as found in the Declaration of Independence, the Constitution, and the Bill of Rights, particularly the First Amendment, are compatible with Catholicism.[70] But many scholars overlook the importance of

68. For the many problems in peoples' lives caused by the sexual revolution, see Mary Eberstadt, "The Vindication of Humanae Vitae," *First Things* (August 2008): https:// www.firsthings.com/article/ 2008/08/002-the vindication-of-ihumanae-vitaei; and *Adam and Eve after the Pill: Paradoxes of the Sexual Revolution* (San Francisco: Ignatius Press, 2012).

69. The Church has provided a response to this "personally opposed but" approach, but, no surprise, it has been rejected by those same politicians. See Congregation for the Doctrine of Faith, *Doctrinal Note on Some Questions Regarding the Participation of Catholics in Political Life*, 2004, nos. 4, 6, website of the Holy See, http://www.vatican.va/roman_curia/congregations/cfaith/documents/rc_con_cfaith_doc_20021124_politica_en.html; and St. John Paul II, *Evangelium Vitae*, 1995, nos. 68–74, esp. nos. 68–69.

70. Murray, *We Hold These Truths*, 3–123.

the ninth chapter, where Murray appears to modify his support for the American experiment.[71] This chapter, "Are There Two or One? The Question of the Future of Freedom," is about, as the title implies, the two-powers doctrine and the nature of freedom.[72] In it, Murray argues that the modern political project (of which America appears to be an example) denies the two-powers doctrine. For Murray, this doctrine is rooted in the principle of *libertas ecclesiae* (the freedom of the Church), which manifests itself in a twofold manner. The first concerns the Church as the spiritual authority that has care for souls. She teaches, rules, sanctifies, and does all that is necessary to fulfill these purposes. This first freedom includes immunity for the Church from politicization. In other words, the Church should not be subordinate to or an instrument of the state, because its spiritual authority would thereby be hindered.[73] The second considers the Christian people themselves, who should have freedom of access to Church teaching, to obey her laws, and receive the sacraments of grace in order to attain supernatural life and live in society fruitfully according to reason and conscience, and that "all the intra-political sacrednesses (*res sacra temporalibus*) be assured of their proper immunity from politicization." This includes all those things in the temporal life of man.[74]

The superior purpose for which the Church exists has historically resulted in two political consequences. The first is that the freedom of the Church served as the limiting principle on the power of government: "It furnished, as it were, a corporate or social armature to the sacred order, within which *res sacra homo* (the sacred person) would be secure in all the freedoms that his sacredness demands."[75] The second consequence is that the Church, as the People of God, "furnished the ultimate directive principle of government.... the Church ... stood between the body politic and the public political power, not only limiting the reach of the power over the people, but also mobilizing the moral consensus of the people and bringing it to bear upon the political power, thus to insure that the king [the state], in the fine phrase of John of Salisbury, would 'fight for justice and for the freedom of the people.'"[76]

71. On this I am indebted to the scholarship of Kenneth Craycraft, *The Myth of American Religious Freedom* (Dallas: Spence Publishing, 2001), 102–20.

72. Murray, *We Hold These Truths*, 197–217.

73. Murray, *We Hold These Truths*, 203.

74. Murray, *We Hold These Truths*, 203.

75. Murray, *We Hold These Truths*, 205.

76. Murray, *We Hold These Truths*.

Thus the Church is the corporate public witness to the truth of the sacred order and the witness to all of the moral truths and principles upon which the state is based. The Church counterbalances the state's power, helping form the consciences of the faithful and all others living in society. The Church also provides the spiritual substance of society.[77] But "modernity [of which the American experiment is an example] dropped the phrase [the freedom of the Church] out of its political vocabulary and eliminated the thing from its political edifice and installed in its place a secular surrogate, with [the negative] results that we now begin to see."[78] The individual private conscience is the surrogate that is supposed to mediate the "moral imperatives of the transcendent order of justice," transmitting them to the public power (the state) and thereby promoting freedom and justice in the political order.[79]

Without the Church as that counterbalancing public authority and witness, the state creates the ethos of society and becomes its highest teacher.[80] The democratic order becomes a monism of power with a secular substance:[81] "*One there is* whereby this world is ruled-the power in the people, expressing itself in the preference of a majority; and *beyond or beside or above this power there is no other.*"[82] Murray recognizes that religion is accepted only when it is privatized, and the Church is accepted so long as it is considered a voluntary organization, which does not impinge on the monistic public order.[83] The non-impingement on public order is key, for it reorders the hierarchy. Instead of obeying God rather than men, the state wants you to obey men rather than

77. About 115 years earlier, in 1845, the prominent Catholic thinker Orestes Brownson basically recognized what Murray did, and so he claimed that only Catholicism (and not Protestant denominations) can sustain popular liberty (democracy) in America because the Church—through its moral teachings and graces—guides the person in growing in virtue, a virtue that is necessary for everyone in American democracy. "Catholicity Necessary for Sustaining Popular Liberty," *Brownson Quarterly Review* (October 1845): http://orestesbrownson.org/108.html.

78. Murray, *We Hold These Truths*, 201.

79. Murray, *We Hold These Truths*, 206.

80. Murray, *We Hold These Truths*, 209.

81. Murray, *We Hold These Truths*. By the term "secular substance," I mean a bad secular substance that is contrary to the Gospel and the natural moral law.

82. Murray, *We Hold These Truths*, 208, emphasis added. See Hamburger, *Separation of Church and State*, 436. We can see this in the US Supreme Court's claim: "We are not final because we are infallible, but we are infallible only because we are final," wrote Justice Jackson in *Brown v. Allen* 344 U.S. 443 (1953), thereby illustrating that the Supreme Court is effectively a replacement for the Magisterium in adjudicating constitutional matters that pertain to moral issues).

83. Murray, *We Hold These Truths*, 210. This theory of the voluntary and subordinated church is seen in John Locke, *A Letter Concerning Toleration*, ed. James Tully (Indianapolis: Hackett, 1983), 48–50.

God, claiming for Caesar what is God's by "redefining" the moral order. The state is not neutral with respect to the moral order.

Without the Church acting as the public body to provide needed spiritual substance and guidance, the monistic state becomes the final arbiter of the moral law. The grave problem with this is that there is no external authority (foreign power) to which that one could or should appeal. As we have seen, this is precisely what much of the consistent anti-Catholic sentiment has been rooted in.[84] The guidance that a Catholic receives from the Church to help him exercise his freedom properly has historically been seen by non-Catholic Americans as contrary to the ideal of American freedom. The Catholic claim that everyone must follow the truth of the human person and the moral law,[85] as given by Christ through his Church, further fuels the charge that Catholics are out to restrict American rights and liberty and impose Catholic morality on America.[86]

It is one thing for those outside the Church to make these accusations, but the underlying problem today is that many Catholics make these charges moot (at least for them) by not believing in and adhering to the Church's teachings. Instead, they conform to the teachings of the American *zeitgeist*, or at least the worst and incompatible aspects of that spirit, that is, the Americanist tendency about which Leo XIII was so concerned. To understand how much American culture has transformed Catholics and not vice versa, consider that a majority of American politicians who identify as Catholics support positions contrary to the Church's immutable moral teachings. Similarly, regarding some American laws, a majority of Catholic voters oppose immutable Church teaching, and in other cases, a near majority does.[87]

84. All of the major philosophers who promoted the modern political project and its notion of freedom (Machiavelli, Hobbes, Locke, Rousseau) have seen the Church and Catholicism as obstacles and wanted to minimize or eliminate their influence on politics.

85. Orestes Brownson states that because the Church teaches that all Americans need to adhere to the moral truths taught by the Church to grow in virtue, the mistaken charge arises that Catholics—through the leadership of the pope—are out to control the government ("Catholicity Necessary"). Brownson later expressed concern that Catholics, especially the Irish, were not assimilating enough to American culture. See McGreevy, *Catholicism and American Freedom*, 45–46.

86. Catholics have taken on a new American civil religion. See Olsen, *On the Road*, 148.

87. There still are many who do not succumb to the false morality of the culture, hence the resistance to it gives rise to the phenomena called "culture wars." Michael Lipka, "Majority of U.S. Catholics' Opinions Run Counter to Church on Contraception, Homosexuality," Pew Research Forum, September 19, 2013, http://www.pewresearch.org/fact-tank/2013/09/19/majority-of-u-s-catholics-opinions-run-counter-to-church-on-contraception-homosexuality/; "Religious Landscape Study: Catholics,"

Although we have focused on the rejection of the Church's moral teachings on human life, marriage and family, and sexual matters in general, there are other areas where Catholic teachings appear to be rejected or redefined to fit a particular political ideology of the spirit of the age. These concern the Church's teachings on economics, whereby Catholics tend to identify as "liberal" or "conservative" first and then interpret, or accept or reject, the teachings in light of these political identities and ideologies.[88] A recent example of this occurred in 2009 with the release of Pope Benedict XVI's social encyclical *Caritas in Veritate*, whereby Catholics who called themselves liberal and conservative identified passages to use to support their own political ideology and criticize their opponents.[89] What this "liberal" and "conservative" Catholic divide masks is the real possibility that both sides err by accepting a false notion of freedom, that is, one untethered to the truth of the human person and moral law, which so much of the modern Church's social and political teachings have sought to counter, especially as exemplified by Leo XIII in many of his encyclicals.[90] Admittedly, when the economic and political ideologies are translated into specific economic (or other) policy preferences, it is more difficult to determine where they are contrary to the Church's teachings. The reason for this is that specific policy positions in economic areas are mostly a matter of prudential judgment. Many policy preferences could be better or worse, without any one of them violating the social and moral teachings of the Church.

In contrast, it is much easier to determine where the policy decisions regarding human life, marriage and family, human sexuality, and religious free-

---

Pew Research Forum, accessed March 28, 2023, http://www.pewforum.org/religious-landscape-study/religious-tradition/catholic/. In a felicitous turn of events, it is ironic that some contemporary evangelical Protestants who adhere to orthodox Christian and natural/moral law norms on some issues (as the seventeenth- through nineteenth-century Protestants did) have made common political cause with faithful Catholics.

88. Unfortunately, this important problem cannot be adequately addressed in this chapter, but I look to address it in a future publication. I merely introduce it here since it is connected to the overall argument.

89. An example of picking and choosing Church teachings should be accepted is from a prominent self-identified conservative, who marked the passages he rejected with a red pen while marking with a gold pen the passages he accepted. See George Weigel, "*Caritas in Veritate* in Gold and Red: The Revenge of Justice and Peace (or So They May Think)," *National Review*, July 7, 2009, https://www.nationalreview.com/2009/07/caritas-veritate-gold-and-red-george-weigel/.

90. See Patrick Deneen, *Why Liberalism Failed* (New Haven, CT: Yale University Press, 2018), 43–63, 77–87, for this point about the shared notion of freedom by liberals and conservatives.

dom, are contrary to Church teachings and promote a false understanding of freedom because they involve areas of fundamental moral and legal principles and are not based upon prudential judgment.[91] As a result, they are detrimental to a good and just political order in themselves.[92]

Conclusion

If the Catholic Church is to be the "pillar and bulwark of truth" (1 Tim 3:15) in America (including in American politics) to help fulfill Christ's Great Commission to "make disciples of all nations" (Mt 28:18–20), all of her members—bishops, priests, religious, and laity alike—must be humble and docile to discover and assent to the Church's teachings, joyfully living them out as a witness to an often-hostile culture. They must renew their minds according to the Gospel (Rom 12:2). Only then can one be prepared to carefully discern which American principles, tendencies, customs, and mores are harmful to the Faith of Catholics, and/or serve as an obstacle or aid to evangelizing, including enculturating the Gospel.

This primary allegiance of Catholics to God, his Church, and his teachings will probably always lead to charges of deficient loyalty or allegiance to the state's laws and policies. In other words, there *is* some truth to long-standing anti-Catholic claims that the Catholic understanding of freedom—linked as it is to adhering to the truth of the human person and the moral life as taught by the Church—is different in key ways from the dominant American culture, both past and present. The problem with these critical claims is that they fail to recognize that being guided and shaped by God and his Church is not contrary to freedom, but in fact enables one to flourish in authentic freedom. To recognize this reality, and strive to live up to it, is the very challenge Catholics face in giving faithful and fruitful witness to America.[93] But fidelity in

91. The clearest example of this is abortion. The teaching is not only that abortion, the killing of a human being, is always morally wrong, but also that it can never be legitimized by law and must be illegal. See St. John Paul II, *Evangelium Vitae*, nos. 72–73, website of the Holy See, http://www.vatican.va/content/john-paul-ii/en/encyclicals/documents/hf_jp-ii_enc_25031995_evangelium-vitae.html.

92. For the problems caused by the sexual revolution, see Mary Eberstadt, *Adam and Eve after the Pill: Paradoxes of the Sexual Revolution* (San Francisco: Ignatius Press, 2012).

93. To avoid a misperception that I am reducing the Christian life to mere teachings or laws, I note that the life of Christ encompasses a sacramental covenant relationship with God in his Church, living a prayerful life of grace in the Holy Spirit, for which the Church's orthodox teachings and their acceptance by Catholics are necessary but not sufficient.

the present might not guarantee future success in transforming the culture according to the Gospel. Faithfulness does not necessarily include success in a worldly sense. It will lead to spiritual success, which ultimately entails eternal life in heaven. It is *that* success which is the only future really worth hoping for ourselves—and for our fellow American citizens.

CHAPTER 2

The Downside of Constitutional "Protection" for Religious Liberty

Can Constitutional Protection for Religious Liberty Actually Undermine It?

GARY GLENN

This chapter's provocative title is meant to prepare the reader to recover, take seriously, and learn from an all-but-forgotten founding debate concerning the Constitution and religious liberty. The debate occurred in 1789 during the First Congress over James Madison's proposed constitutional amendments, which were intended to protect religious liberty. Some Anti-Federalist representatives articulated pertinent criticisms about the merits of the proposed amendments. Madison had proposed them pursuant to Anti-Federalist demands in the states' ratifying conventions.[1] Anti-Federalists, however, such as Representative Peter Sylvester of New York, "feared" that the proposed language could too readily be interpreted to harm religion and religious liberty.[2] Sylvester feared that it might be used "to abolish religion altogether."[3] Representative Benjamin Huntington of Connecticut was also concerned that it would be "extremely hurtful to the cause of religion."[4]

1. See Ellis West, *The Religion Clauses of the First Amendment* (Lanham, MD: Lexington Books, 2011), 57–88.

2. Rep. Peter Sylvester of New York used the term "feared." "Congressional Debates: Religious Amendments, 1789," The Constitutional Principle: Separation of Church and State, August 15, 1789, http://candst.tripod.com/1stdebat.htm; hereafter abbreviated as *CD*.

3. *CD*, August 15, 1789.

4. *CD*, August 15, 1789.

Both the pedigree and the substance of these forgotten arguments suggest the following question: Could it be that the explicit constitutional protection of religious liberty might actually permit and even facilitate harming religion to some degree? If so, this insightful suspicion might be instructive in unexpected ways, both in itself and with regard to the present and prospective constitutional situation of religious liberty.

The Anti-Federalist Criticisms of the Proposed Constitutional Religious Amendments

Madison had sent to Paris a copy of the proposed Constitution for Thomas Jefferson. Jefferson responded on December 20, 1787, generally praising the Constitution but recommending the addition of a bill of rights guaranteeing "freedom of religion, freedom of the press, protection against standing armies, restriction against monopolies, the eternal and unremitting force of the habeas corpus laws, and trials by jury in all matters of fact triable by the laws of the land and not by the law of Nations."[5] Madison replied to Jefferson on October 17, 1788:

> There is great reason to fear that a positive declaration of some of the most essential rights could not be obtained in the requisite latitude. I am sure that the rights of conscience in particular, if submitted to public definition, would be narrowed much more than they are likely ever to be by an assumed power. One of the objections in New England was that the Constitution, by prohibiting religious tests, opened a door for Jews, Turks and infidels.[6]

Madison suggested that a broader protection for "rights of conscience" was possible after the Constitution was adopted. Madison believed that when Federalists (i.e., advocates of the Constitution) assumed power, they would be able to define the rights of conscience more expansively than if Anti-Federalists had defined them. Madison, unfortunately, is not more explicit in his letter. It is unclear what his specific concern is. It is also un-

5. Thomas Jefferson, "To James Madison, December 20, 1787," in *The Papers of Thomas Jefferson*, ed. Julian P. Boyd (Princeton, NJ: Princeton University Press, 1955), 12:440.

6. James Madison, "To Thomas Jefferson, October 17, 1788," in *James Madison: Writings*, ed. Jack N. Rakove (New York: Library of America, 1999), 420.

certain how "rights of conscience" might be so "narrowed." It is possible to suspect, however, that he perhaps has in mind the right to not believe in God or the right to profess no religion.

What did the Anti-Federalists in the ratification debate want the Constitution to do about religion? One modern source posits:

> Anti-Federalists argued [that] the diversity of religion tolerated by the Constitution would prevent the formation of a political community with shared values and interests. The Constitution contained no provisions for government support of churches or of religious education, and Article VI explicitly forbade the use of religious tests to determine eligibility for public office. This caused many, like Henry Abbot of North Carolina, to fear that government would be placed in the hands of "pagans . . . and Mahometans [Muslims]."[7]

Herbert J. Storing provides the most complete modern presentation of the Anti-Federalist position concerning the Constitution and religion, however:

> Many Anti-Federalists were concerned with the maintenance of religious conviction as a support of republican government. "Refiners may weave as fine a web of reason as they please, but the experience of all times," Richard Henry Lee wrote to James Madison in 1784, "shews Religion to be the guardian of morals." The opinions of men need to be formed "in favour of virtue and religion . . ." Religious support of political institutions is an old idea, and here again the Anti-Federalists tended to be the conservatives.[8]

In other words, the Anti-Federalists articulated the following reservations concerning the relation of the proposed Constitution and religion: (1) that the proposed Constitution sufficiently supported *neither* religious freedom *nor* religion as such; (2) that governmental support for religion was necessary to make religion politically effective; and (3) that without politically effective religion, republican government would lack sufficient moral ties and hence

7. Isaac Kramnick, "The Great National Discussion: The Discourse of Politics in 1787," in *What Did the Constitution Mean to Early Americans?*, ed. Edward Countryman (Boston: Bedford / St. Martins, 1999), 52, quoted in "The Ratification of the Constitution," Lumen American Government, accessed June 1, 2020, https://courses.lumenlearning.com/amgovernment/chapter/the-ratification-of-the-constitution/.

8. Herbert J. Storing, *What the Anti-Federalists Were For* (Chicago: University of Chicago Press, 1981), 22.

lack the unity made possible by those ties. In other words, without unity, republican government would not work.[9]

In contrast, the Federalists thought that a multiplicity of sects (if properly structured institutionally) was sufficient to protect religious liberty.[10] They also followed Enlightenment thinkers in regarding religion as a "worn out trick" that was unnecessary for a successful republican government. As Storing notes, reliance on this multiplicity is what the Anti-Federalists refer to as "an artful collusion of interest."[11]

Proposed Constitutional Amendments Concerning Religion

In order to get the Constitution ratified, the Federalists had to promise the Anti-Federalists that, if the Constitution were adopted, they would introduce amendments to appease their objections and concerns. Accordingly, James Madison introduced such amendments in a speech to the First Congress on June 8, 1789.

Three of these amendments concerned religion. The first read, "The civil rights of none shall be abridged on account of religious belief or worship, nor shall any national religion be established, nor shall the full and equal rights of conscience by in any manner, or on any pretext infringed." The second stated, "The right of the people to keep and bear arms shall not be infringed; a well-armed, and well-regulated militia being the best security of a free country: but no person religiously scrupulous of bearing arms, shall be compelled to render military service in person." A third claimed, "No state shall violate the equal rights of conscience, or the freedom of the press, or the trial by jury in criminal cases."[12] The first two amendments, but not the third, were proposed by state ratifying conventions. No state had proposed giving the federal constitution power to interfere with the states' powers concerning rights of conscience.

9. See the section at end of this chapter titled "The Possible Contemporary Relevance of Anti-Federalist Concerns about Religion."

10. "In a free government the security for civil rights must be the same as that for religious rights. It consists in the one case in the multiplicity of interests, and in the other in the multiplicity of sects." James Madison, "Federalist #51," in *The Federalist Papers,* ed. Charles R. Kesler (New York: Signet Classics, 2003), 321.

11. Storing, *What the Anti-Federalists Were For,* 22.

12. *CD,* June 8, 1789.

In his June 8, 1789, speech introducing the amendments, Madison asserted that religious freedom is a natural right. He claimed, "The people have certain natural rights which are retained by them when they enter into society, such are the rights of conscience in matters of religion."[13] One of Madison's proposed amendments was revised by the House Committee of Eleven—a committee that included Madison—and reported to the full House as "no religion shall be established by law, nor shall the equal rights of conscience be infringed." The debate on this amendment began on August 15. Representative Peter Sylvester immediately expressed "some doubts of the propriety of the mode of expression" because the language "was liable to a construction different from what had been made by the committee. He feared it might be thought to abolish religion altogether."[14] He did not explain how the latter interpretation might be possible.

Sylvester's "fear" appeared somewhat plausible, however, since the immediately ensuing debate produced proposals for rewording the language to remedy the fear. "Mr. [Elbridge] Gerry said it would read better if it was no religious doctrine shall be established by law," but "Mr. [Roger] Sherman thought the amendment altogether unnecessary, inasmuch as Congress had 'no authority whatever delegated to them by the Constitution to make religious establishments; he would, therefore, move to have it struck out.'" Representative Daniel Carroll, a Catholic Federalist, replied that since "many sects have concurred in the opinion that they are not well secured under the present constitution, [Carroll] said he was much in favor of adopting the words [because] it would tend more towards conciliating the minds of the people to the government than almost any other opinion he heard proposed."[15]

Representative Madison replied to these arguments in the following way:

13. *CD*, June 8, 1789. Four years earlier, in Virginia's *Memorial and Remonstrance Against Religious Assessments* (1785), Madison had elaborated this argument as follows. "It is the duty of every man to render to the Creator such homage and such only as he believes to be acceptable to him. This duty is precedent, both in order of time and in degree of obligation, to the claims of Civil Society. Before any man can be considered as a member of Civil Society, he must be considered as a subject of the Governour of the Universe: And if a member of Civil Society, who enters into any subordinate Association, must always do it with a reservation of his duty to the General Authority; much more must every man who becomes a member of any particular Civil Society, do it with a saving of his allegiance to the Universal Sovereign. We maintain therefore that in matters of Religion, no man's right is abridged by the institution of Civil Society and that Religion is wholly exempt from its cognizance." Madison, *Writings*, 30.

14. *CD*, August 15, 1789.

15. *CD*, August 15, 1789.

> He apprehended the meaning of the words to be, that Congress should not establish a religion, and enforce the legal observation of it by law, nor compel men to worship God in any manner contrary to their conscience. Whether the words are necessary or not, he did not mean to say, but they had been required by some of the state conventions, who seemed to entertain an opinion, that under the clause of the Constitution, which gave power to Congress to make all laws necessary and proper to carry into execution the constitution, and the laws made under it, enabled them to make laws of such a nature as might infringe the rights of conscience, and establish a national religion; to prevent these effects he presumed the amendment was intended, and he thought it as well expressed as the nature of the language would admit.[16]

Sylvester's fear is explicitly supported by Huntington, who thought "that the words might be taken in such latitude as to be extremely hurtful to the cause of religion."[17] Yet Huntington's argument is stronger than Sylvester's because he gives an example:

> The ministers of their congregations to the eastward were maintained by contributions of those who belong to their society; the expense of building meeting houses was contributed in the same manner. These things were regulated by laws. If an action was brought before a federal court on any of these cases, the person who had neglected to perform his engagements could not be compelled to do it; for a support of ministers or buildings of places of worship might be construed into a religious establishment.[18]

Thus Huntington foresaw how the language purportedly intended by its authors to prohibit a religion from being "established by law" could be "construed into" a hindrance of religion as such by construing any or all governmental support (even by courts enforcing contractual obligations) as "a religious establishment." "Construed into" is particularly instructive language because it shows that the Anti-Federalists were concerned with constitutional interpretation. The Anti-Federalists expressed the concern that "religious establishment" does not have a sufficiently fixed legal meaning. Given the

16. *CD*, August 15, 1789.

17. *CD*, August 15, 1789.

18. *CD*, August 15, 1789. Huntington had supported ratification of the Constitution and so had not been an Anti-Federalist. But he seems, in the First Congress debate on religion, to have been supportive of Anti-Federalist concerns.

"latitude" or "imprecision" of its meaning, its insertion into the Constitution would give a federal court carte blanche to construe it in such a way as to hinder the legitimate interests of religion. In this case, it could be a federal court refusing to enforce contracts to support the costs of church buildings and operations.

The legitimacy of Huntington's concern about the amendment's language is apparent when one examines the jurisprudence of the second half of the twentieth century. During the Warren Court, the prohibition against "establishment" was construed into prohibiting such traditionally acceptable actions as prayer in public schools. This interpretative revolution over time transformed public constitutional support for religious liberty into requiring governmental neutrality between religion and non-religion, and eventually requiring a secular public life.[19] Accordingly, the possibility of undermining public support for religion was apprehended during the First Congress debate by those who wanted the Constitution to better protect *both* the interests of religion and religious liberty.

The debate thus involved more than simply protecting a predefined and universally agreed upon term such as "religious liberty." Several issues were at stake, including (1) how to articulate what religious liberty is; (2) how to protect the cause of religion; (3) how to recognize and protect the legitimate interest of churches in preserving themselves—in particular to avoid establishment language that might be "construed into" constitutionally forbidding any use whatsoever of government to support religion; and (4) how to avoid language that would "patronize those who professed no religion at all."[20] Finally, the debate also touched upon whether the Constitution and its federal government is supportive of religion and churches, or whether it is to be neutral between religion and non-religion, as in the language of twentieth-century jurisprudence.

19. The seed of this secularism was planted by the court's declaring, in *Everson v. Board of Education* (1947), without evidence or precedent, that the Establishment Clause mandated government neutrality concerning religion. The first blossoming was finding unconstitutional government-sponsored religious instruction in public schools as a means to combat growing juvenile delinquency in *McCollum v. Board of Education* (1948). The mature fruit became visible for all to see in finding unconstitutional publicly sponsored prayer and Bible reading in public schools in *Engel v. Vitale* (1962) and *Abington v. Schempp* (1963), respectively. Gary D. Glenn and John Stack argue this development more thoroughly in "Is American Democracy Safe for Catholicism?," *Review of Politics* 62, no. 1 (Winter 2000): 5–29; reprinted in Daniel Philpott and Ryan T. Anderson, eds., *A Liberalism Safe for Catholicism? Perspectives from the Review of Politics* (Notre Dame, IN: University of Notre Dame Press 2017).

20. *CD*, August 15, 1789.

What Did "Establishment" of Religion Mean in the First Congress Debates? A Short but Not Sufficient Answer: Nothing Unambiguous

If one attempts to ascertain what was meant by a religious "establishment" in the thirteen states at the time of the Constitution's adoption, one will see that it had no clear unequivocal *legal* meaning. Different states used the term interchangeably to support, encourage, and *require* religion for certain specific purposes. The variety and complexity of the term "establishment" lasted well into the mid-nineteenth century.[21] Thus the following questions arise:

1. Did "establishment" mean the use of taxation to fund the building and maintaining of churches? Did it mean the use of tax revenues to pay ministers? If so, was it still "establishment" if all churches were equally supported? Or was it "establishment" only if a particular church was supported while others were not?
2. Did "establishment" mean the use of civil law to put into place requirements for voting or serving in the legislature? Did it refer to religious tests that required one to be a Christian or a Protestant?
3. Did "establishment" involve a legal requirement to attend church services on Sunday?
4. Did "establishment" mean that only marriages performed in a particular denominational church (e.g., Episcopal, Congregational, Protestant) would be recognized by the state?
5. Did "establishment" imply that a state had to legislate *all* (or only some of) the foregoing things in order to have a religious "establishment"?

The problem is that the word "establishment" was able to signify all of these scenarios in the states. That is to say, the word "establishment" was radically equivocal. The equivocalness is the problem that prompted the Anti-Federalist "fear" of the proposed language "no religion shall be established by law." Therefore, contrary to the intention of the advocates of adding that language, its addition to the Constitution might give to the courts and

21. A state-by-state listing of the relevant provisions of each state constitution respecting religion can be found here: "Religion in the Original 13 Colonies: Text from Historical Documents Showing State Support of Religion," Pros and Cons of Controversial Issues, accessed June 1, 2020, http://undergod.procon.org/view.resource.php?resourceID=000069.

other people in power greater power to harm religion than what might already be either implied in (or could be "construed into") the unamended Constitution.[22] The Anti-Federalists were not alone in acknowledging that improper language could unintentionally extend the power of government. Madison, after all, in his October 17, 1788, letter to Jefferson, had apprehended the same concern about the rights of conscience when he wrote: "My own opinion has always been in favor of a bill of rights; provided that it be so framed as not to imply powers not meant to be included in the enumeration."[23]

Therefore the First Congress debate is centrally, but not exclusively, about what an "established" religion is or could be "construed" to suggest. It also centers on how to prohibit "established" religion, without removing the federal government entirely from support for religion and religious liberty. One could fairly summarize the debate thusly: religion and religious liberty, good; establishment of religion, bad. The debate is about whether the language permits the government to support religion and religious liberty but not establish religion.

Huntington raised this issue when he stated that Madison's proposed establishment clause might be "construed into" something "extremely hurtful to the cause of religion." Similarly, he pointed to this issue when he expressed his fear that the proposed language might support non-religion. He thereby defined the parameters of the debate in a helpful way. He hoped that "the amendment would be made in such a way as to secure the rights of conscience, and the free exercise of religion, but not to patronize those who professed no religion at all."[24] It looks like Huntington foresaw the late twentieth-century judicial theory that the Establishment Clause of the First Amendment requires government to support only non-religion and to forbid it to support religion.[25]

22. Madison acknowledged that this "construed into" problem had been a/the source of state ratification demands to better protect religious freedom. In the August 15 debate, Madison had said, "Whether the words are necessary or not, he did not mean to say, but they had been required by some of the state conventions, who seemed to entertain an opinion, that under the clause of the Constitution, which gave power to Congress to make all laws necessary and proper to carry into execution the constitution, and the laws made under it, enabled them to make laws of such a nature as might infringe the rights of conscience, and establish a national religion; to prevent these effects he presumed the amendment was intended, and he thought it as well expressed as the nature of the language would admit." See *CD*, August 15, 1789.

23. Madison, "To Thomas Jefferson," in *Writings*, 420.

24. *CD*, August 15, 1789.

25. The court announced this understanding in *Everson v. Board of Education:* "The 'establishment

Representative Samuel Livermore of New Hampshire shared the fears of Huntington and Sylvester about how the proposed language could be "construed into" harming either or both religion and religious liberty. Accordingly, he "thought it would be better if it were altered, and made to read in this manner, that Congress shall make no laws touching religion, or infringing the rights of conscience."[26] "Touching" is a more precise word. Livermore hoped that the word would neither hinder religion nor enflame a debate concerning constitutional interpretation. Accordingly, Livermore's proposed language was adopted at the end of August 15 debate by a vote of 31–20.[27]

This solution to the foregoing problem did not survive. The "touching" language was soon dropped for reasons having to do with the next matter of debate. On August 17, the topic was Madison's proposal that "no person religiously scrupulous shall be compelled to bear arms." There was a long, substantive, and instructive debate. Yet whatever one's opinion about whether such exemptions were just or unjust, good or bad, practical or impractical, it is hard to see any way in which the language could not "touch" religion. Even to decide not to grant an exemption would, in a manner, "touch" religion.

At the end of debate on August 17, the amendment concerning those "religiously scrupulous of bearing arms" was retained by the narrow defeat, in a 22–24 vote, of a motion to "strike out the whole clause."[28] Perhaps, in contrast to their adoption of Livermore's "no laws touching" language two days earlier, this debate had made clear to the House that a majority *wanted* the federal government to be able to "touch" religion in certain ways. For example, the First Congress was open to coercing the religiously scrupulous to bear arms. This view is supported by the fact that Egbert Benson of New York, who

---

of religion' clause of the First Amendment means at least this: neither a state nor the Federal Government can set up a church. Neither can pass laws which aid one religion, aid all religions, or prefer one religion over another. Neither can force nor influence a person to go to or to remain away from church against his will or force him to profess a belief or disbelief in any religion. No person can be punished for entertaining or professing religious beliefs or disbeliefs, for church attendance or non-attendance. No tax in any amount, large or small, can be levied to support any religious activities or institutions, whatever they may be called, or whatever form they may adopt to teach or practice religion. Neither a state nor the Federal Government can, openly or secretly, participate in the affairs of any religious organizations or groups, and vice versa. In the words of Jefferson, the clause against establishment of religion by law was intended to erect 'a wall of separation between church and State.'" Everson v. Board of Education 330 U.S. 1, 15–16 (1947).

26. *CD*, August 15, 1789.

27. *CD*, August 15, 1789.

28. *CD*, August 17, 1789.

voted against the "religiously scrupulous" amendment, made it explicit that they wished to "leave it to the benevolence of the Legislature, for, modify it as you please, it will be impossible to express it in such a manner as to clear it from ambiguity . . . the Legislature will always possess humanity enough to indulge this class of citizens in a matter they are so desirous of; but they ought to be left to their discretion."[29]

The problem now appeared to be one of language to permit government to "touch" religion in such a supportive way as to grant exemptions to those who would later be called "conscientious objectors" but not to have an "establishment" of religion. Moreover, this delicate issue had to be resolved without patronizing "those who professed no religion at all."

The same Anti-Federalist distrust of how the provision might be construed surfaced early in this August 17 debate concerning Madison's proposal that "no person religiously scrupulous of bearing arms, shall be compelled to render military service in person." Representative Gerry of Massachusetts argued:

> I am apprehensive, sir, that this clause would give an opportunity to the people in power to destroy the constitution itself. They can declare who are those religiously scrupulous and prevent them from bearing arms. [The purpose] of a militia . . . is to prevent the establishment of a standing army, the bane of liberty. [U]nder this provision, together with their other powers, Congress could take such measures, with respect to a militia as to make a standing army necessary. Whenever Governments mean to invade the rights and liberties of the people, they always attempt to destroy the militia, in order to raise an army upon their ruins.[30]

To remedy this problem, Gerry "wished the words to be altered so as to be confined to persons belonging to a religious sect scrupulous of bearing arms."[31]

Gerry's remedy would solve the problem he foresaw on the assumption that there would probably never be enough persons belonging to pacifist religious sects to enable those in power to destroy the militia's ability to maintain itself. In contrast, without such a restriction, *anyone* could claim they were "religiously scrupulous of bearing arms" thereby undermining state militias.

Representative James Jackson of Georgia objected to the proposed "reli-

29. *CD*, August 17, 1789.
30. *CD*, August 17, 1789.
31. *CD*, August 17, 1789.

giously scrupulous" amendment on grounds of justice. If it was adopted, he argued:

> One part [of the people] would have to defend the other in case of invasion. Now this, in his opinion, was unjust, unless the constitution secured an equivalent: for this reason he moved to amend the clause, by inserting at the end of it, "upon paying an equivalent" to be established by law.[32]

Representative William Smith of South Carolina supported Jackson's proposal to "amend the clause" by pointing out that it was included in the exemption amendments proposed by the Virginia and Carolina ratifying conventions. Jackson agreed that these conventions had recommended the "upon paying an equivalent" language.

After further debate, it was moved by Representative Egbert Benson of New York to strike out the words "but no person religiously scrupulous shall be compelled to bear arms." The interesting reason given was that this is

> No natural right, and therefore ought to be left to the discretion of the Government. If this stands part of the constitution, it will be a question before the Judiciary on every regulation you make with respect to the organization of the militia, whether it comports with this declaration or not. It is extremely injudicious to intermix matters of doubt with fundamentals. . . . the Legislature will always possess humanity enough to indulge this class of citizens in a matter they are so desirous of; but they ought to be left to their discretion.[33]

This motion to strike out these words was narrowly defeated, 22 in favor and 24 against. They remained in the amendment. That was the end of debate on the "religiously scrupulous" amendment for now.

On August 20, an amendment from the Committee of the Whole was revised to read: "Congress shall make no law establishing religion, or to prevent the free exercise thereof, or to infringe the rights of conscience." Slight-

32. *CD*, August 17, 1789.

33. *CD*, August 17, 1789. Given the seeming New England locus of the ratification debate critique of how the proposed Constitution dealt with religion and religious liberty, it is worth noting how this locus continued in the First Congress debate. Huntington and Sherman were from Connecticut; Gerry from Massachusetts. Even the two New York representatives (Benson from Upper Red Hook, and Sylvester from Kinderhook) hailed from towns twenty-eight miles apart in the eastern part of the state, within a few miles of the western borders of Massachusetts and Connecticut. Only Thomas Scott of Pennsylvania and Daniel Carroll from Maryland were distant from New England.

ly revised, this was the form sent to the Senate on August 24 as "Congress shall make no law establishing religion or prohibiting the free exercise thereof, nor shall the rights of Conscience be infringed." Notwithstanding the Anti-Federalist concerns about how "establishment" might be "construed," the House approved that language. The "religiously scrupulous" amendment was also approved and sent to the Senate as follows. "A well-regulated militia, composed of the body of the People, being the best security of a free State, the right of the People to keep and bear arms, shall not be infringed, but no one religiously scrupulous of bearing arms, shall be compelled to render military service in person." The "no state" religion amendment was also sent in this form: "No State shall infringe the right of trial by Jury in criminal cases, nor the rights of conscience, nor the freedom of speech, or of the press."[34]

How the Senate Handled the Proposed House Amendments

The Senate did not keep a record of the floor debate; there is only the official record of motions made, the votes, amendments to the motions, and the like. The Senate's consideration of the proposed House Amendments began September 3. The first religion amendment to be considered was "Congress shall make no law establishing religion, or prohibiting the free exercise thereof; nor shall the rights of conscience be infringed." After much debate, and many proposed amendments, the Senate eventually adopted this amendment, but only after striking out "nor shall the rights of conscience be infringed." There are no records that provide a clear answer why the protections for conscience were opposed.[35]

In general, "religious freedom," "religious liberty," and "rights of conscience" seem to be used interchangeably throughout the consideration of these amendments. A good example of this is Madison's response to Jefferson's letter dated December 20, 1787, in which Jefferson had recommended a bill of rights to protect "religion" (among other rights). Madison responded on October 17, 1788, arguing that "the rights of conscience in particular, if submitted to public definition, would be narrowed much more than they are likely ever

34. *CD*, August 24, 1789.
35. *CD*, September 3, 1789.

to be by an assumed power."[36] Admittedly, Madison's response might have a different meaning. He might have been substituting "rights of conscience" for "religion," thereby correcting Jefferson's suggestion. I know of no evidence to support this possibility, however.

Nevertheless, suppose that "religion" referred to the relation of civil law to sects or churches, while "rights of conscience" referred to the relation of civil law to individual beliefs. The latter would then have a more individual connotation, while the former would have a more institutional meaning. Madison might be suggesting to Jefferson that Americans should be more concerned with the latter than the former. "Religion," after all, raises the thorny, and difficult to resolve, problems of what constitutes institutional "establishment." It also partly concerns the relation of the federal constitution to state religious establishment. In contrast, "rights of conscience" might be dealt with more easily than the problems concerning religion. The reason Madison might prefer "rights of conscience" language is his conviction that individuals have a natural right to freedom of religious belief. It is equally clear that churches do not have any natural rights, and the connection of individual natural rights to the existence of churches is unclear and controversial. Although this may be speculation, after the September 3 debate, the Senate was willing to keep the prohibition against "establishing" religion but not the rights of conscience language.

On September 9, the Senate again took up the proposed House amendment concerning establishment. In addition to the "rights of conscience" language that the Senate had already rejected on September 3, this September 9 debate substituted "establishing articles of faith, or a mode of worship" in place of "establishing religion." It also substituted "or prohibiting the free exercise of religion" in place of "or prohibiting the free Exercise thereof ["thereof" referring to religion]." The amendment then was approved as "Congress shall make no law establishing articles of faith, or a mode of worship, or prohibiting the free exercise of religion, or abridging the freedom of speech, or the press, or the right of the people peaceably to assemble, and petition to the government for the redress of grievances." At the same time, the Senate also deleted "but no one religiously scrupulous of bearing arms shall be compelled to render military service in person" from the amendment concerning the militia.[37]

36. Madison, "To Thomas Jefferson," in *Writings*, 420.

37. *CD*, September 9, 1789.

On September 19–23, the House rejected the Senate's changes to the "Congress shall make no law" amendment. Specifically, it rejected the Senate's deletion of the "rights of conscience" language and its substitution of "One Religious Sect or Society in preference to others" in place of "Religion or prohibiting the free exercise thereof." On September 21, the House agreed to accept the Senate's deletion of "but no one religiously scrupulous of bearing arms shall be compelled to render military service in person." It called for a conference committee with the Senate on these and other disagreements regarding constitutional amendments. When the Senate received the House responses, it decided to "recede" from its version of the "Congress shall make no law" amendment but to insist on the others.[38]

The result of the conference committee was that on September 24, the following language was agreed to by both houses. "Congress shall make no law respecting an establishment of religion, or prohibiting the free exercise thereof; or abridging the freedom of speech, or of the press; or the right of the people peaceably to assemble, and to petition the government for a redress of grievances." On September 28, this language was sent to the states for ratification. Thus the following phrases, which had been part of the religion amendments at various stages, were ultimately rejected: "rights of conscience," "establishing articles of faith, or a mode of worship" (in place of "establishing religion"), and "no person religiously scrupulous shall be compelled to bear arms."[39]

One cannot say with certainty why the rights of conscience language was rejected. What is certain is that the Senate tried and failed several times to approve the amendment "Congress shall make no law establishing religion, or prohibiting the free exercise thereof; nor shall the rights of conscience be infringed," but it passed the amendment only when "rights of conscience" was removed.[40] This language seems to have been unacceptable to the Senate. After all, it would require the federal government to define the "rights of conscience." The government would come dangerously close to defining what individual rights of conscience are in matters of religion. This raises a question: Might they have feared giving this power to a government that was so distant from the states in which the people lived? The plausibility of this speculation

38. *CD,* September 21 and 24, 1789.
39. *CD,* September 3 and 9, 1789.
40. *CD,* September 28, 1789.

is strengthened by the fact that the Senate was elected by the state legislatures and hence represented the state governments. In contrast, the people of the states elected the House, and so it represented them. Thus the House could be comfortable with the "rights of conscience" language than the Senate.

The Possible Contemporary Relevance of Anti-Federalist Concerns about Religion

One wonders today whether our contemporary political divisions have become increasingly impervious to compromise. For example, our political life may no longer have a basis for political unity that is sufficient to overcome some political disagreements. Compromise does not occur because the opposing sides do not share a common moral ground that transcends their policy disagreements. This formulation gives practical contemporary weight and relevance to the Anti-Federalist argument that religion is necessary to provide that common moral ground.

In the Founding debate, the Anti-Federalist assertion that religion had a positive political effect contrasted with the Federalist temptation of seeing religion primarily as a source of political conflict. That is to say, if the Anti-Federalists were correct that religion is necessary (amidst political divisiveness and conflict) to make political unity possible, then it would not be *sufficient* (either in the founding debate or for contemporary political analysis) to regard religion *only* as a source of political or social conflict. Thus we need to reexamine how to foster that positive political effect of religion without unnecessarily fostering religious conflict and oppression. The whole truth rests neither with the political opinion that religion is merely a political problem to be avoided, nor with the political opinion that religion is to be fostered by society and government. This point only reveals what needs to be examined; it does not immediately provide insight on how to achieve both of these partly conflicting political purposes. It does not even show us that it is possible to do so. Nor is the contradiction between religion's purported political necessity and its problematic political consequences solved merely by formulating it. Yet one must be aware that the contradiction is suggested by the following: if we follow the Federalists in denying that religion is necessary for political unity, then we need to figure out what alternative makes such unity possible.

Put another way, when we confront an apparently insoluble political conflict, what other institution than religion might make it possible for us to have the kind of political, social, and moral unity necessary to live together in the same political order? If the love of fellow citizens, rooted in the love of God, is not recognized by *all* sides as that which binds together warring political factions, it is not implausible to suspect that some kind of state of war will exist either indefinitely or occasionally between those factions. The rights of religious communities and even the common political good may be trampled upon by the government.

The Federalist multiplicity of interest solution may work well enough when social peace, political unity, and mutual recognition of rights can be assumed or taken for granted. But when they cannot be assumed or taken for granted, what other institution besides religion can persuade the conflicting political interests to place their own and their opponents' mutual well-being *above* their partisan interests? Of course, it is possible that religion cannot so persuade either in all such circumstances. The Anti-Federalists did not assume that it could, but they knew of nothing that could take its place in cultivating and achieving political unity in the face of otherwise apparently insoluble political conflict.

It is therefore instructive for contemporary readers to ask themselves whether, or to what extent, the United States currently has "a political community with shared values and interests." The recent government shutdowns suggest that what divides us politically may be stronger than whatever shared values and interests we might have thought we had. Given the declining influence of religious belief, if what divides us politically is stronger than our shared political values and interests, does that not to some extent support the Anti-Federalist argument about the importance and necessity of religious conviction as a support for preserving a republican political community and government? Obviously, the Anti-Federalists did not argue that religious conviction would be *sufficient* for such purposes, but it does not seem beyond serious consideration for us to be open to its *necessity*.

Conclusion

This study may seem odd to many contemporary students of American politics because it unexpectedly uncovers, in an almost forgotten founding debate, insight that sheds light on contemporary political issues. Careful attention to Anti-Federalist criticisms about Madison's proposed constitutional amendments, which purportedly intended to protect religious liberty, highlights our contemporary problem of apparently uncompromisable political disagreement. If this study has succeeded in showing that this founding debate is relevant to this contemporary issue, it is because the debate turned to some extent on permanent problems of political life intrinsic to popular government. We cannot assume that the present apparently insoluble political conflict is a consequence of unprecedented or historically unique circumstances.

The Federalists believed that popular government depended decisively on strong central government and saw the political relevance of religion only as problematic. The Anti-Federalists countered that popular government depended decisively on the pre-political unity of shared moral and religious beliefs that were strong enough to survive political disagreements. If we see that these different emphases persist down to our own time, perhaps that is because they are part of the nature of the political life of popular government.

CHAPTER 3

Two Rival Versions of Religious Liberty

KENNETH L. GRASSO

> "Everything is open to question" may seem a natural intellectual principle to those raised between 1970 and 2000 . . . But most cultures, for most of human history, haven't acted this way. Maybe that's because such openness represents an unstable equilibrium, possible only in the liminal moment between the eradication of an existing orthodoxy and the establishment of a new one.
>
> —Megan McCardle

> *The culture wars are over; they lost, we won. . . .* For liberals, the question now is how to deal with the losers in the culture wars. That's mostly a question of tactics. My own judgment is that taking a hard line ("You lost, live with it") is better than trying to accommodate the losers, who—remember—defended, and are defending, positions that liberals regard as having no normative pull at all. Trying to be nice to the losers didn't work well after the Civil War . . . (And taking a hard line seemed to work reasonably well in Germany and Japan after 1945).
>
> —Mark Tushnet, William Nelson Cromwell Professor of Law, Harvard Law School

Confronted with the "new intolerance" that has emerged in recent decades, practicing Catholics and other religious believers have tried to secure the legal and social space necessary for themselves and their institutions to live in accordance with their beliefs (and to profess those beliefs publicly) by appealing to America's historic commitment to religious freedom.[1] Whether this strate-

1. Mary Eberstadt, *It's Dangerous to Believe: Religious Freedom and Its Enemies* (New York: Harper, 2016).

gy succeeds, however, will depend both on the durability of this commitment to and on our understanding of the nature and scope of this principle.

The fact is that in America today, religious liberty—or at least religious liberty as Americans have traditionally understood it—is under assault, and its adversaries seem to have the momentum. This is a truly remarkable development. After all, even if we have not always been completely faithful to it in practice, the idea of religious liberty has long been central to America's self-understanding. It is made even more remarkable by the fact that it has happened so quickly: only a quarter century ago, the Religious Freedom Restoration Act passed both houses of Congress virtually unanimously.

Before turning our attention to this development, it is necessary to be clear on two preliminary points. First, as Robert P. George has explained, religious liberty can be defended

> on various grounds. Some argue for religious freedom on the basis of the controversial religious view that all religious are "equally" true or untrue; or the equally controversial view that religious truth is purely a subjective matter; or the pragmatic political ground that religious freedom is a necessary means of maintaining social peace in the face of religious diversity; or the political-moral view that religious liberty is part of the right to personal autonomy; or the religious-political view that "religion," if a value at all, is a value with which government lacks the jurisdiction or competence to deal. There are other arguments as well.[2]

Religious liberty, in other words, is by no means a univocal concept. There are competing theories of religious liberty that derive from different understandings of the nature of man, the human good, the proper structure of human social relations, the proper role of the state in the overall economy of human social life, the nature and epistemological status of religious truth, and the proper organization of man's spiritual life. These various theories, in turn, have profoundly different implications for our understanding of this liberty's nature and scope.

Second, religious liberty is by its very nature limited in its scope. "Every liberty," as Ross Douthat reminds us, "has its limits." No one, for example, proposes that we "allow people to exercise beliefs that require, say, forced mar-

2. Robert P. George, *Making Men Moral: Civil Liberties and Public Morality* (Oxford: Clarendon Press, 1993), 219–20.

riage or honor killings."[3] Likewise, no one argues that the right to religious liberty includes the right to engage in human sacrifice. What these limits are will stem from our understanding of religious liberty and the background assumptions that inform it. The real issue we face, therefore, is not whether there should be limits to religious liberty, but what principles—what background understandings of the nature of man, the human good, and the role of government—should guide our thinking about these limits.

American Religious Liberty: The First Tributary

How, then, can the ongoing collapse of America's commitment to religious liberty—or at least religious liberty as Americans have traditionally understood—be explained? The answer, I would suggest, is to be found in an ambiguity that has characterized the American idea of religious liberty from the earliest days of the republic. As George Marsden has recently reminded us, the American republic was launched by an alliance between "the secular heirs of the enlightenment and the religious heirs of frontier revivalism."[4] In the founding era, as he notes, Christianity—or at least Protestantism—and the Enlightenment were "almost always seen not as contradictory but as complementary."[5] But these were not the only parties to the alliance. Insofar as it was also influenced by the English heritage, it was shaped by a constitutional tradition whose roots lay deep in the Catholic Middle Ages.[6] Thus, as Ellis Sandoz shows, the American founding was rooted in an "eclectic synthesis" that "partook of the whole amplitude of Western civilization" and thus included "classical," "biblical," and "modern" elements.[7] Given the "eclectic" character of this synthesis, it is not surprising that, as Yuval Levin points out, the principles of American religious liberty "are themselves not perfectly coherent."[8]

Leaving aside pragmatic considerations (e.g., the necessity of securing civil peace in an environment of far-reaching religious pluralism) and America's

3. Ross Douthat, "Defining Religious Liberty Down," *New York Times*, July 29, 2012, https://www.nytimes.com/2012/07/29/opinion/sunday/douthat-defining-religious-liberty-down.html.

4. George Marsden, *The Twilight of the American Enlightenment* (New York: Basic Books, 2014), 121.

5. George Marsden, *Religion and American Culture*, 2nd ed. (Fort Worth, TX: Harcourt, 2001), 43.

6. On the premodern influences on the American founding, see Ellis Sandoz, *A Government of Laws: Political Theory, Religion and the American Founding* (Columbus: University of Missouri Press, 2001).

7. Sandoz, *Government of Laws*, xiii, 151.

8. Yuval Levin, "The Perils of Religious Liberty," *First Things* (February 2016): 31.

federal character, and at the risk of oversimplifying, one might say that the American idea of religious liberty had two intellectual tributaries. The first of these tributaries was the revolution in human self-understanding wrought by Christianity.

To begin with, there was the Christian distinction between the sacred and the secular, and the dyarchical understanding of society in which it issued. The social orders of the ancient world had a monistic character. As Ernest Barker reminds us, the small and intimate society of the *polis* "was something more than a political system"; its purposes "went far beyond the legal purpose of detailing and enforcing a body of rules for the control of legal relations." In fact, the *polis* "was State and Society in one, without distinction or differentiation; it was a single system of order, or a fused society-state." Thus it was simultaneously "a religious society," "an ethical society," "an economic concern for the purpose of production and trade," and "a cultural association for the common pursuit of beauty and truth."[9] As "an integrated system of social ethics, which realizes to the full capacity of its members and therefore claims their full allegiance,"[10] it was a "sovereign and all-inclusive association embracing and regulating" human life in all its dimensions: religious, moral, political, economic, familial, artistic, cultural, and scientific.[11] This compact and undifferentiated ontology of social life was characteristic of classical antiquity in general: while the empires of classical antiquity were certainly larger than the Greek *polis*, they shared its all-inclusive, all-embracing character.

Christianity pointed toward a different conception of man and society. In the Christian understanding, as Hugh of St. Victor wrote in the twelfth century,

> there are two lives, one earthly, the other heavenly, one corporeal, the other spiritual ... Each has its own good ... Therefore, in each ... life, powers were established ... The one power is therefore called secular, the other spiritual.... The earthly power has at its head the king. The spiritual power has as its head the supreme pontiff. All things that are earthly and made for the earthly life belong to the power of the king. All things that are spiritual and attributed to the spiritual life belong to the power of the supreme pontiff.[12]

9. Ernest Barker, *Principles of Social and Political Theory* (Oxford: Clarendon Press, 1951), 5–6.

10. "Introduction," in *The Politics of Aristotle,* ed. and trans. Ernest Barker (London: Oxford University Press, 1958), xlvii.

11. Barker, *Principles of Social and Political Theory,* 5.

12. Hugh of St. Victor, "De Sacramentis Christianae Fidei," in *The Crisis of Church and State*

The Christian distinction between the sacred and the secular issued in a dyarchical understanding of society. As John Courtney Murray pointed out, in sharp contrast to the monistic understanding of the structure of social life that prevailed in classical antiquity in which the *polis* (or empire) was simultaneously state, society, and church without distinction or differentiation, the Christian revolution issues in a radically different vision of society in which "the family of mankind . . . is to be organized in two societies, under two laws emanating from two authorities."[13] In the classic formulation of Pope Gelasius I: "Two there are, august Emperor, by which this world is governed, the sacred authority of priests and the royal power."[14]

Under the impact of this revolution, the *polis* or "empire" became the "state" and was forced to share the stage with a new social actor, the Church, an actor that claimed both a greater dignity than it and a God-given freedom vis-à-vis it. Now, in the formulation of *Gaudium et Spes*, "the political community and the Church" must be understood "mutually independent and self-governing" in "proper fields."[15] Deriving from the "divine mandate" conferred on the Church by Christ himself—and pertaining to the Church both "in her character as a spiritual authority, established by the Christ the Lord" and "in her character as a society of men" seeking "to live in society in accordance with the precepts of the Christian faith"—"the freedom of the Church," as *Dignitatis Humanae* (the Second Vatican Council's Declaration on Religious Freedom) affirms, is nothing less than "*the* fundamental principle" that governs "the relations between the Church and governments and the whole civil order."[16]

As Voegelin notes, moreover, insofar "as the spiritual destiny of man in the Christian sense cannot be represented on earth by the power organization of a political society," the state is now "radically de-divinized"—it becomes "temporal."[17] Under the Christian dispensation, in short, the state ceases to

---

1050–1300, ed. Brian Tierney (Englewood Cliffs, NJ: Prentice Hall, 1964; reprint, Toronto: University of Toronto Press, 1988), 94–95.

13. John Courtney Murray, "On the Structure of the Church-State Problem," in *The Catholic Church in World Affairs*, ed. Waldemar Gurian and M. A. Fitzsimmons (Notre Dame, IN: University of Notre Dame Press, 1954), 12.

14. Pope Gelasius, "Letter to Emperor Athanasius," in *Church and State in Early Christianity*, ed. Hugo Rahner (San Francisco: Ignatius Press, 1992), 174.

15. *Gaudium et Spes*, in *The Documents of Vatican II*, ed. Walter Abbott, SJ (New York: Crossroad, 1989), section 76, p. 288.

16. *Dignitatis Humanae*, in *Vatican II: The Conciliar and Post-Conciliar Documents*, section 13, p. 693.

17. Eric Voegelin, *The New Science of Politics* (Chicago: University of Chicago Press, 1952), 107.

be the ultimate milieu of human perfection or the authoritative interpreter or representative of man's nature and destiny, of God's will for humanity. It loses the responsibility for the care of souls and for shepherding man to his ultimate destiny. Indeed, there now exists a wide array of human concerns that lie beyond the jurisdiction of the state.

The result, as Francis Oakley observes, is "an almost wholly unprecedented reduction of the state to the position of a merely secular entity," and the appearance of "something new in the history of mankind, of a society in which the state is stripped of its age-old religious aura, and its overriding claims . . . [are] balanced and curtailed by the claims of a rival authority; a society distinguished therefore by an established institutional dualism and racked by the internal tensions resulting therefrom."[18] It is here that we discern the beginning of Western civilization's commitment to the ideal of the rule of law and limited government.[19]

But Christianity changed more than our understanding of the ontological structure of social life: it changed our understanding of man and of the individual's relationship to society. The Christian affirmation of the dignity and transcendent destiny of the individual human person broke, as Fustel de Coulanges pointed out in his classic study, the "absolute empire" of the city over the individual.[20] Individuals could no longer be viewed as mere instruments to be used for civic purposes and now must be treated as ends rather than means. By virtue of his transtemporal destiny, the human person now transcends the body politic and possesses a sacredness that must be respected. In light of this anthropology, as Glenn Tinder writes, "no one belongs at the bottom, enslaved, irremediably poor, consigned to silence."[21]

Furthermore, insofar as human beings were now understood as persons—beings who possess intelligence and free will and who are privileged to bear responsibility—it followed that a rightly ordered society could not treat human beings merely as passive elements in the ordering of social life but must respect the subjectivity and thus the freedom of the human person, "the fact

18. Francis Oakley, *Kingship and the Gods: The Western Apostasy*, 1968 Smith History Lecture (Houston: University of St. Thomas, 1968), 48–49.

19. As Francis Canavan notes, "the state and its organs of government . . . come to have limited powers because they have limited goals and functions." "John Courtney Murray and Vatican II," in *John Courtney Murray and the American Civil Conversation*, ed. Robert P. Hunt and Kenneth L. Grasso (Grand Rapids, MI: Eerdmans, 1992), 168.

20. Fustel de Coulanges, *The Ancient City* (Garden City, NY: Doubleday Anchor Books, n.d.), 394.

21. Glenn Tinder, *The Political Meaning of Christianity* (San Francisco: Harper, 1991), 32–33.

that," in Francis Canavan's words, "the person is a subject who acts, and this by his own free choice, rather than an object who is acted upon."[22]

This new understanding of the person, as Robert Louis Wilken has recently reminded us, has profound implications in the sphere of religion. Religion could no longer be seen as "simply an affair of ancient rituals and ceremonies; it has to do with an inner disposition." As Lactantius noted in the early fourth century, "the worship of God . . . requires full commitment and faith." Thus "it cannot be coerced. It is a matter to be dealt with by words not by blows. For it has to do with the will."[23]

Finally, the intellectual revolution spurred by Christianity also caused a far-reaching development in thinking about natural law. This idea long predated Christianity. Nevertheless, under the impact of Christianity, the natural law tradition flourished and received arguably its most developed expression. While not all expressions of the Christian tradition embraced the idea of natural law, there seems to be an affinity between the Christian vision of a divinely created and ordered universe and man as a creature made in the image and likeness of God, and the metaphysical realism that lies at the heart of the natural law tradition. In this view, as Murray writes, there exists "a rational order of truth and justice, which man does not create, since it is a reflection of the Eternal Reason of God, but which man can discover since he himself is made in the image of God."[24] Politics thus becomes part of the moral universe, law comes to be understood as an expression of reason rather than sheer will, and government is understood to be bound by the dictates of a universal and divinely ordained moral law accessible to human reason.

By stripping the state of its age-old religious aura, restricting its jurisdiction to temporal matters, compelling it to respect the independence and autonomy of the church, insisting on the dignity of the human person and the essential freedom of the act of faith, and fostering an approach to politics that subjects government to the dictates of a divinely ordained universal moral law, Christianity helped lay the groundwork not only for the emergence of the idea of religious liberty, but also more broadly to the ideal of limited, constitu-

22. Francis Canavan, "The Image of Man in Catholic Thought," in *Catholicism, Liberalism and Communitarianism*, ed. Kenneth L. Grasso, Gerard V. Bradley, and Robert P. Hunt (Lanham, MD: Rowman & Littlefield, 1995), 19.

23. Robert Louis Wilken, *The Christian Roots of Religious Freedom* (Milwaukee, WI: Marquette University Press, 2014), 15.

24. John Courtney Murray, "Freedom, Responsibility and the Law," *Catholic Lawyer* 2 (July 1956): 215.

tional government. To say this, it should be stressed, is not to suggest that all of this happened immediately. It took centuries for the social consequences of this new vision of man and the universe to be understood and even longer for these consequences to be successfully institutionalized, for older social forms and arrangements to be supplanted by newer ones.

Before moving to our second tributary, it is essential to emphasize four characteristics of this intellectual horizon that have far-reaching implications of the understanding of religious liberty in which it issues. The first is its insistence on *taking religion seriously*. Man, in this view, is *homo religious*, and as Peter Berger remarks, it would require "something close to a mutation of the species to extinguish" the "religious impulse for good."[25] Religion, moreover, is not only a central, essential, and foundational element in the lives of individuals, but also a central, essential, and foundational element of the social order. As Tocqueville notes, a functioning society requires a consensus—"for society to exist . . . all the minds of the citizens must always be brought and held together by some principal ideas. Indeed, "without common ideas" there could be no "social body."[26] This consensus, in turn, necessarily has a religious dimension:

> There is hardly any human action . . . that is not born out of a very general idea that men have conceived of God, of God's relationship with humanity, of the nature of their soul and of their duties toward their fellows. You cannot keep these ideas from being the common source from which all the rest flows.[27]

In Voegelin's formulation, a "social order" involves more than mere "pragmatic" considerations concerning "survival in the world" but must be ultimately understood as "an attunement of man with the order of being."[28]

Second, this view insists there is such a thing as religious truth, that this truth is of the utmost importance, and that the duties it imposes bind us unconditionally and take precedence over all other duties and commitments. As *Dignitatis Humanae* affirms, "it is in accordance with their dignity as per-

25. Peter Berger, "The Desecularization of the World: A Global Overview," in *The Desecularization of the World: Resurgent Religion and World Politics*, ed. Peter L. Berger (Washington, DC: Ethics and Public Policy Center, 1999), 13.

26. Alexis de Tocqueville, *Democracy in America,* ed. Eduardo Nolla, trans. James T. Schliefer (Indianapolis: Liberty Fund, 2010), vol. 2, part 1, chap. 2, p. 713.

27. Tocqueville, *Democracy in America*, vol. 2, part 1, chap. 5, p. 743.

28. Eric Voegelin, *The World of the Polis* (Baton Rouge: Louisiana State University Press, 1957), 2.

sons—that is, beings endowed with reason and free will and therefore privileged to bear personal responsibility—that all men are impelled by nature and bound by a moral obligation to seek the truth, especially religious truth. They are also bound to adhere to the truth, once it is known, and to order their whole lives in accord with the demands of truth."[29] Every man, in other words, "has the duty . . . to seek the truth in matters religious" and "to adhere to it" so "that he may come to God, for whom he was created"[30] In the New Testament's formulation, "We must obey God rather than men."[31]

The third is what might be called the social character of its understanding of religion. As Steven D. Smith observes, under the impact of Protestantism with its more individualistic ecclesiology, "the position and functions" of the church "came to be transferred to the individual and his or her conscience,"[32] and "the individual conscience [effectively] *became* the church."[33] In this way, the campaign to keep "the church independent of secular jurisdiction" was "partially rerouted into as a commitment to keeping the *conscience* free from secular control."[34] Nevertheless, even here the church remained a central and critically important religious and social institution, and religion was understood to have an essential communal and public dimension.

And insofar as religion necessarily has a public character, religious freedom necessarily encompasses the right to the public expression of religious beliefs and to the establishment of religiously inspired institutions. As *Dignitatis Humanae* puts it: "The social nature of man . . . requires that he should give external expression to his internal acts of religion: that he should share with others in matters religious; that he should profess his religion in community." Religious freedom thus encompasses the right to establish "religious communities" and to "establish educational, cultural, charitable and social organizations" inspired by faith, as well as the right of these communities to "govern themselves according to their own norms" and to publicly "witness" and bring their faith to bear on social and political matters.[35]

29. *Dignitatis Humanae*, 2, 679.

30. *Dignitatis Humanae*, 3, 680–81.

31. Acts 5:29.

32. Steven D. Smith, *The Disenchantment of Secular Discourse* (Cambridge, MA: Harvard University Press, 2010), 123.

33. Steven D. Smith, *The Rise and Decline of American Religious Freedom* (Cambridge, MA: Harvard University Press, 2014), 37.

34. Smith, *Disenchantment of Secular Discourse*, 123.

35. *Dignitatis Humanae*, 3, 681, and 4, 682–83.

Finally, there is this understanding of religious liberty's theological character: its roots in the Christian vision of reality. Its conception of human dignity, for example, is rooted in its vision of man as a being created in the image of God, united to God through the Incarnation, and called to eternal participation in the life of the persons of the Holy Trinity. Similarly, its distinction between the sacred and secular is rooted in Christ's injunction to render unto God what is God's and unto Caesar what is Caesar's, and God's establishment of the Church. As Charles Taylor notes, the concept of the "[s]ecular itself is a Christian term, that is, a word that finds its original meaning . . . in a Christian context," in the context of a vision of a divinely created, ordered, and governed universe.[36] "'The secular,'" as Nomi Stolzenberg points out, was "originally a *religious* concept" that "served the function of distinguishing religious from nonreligious domains. But nonreligious did not . . . exist outside the religious framework." Indeed, the spiritual and the secular "referred to different institutions, different jurisdictions." The secular world was simply "a specialized area of God's domain."[37]

Although they took centuries to emerge, Christian ideas about the distinction between church and state, the freedom of the church, the dignity of the human person, and the personal character of faith provided the materials out of which a distinctive understanding of religious liberty could be fashioned, provided the materials that, as Gerard V. Bradley notes, made such liberty not just "conceivable," but also "desirable."[38]

The Second Tributary: Enlightenment Liberalism

The second tributary is what might be called Enlightenment Liberalism. Now, the term *liberalism* is often used to designate a broad institutional orientation that encompasses a commitment to government that is limited in its scope, subject in its operations to the rule of law and incorporating in its public law guarantees to the protection of the rights of individuals and of the autonomy of the institutions of civil society. Inasmuch as these institutions and practices

36. Charles Taylor, "Modes of Secularism," in *Secularism and Its Critics* (New York: Oxford University Press, 2005), 32.

37. Nomi Stolzenberg, "The Profanity of Law," in *Law and the Sacred*, ed. Austin Sarat, Lawrence Douglas, and Martha Merrill Umphrey (Stanford, CA: Stanford University Press, 2007), 30–31, 73.

38. Gerard V. Bradley, "Beyond Murray's Articles of Peace and Faith," in *John Courtney Murray and the American Civil Conversation*, 199.

can be projected from the premises of a variety of different political philosophies, liberalism in this sense does not entail a commitment to a particular intellectual tradition, to what Rawls calls a particular "comprehensive doctrine."[39]

Enlightenment Liberalism in the sense I am employing the term here is more than just a commitment to a particular set of political practices. Rather, it is a particular model of politics originating in seventeenth-century England and associated with past thinkers like Hobbes, Locke, Kant, and Mill, and today's thinkers like Rawls, Nozick, and Dworkin. As Roberto Mangabeira Unger observes, for "its true nature" to be understood, Enlightenment Liberalism "must be seen all of a piece, not just as a set of doctrines about the disposition of power and wealth, but as a metaphysical model of mind and society," as a "metaphysical system," at the heart of which is found a body of premises about the nature of human person, the structure of reality, nature, and capabilities of human reason.[40]

The core premises constitutive of Enlightenment Liberalism as a distinctive intellectual tradition—in particular, its individualism, rationalism, and nominalism—do not entail a single position on the whole range of issues addressed by political theory; they do not tell us, for example, whether to embrace the nightwatchman state as opposed to the welfare state, monarchy as opposed to democracy, and the like. Nevertheless, the number of positions these premises allow for are "limited." They act to preclude certain options, "determine and limit the possibilities" of its political theorizing, and push the thought of its proponents in certain directions.[41]

The intellectual horizon against which Enlightenment Liberalism's thinking on religious liberty unfolds exhibits certain continuities with the Christian intellectual tradition. One thinks here immediately of its exaltation of the in-

39. John Rawls, *Political Liberalism,* expanded ed. (New York: Columbia University Press, 2005), 13 and passim.

40. Roberto Unger, *Knowledge and Politics* (New York: Free Press, 1975), 6, 11.

41. Unger, *Knowledge and Politics,* 6. This volume provides an insightful overview of the interplay of Enlightenment Liberalism's metaphysical commitments and its thinking about man and society. For briefer accounts, see Francis Canavan, "From Ockham to Blackmun," in *Courts and the Culture Wars,* ed. Bradley C. S. Watson (Lanham, MD: Lexington Books, 2002), 3–14; Kenneth L. Schmitz, "Is Liberalism Good Enough?," in *Liberalism and the Good,* ed. R. Bruce Douglass, Gerald M. Mara, and Henry Richardson (New York: Routledge, 1990), 86–104; and Schmitz, "Liberal Liberty and Human Freedom," *Chesterton Review* 20 (May–August 1994): 213–27. For a brilliant account of the impact of Enlightenment Liberalism's rationalism on its theory of politics, see Thomas A. Spragens Jr., *The Irony of Liberal Reason* (Chicago: University of Chicago Press, 1981).

dividual and the aura of sanctity with which liberal thinkers tend to surround the individual human person. But these continuities are not the whole story. As Christopher Dawson points out, liberalism must ultimately be seen as a "partial and one-sided" appropriation of the Christian tradition.[42] What liberalism did was to lay claim to certain of the human and cultural consequences of Christianity—above all, what might be called its "individualism"—while rejecting Christian doctrine and the broader vision of the nature and destiny of the human person which informed the Christian tradition. The result was something new and revolutionary. As Reinhold Niebuhr pointed out, for example, when transplanted to the soil of Enlightenment "rationalism," the Christian exaltation of the individual mutated into "a new concept of individual autonomy, which is known in neither classicism nor Christianity" and which takes "the idea of individuality beyond the limits set for in the faith . . . and by the idea of the creatureliness of man."[43]

Despite some elements of continuity, the intellectual horizon against which Enlightenment Liberalism's thinking on religious liberty unfolded differed in important respects from that against which Christian thinking on the subject unfolded. From the outset, for example, the former theories were far more individualistic in their focus than the latter. Not surprisingly, therefore, the result was theories of religious liberty that differed in important respects.

Locke's seminal theory of religious toleration provides a case in point. There are certainly elements of continuity. One thinks of the pivotal role played in Locke's doctrine of toleration by the distinction between church and state and the sacred and the temporal, and the freedom of the act of faith. The state, he argues, is "a society of men constituted only for the procuring, preserving, and advancing their own civil interests," by which he means "life, liberty, health, and indolency of body; and the possession of outward things, such as money, lands, houses, furniture." The church, in contrast, is "a free and voluntary society" of men who have joined "themselves together of their own accord" for "the public worshipping of God, in such manner as they judge acceptable to him, and effectual to the salvation of their souls."[44] Thus

42. Christopher Dawson, *Religion and the Modern State* (New York: Sheed & Ward, 1935), xxi.

43. Reinhold Niebuhr, *The Nature and Destiny of Man* (New York: Charles Scribner's Sons, 1941), 1:57, 1:61.

44. John Locke, *Letter Concerning Toleration*, in *The Works of John Locke*, vol. 6 (London: Thomas Tegg et al., 1823; reprint, Germany: Scientia Verlag Aalen, 1963), 9–10, 13.

"he jumbles Heaven and Earth together, the things most remote and opposite, who mixes these Societies; which are in their Original, End, Business, and in every thing, perfectly distinct, and infinitely different from each other."[45]

Likewise, he maintains that "true and saving religion consists in the inward persuasion of the mind without which nothing can be acceptable to God." Thus "if we are not fully satisfied in our own mind" that the religion we profess "is true and . . . well-pleasing unto God, such profession and such practice . . . are indeed great obstacles to our salvation."[46]

Furthermore, there is the vision of human dignity and equality that animates his whole political theory: his famous insistence that men are born free, equal, and independent, that they are "the workmanship of one omnipotent and infinitely wise maker" to whom they belong ("they are his property whose workmanship they are"), a status that confers upon them the "rights" to "life, liberty and estate."[47] As countless commentators have shown, the roots of this vision are found in Locke's Christian theology.[48]

Finally, there is the moral and metaphysical realism that undergirds Locke's account of political life. His political theory takes its bearings from a vision of created and a natural moral law discernable by human reason. As Locke insists in the *Essay*, "'Tis as certain that there is a God, as that the opposite Angles, made by the intersection of two straight Lines, are equal. There was never any rational creature, that set himself sincerely to examine the truth of these Propositions, that could fail to assent to them."[49] "The idea of a Supreme Being, infinite in power, goodness, and wisdom, whose Workmanship we are, and on whom we depend; and the Idea of ourselves, as understanding rational beings," in turn, "would, I suppose, if duly considered and pursued, afford such Foundations of our Duty and Rules of Action, as might place *Morality amongst the Sciences capable of demonstration.*"[50] This certainty about God and the "law of nature" lies at the heart of Lockean politics. As Thomas

45. Locke, *Letter Concerning Toleration*, 21.

46. Locke, *Letter Concerning Toleration*, 10–11.

47. John Locke, *Two Treatises of Government*, critical ed. with an introduction and scholarly apparatus by Peter Laslett (Cambridge: Cambridge University Press, 1963), Treatise 2, chap. 2, section 6, p. 311; and Treatise 2, chap. 7, section 87, p. 367.

48. See, e.g., Jeremy Waldron, *God, Locke and Equality: Christian Foundations in Locke's Political Thought* (Cambridge: Cambridge University Press, 2002).

49. John Locke, *An Essay Concerning Human Understanding*, ed. Peter Nidditch (Oxford: Clarendon Press, 1975), book 1, chap. 4, section 16, pp. 94–95.

50. Locke, *Essay Concerning Human Understanding*, book 4, chap. 3, section 18, p. 549.

A. Spragens remarks, removing them from Locke's political theory "would not be like deleting the olive from the martini; it would be like forgetting the gin."[51]

But there are strong elements of discontinuity as well. To give but a few illustrations, there is the underlying voluntarism and individulism that pervades Locke's political thought and his highly restricted conception of the state and its role in the overall scheme of human life. The state's jurisdiction is limited to men's "civil interests," understood as "life, liberty, health, and indolency of body; and the possession of outward things, such as money, lands, houses, furniture."[52]

The same voluntarism and individualism permeate his account of the church as well.

"The care of each man's salvation," he writes, "belongs only to himself."[53] This individualism fnds expression in an ecclesiology that reduces the church to a purely human institution whose sole foundation is human consent which plays no essential role in the economy of salvation. "No body," he insists, "is born a Member of any Church" or "by nature is bound unto any particular Church or Sect." For Locke, the church is simply "a free and voluntary" society of men who have joined "together of their own accord in order to then public worshipping of God." While "some enter into company for trade and profit: others, for want of business, have their clubs for claret. Neighborhood joins some, and religion others."[54]

For Locke, as Fraser writes, visible churches were "accidents of religion, not part of its essence, which in personal faith and conduct, and might flourish under any ecclesial organization or even apart from all organized religious societies."[55] Not surprisingly, given his ecclesiology, Locke's account leaves little or no room for a sacramental understanding of religion. His approach here can be gleaned from his remark that "there is no Civil Injury done unto the excommunicated Person, by the Church-Minister's refusing him that Bread and Wine, in the Celebration of the Lord's Supper, which was not bought with his, but other mens Money."[56] He seems deeply suspicious of any church

51. Spragens, *Irony of Liberal Reason*, 206.
52. Locke, *Letter Concerning Toleration*, 9–10.
53. Locke, *Letter Concerning Toleration*, 41.
54. Locke, *Letter Concerning Toleration*, 13, 49.
55. Alexander Campbell Fraser, *Locke* (Philadelphia: J. B. Lippincott, 1890), 68.
56. Locke, *Letter Concerning Toleration*, 17.

making exclusive claims to the possession of religious truth or the means of salvation, or which is hierarchical in form or dogmatic in doctrine.

Likewise, there is Locke's understanding of the epistemological status of religious faith. While Locke maintains that "there is but one truth, one way, to heaven,"[57] the fact is that "to certain knowledge of the true religion," we "can in this world never arrive."[58] We must distinguish, Locke insists, between "knowledge," "properly so-called," and mere "belief" or "opinion." Knowledge, in the strict sense of the term, he argues, is restricted to those "truths" that are either "self-evident" or capable of "strict demonstration," and "matters of fact."[59] The highly limited scope of human knowledge becomes apparent when it is reflected that by "strict demonstration," by which Locke means demonstration in accordance with the canons of a highly rationalistic and rigorously mathematical model of reason. Our knowledge of matters of fact is also highly restricted: "matters of fact are not capable of being any way known but to the bystanders."[60] Matters of fact are known, in the strict sense of the this term, only to actual eyewitnesses to them. Belief, however, is synonymous with faith or opinion and means, "any degree of persuasion even to the highest degree of assurance." Thus "believing [even] in the highest degree of assurance, is not knowledge."[61]

A revealed religion's claim to truth rests upon not self-evident propositions but upon matters of historical fact. Christianity's claim to truth, for instance, is built upon a historical event, namely "that Jesus Christ was put to death at Jerusalem and rose again from the dead." "Now," asks Locke, "do you or I *know* this?" Inasmuch as we ourselves were not eyewitnesses to these events, we do not actually know that these events took place. We *believe* that they did, based upon the testimony of individuals who say that they witnessed them. Thus no matter how "well grounded" our faith in a particular revealed religion is, "faith it is still, and not knowledge, persuasion and not certainty. This is the highest the nature of the thing will permit us to go in matters of revealed

57. Locke, *Letter Concerning Toleration*, 12.

58. John Locke, *A Fourth Letter for Toleration*, in *The Works of John Locke*, vol. 6 (London: Thomas Tegg et al., 1823; reprint, Germany: Scientia Verlag Aalen, 1963), 566.

59. John Locke, *A Third Letter for Toleration*, in *The Works of John Locke*, vol. 6 (London: Thomas Tegg et al., 1823; reprint, Germany: Scientia Verlag Aalen, 1963), 424.

60. Locke, *Third Letter for Toleration*, 424.

61. Locke, *Fourth Letter for Toleration*, 558.

religion."[62] The doctrines of revealed religion are thus relegated to the sphere of subjective opinion.

Finally, Locke's account of religious liberty focuses on the right of individuals to profess their faith and to join with others to worship in accordance with its dictates. There is no mention of the right to establish institutions in which they may join for the purpose of ordering their own lives in accordance with their religious principles, create institutions (be they charitable, social, educational, etc.) inspired and organized in accordance with their faith, or to seek to show the value of their religious vision for the organization of society. As Levin writes, Locke

> extended a generous free exercise right to individuals but not to institutions with a religious character that were not houses of worship, because public institutions—indeed the public square as such—were to have a particular religious character. You can have your own beliefs about God and what He demands of you in such a society, and you can have a fair amount of room to live by those as a private individual. You can even have houses of worship where people like you can congregate and utter various heresies together in peace. But you cannot create other institutions that serve as embodiments of that religion in the society's broader life. *You can say but not do.*[63]

These differences have been amplified over time by the trajectory in which the implications of Enlightenment Liberalism's core premises have pushed its thinking. For our present purposes, I will limit myself to mentioning three of these directions. To begin with, these premises have pushed Enlightenment Liberalism toward a progressively more thoroughgoing, more radical individualism. As Michael Walzer has noted, liberalism is a "strange" and "self-subverting" doctrine that "seems to continually undercut itself . . . and to produce in each generation renewed hopes for a more absolute freedom from history and society alike. Much of liberal political theory from Locke to Rawls, is an effort to fix and stabilize the doctrine in order to end the endlessness of liberal liberation."[64] These efforts have failed, however, and as a result, the

62. Locke, *Third Letter for Toleration*, 144.

63. Yuval Levin, "The Church of the Left," *National Review*, April 3, 2015, https://www.nationalreview.com/corner/church-left-yuval-levin/; my emphasis.

64. Michael Walzer, "The Communitarian Critique of Liberalism," *Political Theory* 18 (February 1999): 14.

history of Enlightenment liberal thought is largely the story of the triumph of will: the triumph of liberalism's commitment to the autonomy of the individual over those elements in liberal thought that had originally restrained it.[65]

This trajectory finds signal expression in the ascendancy of what might be called the liberalism of the sovereign self. From the perspective of this liberalism, as Michael Sandel writes, human beings are viewed as "unencumbered selves," "free and independent" selves who are unbound by "ends we have not chosen—ends given by nature or God, for example, or by identities as members of families, peoples, cultures, or traditions." The self is thus "installed as sovereign, cast as the author of the only obligations that constrain."[66]

A human being, in this view, is simply a sovereign will, an arbitrary center of volition, free to make of himself (or herself) and the world whatever he (or she) chooses. Elevating choice to the status of the human good, this liberalism finds expression in a political morality that, in Taylor's words, affords "absolutely central importance to the freedom to choose one's own mode of life."[67]

From this individualism follows a radically voluntarist conception of social relations. As Canavan notes, Enlightenment Liberalism's nominalism makes it "hard [for it] to entertain the notion of relations as natural." Social relations are understood as external, accidental, adventitious, and contractual, as the essentially arbitrary products of the wills and interests of naturally autonomous individuals. This ontology deprives social institutions of any determinate character and requires that they be understood—and treated in law and public policy—as temporary aggregations of individuals united for reasons of mutual utility.[68] From this perspective, solidaristic communities and institutions—for which religion is a fertile soil—represent potential threats to individual autonomy.

While many proponents of Enlightenment Liberalism have championed a sharply limited state and afforded a central role to markets in ordering social life, the inner dynamism of its commitment to individual autonomy impels it

65. See Kenneth L. Grasso, "The Triumph of Will: Rights Mania, the Culture of Death, and the Crisis of Enlightenment Liberalism," in *A Moral Enterprise: Essays in Honor of Francis Canavan*, ed. Kenneth L. Grasso and Robert P. Hunt (Wilmington, DE: ISI Books, 2002), 221–43.

66. Michael J. Sandel, *Democracy's Discontent: America in Search of a Public Philosophy* (Cambridge, MA: Belknap Press of Harvard University Press, 1996), 12.

67. Charles Taylor, "Atomism," in *Philosophy and the Human Sciences* (Cambridge: Cambridge University Press, 1985), 196.

68. Francis Canavan, *The Pluralist Game: Pluralism, Liberalism and the Moral Conscience* (Lanham, MD: Rowman & Littlefield, 1995), 121.

to employ government both to equalize everyone's chance to live the lifestyle of their choice and to secure the autonomy of the individual in the face of institutions and communities that might endanger it. From the perspective of Enlightenment Liberalism, as Philip Abbott notes, "groups that threaten to close off full and complete individuality" must "be regulated or banned."[69] The state thus expands to emancipate individuals from the claims of solidaristic social institutions.

At the same time, its rationalist conception of reason pushes Enlightenment Liberalism toward a thoroughgoing naturalism. As Murray notes, "the unidimensionality" of the Enlightenment's rationalism leads through "an ineluctable logical process" to a "secularist philosophic monism" that "denies to man, his nature or its law all transcendental reference."[70] In this view, nothing exists beyond—or outside of—the astrophysical universe. It is no accident that the Enlightenment marked the beginning of what one author called "the godless age."[71]

Simultaneously, its rationalism pushes Enlightenment Liberalism toward an ever deeper moral skepticism. Even though many of its early proponents were moral cognitivists, Enlightenment Liberalism's nominalism drives it toward what Spragens describes as value non-cognitivism and what Alasdair MacIntyre describes as moral emotivism.[72] They push it inexorably toward the conclusion that moral judgments express nothing more than individual preferences. In this view, as Canavan notes, "truth is simply what the individual thinks is true," and the "good is only what the individual personally prefers."[73]

If from the beginning theories of religious liberty projected from the premises of Enlightenment rationalism differed in significant respects from those informed by the Christian tradition, these differences have become

69. Philip Abbott, "Liberalism and Social Invention," in *The Liberal Future*, ed. Philip Abbott and Michael B. Levy (Westport: CT: Greenwood Press, 1985), 70.

70. John Courtney Murray, *We Hold These Truths: Catholic Reflections on the American Proposition* (New York: Sheed & Ward, 1960; reprint, Lanham, MD: Rowman & Littlefield, 2005), 323.

71. Lester Crocker, "Presidential Address," in *The Modernity of the Eighteenth Century*, ed. Louis T. Milic (Cleveland, OH: Case Western Reserve University Press, 1971), xviii.

72. See Spragens, *Irony of Liberal Reason*; and Alasdair MacIntyre, *After Virtue*, 2nd ed. (Notre Dame, IN: University of Notre Dame Press, 1984). As Spragens remarks, "epistemological revolutions, like their political counterparts, sometimes devour their own children" (212–13). On the tension between Locke's political theory and his epistemology, see Spragens, *Irony of Liberal Reason*, 203–13.

73. Canavan, *Pluralist Game*, 133.

more pronounced over time by virtue of liberalism's growing secularism, value non-cognitivism, and individualism.

Shedding the theological framework that informed Locke's work, the former theories have assumed a highly secular character, in the modern sense of the term. Now, as Smith remarks, "rather than denoting one realm within an encompassing and ultimately 'religious' reality, secular now describes a comprehensive view of life and the world—a view in which the 'spiritual' or the 'holy' or the 'supernatural' are denied . . . or at least reduced to worldly terms." As far as our understanding of religious liberty is concerned, the results of this new conceptual framework are nothing less than revolutionary. Dissolving the categories of the spiritual and secular or temporal dissolves "the classical problem of church and state." Religious liberty now ceases to be a jurisdictional matter, a question of the respective roles—the respective spheres—of church and state in the overall economy of human existence. At the same time, rather than the two sovereign authorities of which Gelasius spoke, there is now only "one": the state is sovereign, and the "church" becomes simply another voluntary association within it. Thus "the problem of *jurisdiction*" gives way to "a problem of *justice.*"[74]

Moreover, as Canavan points out, this problem of justice will necessarily be conceptualized in a highly individualistic fashion, in terms of a social ontology that views social relations as something "artificial, external, and contractual," which sees the individual human being "as an atom to whom violence is done if he is subjected to a relationship with other humans he [or she] has not chosen," which reduces the political problem to the relationship of "the sovereign state and the sovereign individual" and which is suspicious—even hostile—to "strong, lasting and cohesive communities."[75]

Theories of religious liberty informed by Enlightenment Liberalism's secularism and subjectivism, furthermore, tend to reflect a certain skepticism toward the transcendent, the supernatural, and the miraculous, as well as a distrust of metaphysics and religious truth claims. These theories exhibit a suspicion of religion as such, tending to see it as a source of superstition, alienation, and oppression. Rejecting religious truth claims and thus relegating religious beliefs to what is sometimes called the sandbox of subjectivity, they tend to be particularly hostile to what Smith calls "strong religion"—namely,

74. Smith, *The Disenchantment of Secular Discourse,* 129, 130, 131, my emphasis.

75. Canavan, *Pluralist Game,* 102.

the type of religion that insists that "some people's deeply held beliefs are true while others are false," that "some people are saved and others are not," and that "some ways of living are acceptable to God while others are abhorrent."[76]

In this view, religion—or at least religion that locates the sacred beyond space and time—is something that the human race must leave behind on the road to maturity, enlightenment, and freedom, something that humanity must—and will inevitably—outgrow. And while some people may still feel an emotional or psychological need for the comforts and certainties provided by religious faith, religion must be seen as a purely personal matter concerning only the emotions and conscience of the individual, "a sort of essence . . . or ambient aura that may help to warm the hidden heart of solitary man" in Murray's formulation, but that in the interim between now and its final disappearance must be privatized—restricted to the private realm and strictly forbidden to impinge on public life.[77]

The Triumph of Enlightenment Liberalism and American Religious Liberty

Before turning to America, there are two final points that should be mentioned. The first is that neither theories of religious liberty projected from Christian foundations nor those projected from the premises of Enlightenment Liberalism are neutral in either inspiration or effect. Both embody a broader vision of man and the universe, and both take their bearings from a particular account of the nature of man, the human good, the proper structure of human social relations, the proper role of the state in the overall economy of human social life, the nature and epistemological status of religious truth, and the proper organization of man's spiritual life. These accounts, in turn, lead to public orders that embody different understandings of the human person and human life. These public orders embody public moral judgements and, as Canavan points out, act to set "norms for the whole society," to create "an environment in which everyone has to life," and to exert "a powerful influence on social institutions."[78]

The second is that both theories necessarily place limits on what is en-

76. Smith, *Rise and Decline of American Religious Freedom*, 153.
77. Murray, *We Hold These Truths*, 21.
78. Canavan, *Pluralist Game*, 76.

compassed by a "right to religious freedom," on what such a right means in practice. "In practice," as MacIntyre remarks, "every group sets a limit to its tolerance and in one way or another enforces that limit"; religious liberty is no exception.[79] Locke, for example, may affirm "the duty of toleration," but this duty does not extend to actions done in the name of religion that would "not" be "lawful in "the ordinary course of life" (such as "promiscuous uncleanness" or the "sacrifice [of] infants"); or to religious "opinions contrary to human society, or to those moral rules which are necessary to the preservation of civil society" (the ranks of which include, among other things, Catholicism and atheism).[80] The issue, in short, is not whether there should be limits but what those limits should be. That, in turn, leads us back to the intellectual horizon within each of the theories operate.

Although these points may seem obvious, they need to be emphasized because of the proclivity of some liberal thinkers to assert its alleged neutrality on the question of the human good and of commentators of all stripes to invoke religious liberty as if it was a univocal concept. As MacIntyre and others have pointed out, Enlightenment Liberalism "does indeed have its own broad conception of the good, which it is engaged in imposing politically, legally, socially and economically wherever it has the power to do so."[81] And, as our contemporary debates suggest, there are clearly different understandings of the nature and scope of religious liberty at play in our public life, rooted in divergent understandings of man and the universe.

Against this backdrop, we can begin to come to grips with the contemporary crisis of American religious liberty. The American experiment in self-government and ordered liberty was launched by an alliance between the heirs of the Reformation and the devotees of the Enlightenment. Indeed, as George Marsden pointed out, in early America the two were "almost always seen not as contradictory but as complementary."[82] What made possible this alliance and what Mark Noll terms the "Protestant-Enlightenment synthesis"

79. Alasdair MacIntrye, "Toleration and the Goods of Conflict," in *Ethics and Politics: Selected Essays*, vol. 2 (Cambridge: Cambridge University Press, 2006), 207.

80. John Locke, *Letter Concerning Toleration*, 33, 45. As Voegelin points out, a Lockean society rests on "careful equilibrium between tolerance and intolerance." "Industrial Society in Search of Reason," in *The Collected Works of Eric Voegelin*, vol. 11, *Published Essays, 1953–1965*, ed. Ellis Sandoz (Columbia: University of Missouri Press, 2000), 182

81. Alasdair MacIntrye, *Whose Justice? Which Rationality?* (Notre Dame, IN: University of Notre Dame Press, 1988), 336.

82. George Marsden, *Religion and American Culture*, 2nd ed. (Fort Worth, TX: Harcourt, 2001), 43.

in which it found intellectual expression—an alliance and synthesis that endured well into the twentieth century—was the conservative form that the Enlightenment took in the English-speaking world (as evidenced by the embrace by even deists in the founding era of both moral cognitivism and a secularized version of Christian morality).[83] The American understanding of religious liberty, in turn, took shape against the background of this alliance and was rooted in an amalgam of Christian and Enlightenment principles. Hence the ambiguity that was spoken of earlier. While drawing on the ancient Christian distinction between the spiritual and temporal orders, it was also shaped by the religious individualism and anticlericalism of Enlightenment Liberalism. As Smith observes, although both traditions might use similar language—for example, church and state, religious liberty, and so on—"such language is apt to mislead."[84] It obscures the different meanings each tradition attributes to the terminology both employ and the radically different conceptions of man, society, and the very structure of reality that inform these meanings.

In the course of American history, however, the cultural landscape has changed, and the conflict between the two rival traditions has come into sharp relief. On the one hand, we have the collapse of what might be called American Christendom. As Marsden recently observed, even during the religious revival of the 1950s, American culture was "strikingly secular." In fact, "the underlying beliefs of most Americans, even though they might be expressed in Christian terms," had become "essentially secular," and the "privatization [of religion] was already far advanced."[85] In the decades since, these trends have only intensified. One thinks in this context of the rise of "nones," the deep-seated skepticism of organized religion among the young, the ascendancy of what is sometimes called "moralistic therapeutic deism," and the intensifying efforts to restrict religion—or at least Christianity and Judaism as they have been traditionally understood—to the private sphere.[86]

83. For accounts that emphasize the conservative character of the American Enlightenment, see Henry F. May, *The Enlightenment in America* (Oxford: Oxford University Press, 1069), and Gertrude Himmelfarb, *The Roads to Modernity* (New York: Vintage, 2004).

84. Smith, *Disenchantment of Secular Discourse*, 132.

85. Marsden, *Twilight of the American Enlightenment*, 106, 111–12.

86. For an overview of the decline of Christianity in America and rise of the "nones," see "In U.S., the Decline of Christianity Continues at a Rapid Pace," Pew Research Center, October 17, 2019, https://www.pewforum.org/2019/10/17/in-u-s-decline-of-christianity-continues-at-rapid-pace/. On "moralistic therapeutic deism," see Christian Smith, "On 'Moralistic Therapeutic Deism' as U.S. Teenagers' Actual,

Indeed, as two sociologists of religion have recently pointed out, survey data suggest that while "levels of religious involvement in the United States remain high by world standards," religiosity has in fact "been declining in the United States for decades, albeit slowly and from high levels," and "religious commitment" has been "weakening from one generation to the next." These trends are now so pronounced that America can "no longer be considered" a "decisive counterexample to the secularization thesis."[87]

While many Americans remain devout, today we have experienced the collapse of America's Christian culture. While Christianity continues to be a force in the lives of many Americans, it no longer decisively molds our public culture. Culturally speaking, we live in a largely post-Christian social universe. As Wilken wrote in 2004, "if one uses any measure other than individual adherence (what people say if asked) or even church attendance, it is undeniable that the influence of Christianity on the life and mores of our society is on the wane." Indeed, in the course of his lifetime, the Western world has experienced nothing less than "the collapse of Christian civilization," and "if at first the process of disintegration was slow," it has now "moved into overdrive."[88]

The second development consists in the simultaneous cultural ascendancy and radicalization of the Enlightenment tradition. As described above, the inner dynamism of ideas constitutive of Enlightenment Liberalism as a distinct intellectual tradition have driven it progressively further away from the Judeo-Christian ethic and progressively toward an ethic of human autonomy, a thoroughgoing anthropocentrism.[89] What we have witnessed over the past half century, in short, is not merely the triumph of the Enlightenment strain in American culture over the Christian strain, but the triumph of the Enlightenment strain in a thoroughly radical form, in the form of today's liberalism of the sovereign self.

Our thinking about religious liberty—or at least the thinking of our cultural elites about religious liberty—today unfolds against the backdrop of the

Tacit, de Facto Religious Faith," in *Princeton Lectures on Youth, Church, and Culture, 2005* (Princeton, NJ: Princeton Theological Seminary, 2005).

87. David Voas and Mark Chaves, "Is the United States a Counterexample to the Secularization Thesis?," *American Journal of Sociology* 121, no. 5 (March 2017): 1548.

88. Robert Louis Wilken, "The Church as Culture," *First Things* (April 2004): 32, 31.

89. For accounts of the underlying unity of Enlightenment thought and of the radical (and largely unanticipated) consequences, see Spragens, *Irony of Liberal Reason*; and Lester G. Crocker, *Nature and Culture: Ethical Thought in the French Enlightenment* (Baltimore: Johns Hopkins University Press, 1963).

intellectual horizon of the radical Enlightenment. The consequences of this are nothing short of revolutionary. As we have seen, this means what Bradley calls "the end of church and state,"[90] in the sense of the dissolution of the foundational categories that have informed Western culture's thinking on the subject of religious liberty since the advent of Christianity. Now, rather than discussions of religious liberty focusing on the proper jurisdictions of two divinely ordained institutions—church and state—they take place in the context of a disenchanted universe and a monistic social ontology in which there is but one authoritative institution—the state—and in which man and society are understood in radically individualistic terms.

From this perspective, as Murray writes, "it is within the 'secular state' and by appeal to secular sources that man is to find the interpretation of his own nature and the means to his own destiny." We thus arrive at a vision of the social world in which there is "One Society, with One Law, and with One Sovereign, the politically equal people."[91] In this social universe, churches are nothing more than voluntary associations subject to the regulation of the state, in principle no different from the local Little League or youth soccer association.

What this means, furthermore, is that *religious* liberty ceases to be a distinct category and becomes subsumed in the right to free speech or expressive liberty. Unfolding against the backdrop of a culture informed by a Christian vision of man and the universe, the First Amendment specifically refers to the "free exercise" of religion and implicitly distinguishes it from freedom of speech, freedom of the press, and so forth in the process suggesting that there's something unique about religious liberty. It unfolded, in other words, against the backdrop of a culture informed by a Christian vision of man and the universe, and in which even the few who rejected Christian revelation nevertheless professed some type of ethical monotheism. It took its bearings, in other words, from the idea that there was a God who created man and that, in Madison's words, "every man" has "the duty ... to render ... homage to the Creator such homage and such only as he believes acceptable to him" a "duty [that] is precedent, both in order of time and in degree of obligation, to the claims of Civil Society."[92] In this framework, religious liberty emerges

90. See Gerard V. Bradley, "Church Autonomy in the Constitutional Order: The End of Church and State," *Louisiana Law Review* 49 (1989): 1057–87.

91. Murray, *We Hold These Truths*, 194.

92. James Madison, "A Memorial and Remonstrance against Religious Assessments," in *The Sacred*

as a distinctive and uniquely important form of liberty. Absent it, however, religious freedom is reduced to simply a form of speech or expressive liberty, losing its unique importance, and thus it may be easily overridden in the name of other social goods.

Simultaneously, the naturalism and ethos of radical self-creation that informs this horizon ushers in what Kent Greenawalt describes as "a hostility or sceptical indifference to religion that amounts to a thinly disguised contempt for belief in any reality beyond that discoverable by scientific inquiry."[93] This, in turn, makes it hard for theories unfolding within this horizon to take seriously religion and the religious commitments of believers. Indeed, it ushers in a deep suspicion of religion as a product of ignorance and a source of superstition and oppression. At a minimum, by reducing religion to a matter of subjective opinion or mere feeling, this horizon trivializes religion, reducing it to the status of a mere lifestyle option, nothing more than a hobby analogous to the fondness for golf, stamp collecting, or, as Justice Scalia famously noted, pornography;[94] and the religious commitments of believers, in Sandel's apt formulation, to a matter of choice rather than of conscience.[95]

The thoroughgoing individualism of Enlightenment Liberalism, in turn, causes religion and religious liberty to be conceptualized in a highly individualistic manner. One cannot help but think here of William James's definition of religion as "the feelings, acts and experiences of individual men in their solitude, so far as they apprehend themselves to stand in relation to whatever they may consider the divine."[96] As a result, it produces theories of religious liberty that give short shrift to the social and communal dimensions of religious belief and practice, and thus to religious liberty's social and communal dimensions.

Indeed, not only do theories of religious liberty inspired by Enlightenment Liberalism display a deep-seated blindness to the communal dimension of reli-

---

Rights of Conscience: Selected Readings on Religious Liberty and Church-State Relations in the American Founding, ed. Daniel L. Driesbach and Mark David Hall (Indianapolis: Liberty Fund, 2009), 309.

93. Ken Greenawalt, "Religious Convictions and Lawmaking," *Michigan Law Review* 84 (1985): 356.

94. Lee v. Weisman, 505 U.S. 645 (1992).

95. Michael Sandel, "Freedom of Conscience or Freedom of Choice?," in *Articles of Faith, Articles of Peace: The Religious Liberty Clauses and the American Public Philosophy*, ed. James Davison Hunter and Os Guinness (Washington, DC: Brookings Institution, 1990).

96. William James, *The Varieties of Religious Experience* (Harmondsworth, UK: Penguin, 1882), 31. One also thinks in this context of Whitehead's famous definition of religion as "what the individual does with his solitariness." Alfred North Whitehead, *Religion in the Making* (New York: Macmillan, 1926; reprint, New York: Fordham University Press, 1996), 16.

gious belief, but they also issue in a profound distrust of institutional religion, especially of "strong" religion in an institutional setting. Enlightenment Liberalism's generalized fear of strong, cohesive communities merges with its suspicion of religion as such (especially "strong" religion) to issue in a fear of religion and religious groups as threats to individual autonomy and to the unity and stability of a liberal polity. By virtue of their rejection of some lifestyles and choices, they represent a fundamentally immoral assault on the dignity of others. They are threats to individual autonomy not only because they may shape the making of law and public policy but also because at the deepest level they embody a mistaken and destructive understanding of the human good. By elevating obedience to God above individual self-determination, by rejecting Enlightenment Liberalism's elevation of autonomy to the status of the human good, they psychologically cripple individuals and threaten, in Douthat's phrase, "all that is good and decent."[97] Hence Enlightenment Liberalism's implacable hostility to traditional Christianity and to strong religion more generally.

In any case, since religion is by definition a purely individual, private, personal, and subjective matter, it concerns—or ought to concern—only the conscience and feelings of the individual alone. It follows that religious liberty consists simply in the freedom of worship and belief. It does not extend to institutions other than those that exist simply to worship or express religious belief. Levin, for example, notes how this "highly individualistic understanding of the right of conscience and of the protection of religious practice" informs the Obama administration's Health and Human Services (HHS) mandate. Under these rules, an institution could qualify for a religious exemption only "if 'the inculcation of religious values is the purpose of the organization,' if it 'primarily employs people who share the religious tenets of the organization,' and if it 'serves primarily persons who share the religious tenets of the organization.'" Thus "only houses or worship, or institutions that otherwise serve the direct expression . . . of articles of faith" would qualify for an exemption. Religious liberty would not extend to religious charities, schools, hospitals, and adoption agencies, much less "private institutions run by religious people in the service of their convictions."[98] The free exercise of religion becomes the freedom of the individual to believe whatever he or she chooses and to join with others in wor-

97. Ross Douthat, "Defining Religious Liberty Down," *New York Times*, July 29, 2012, https://www.nytimes.com/2012/07/29/opinion/sunday/douthat-defining-religious-liberty-down.html.

98. Levin, "Perils of Religious Liberty," 31, 32.

ship. It does not extend to the rights of religious groups to establish charities and educational institutions ordered in accordance with their beliefs, much less the right of individuals to operate businesses in accordance with them.

Not surprisingly, given this understanding of religion, these theories culminate in the demand for what is sometimes called "the privatization of religion," in the prohibition of governmental policies that aid or endorse religion, and in the systematic exclusion of religion (and religiously informed moral belief) from public life.[99] They culminate, in other words, in the establishment of what Richard John Neuhaus memorably termed "the naked public square"—the establishment of a public square hermetically sealed to "particularist religious and moral belief."[100]

Since religion, in this view, is a wholly private matter, it has no place in the affairs of the city. While some individuals may feel an emotional or psychological need for the comfort and certainty provided by religious faith and should be free to embrace whatever religion they choose, religious beliefs must be checked at the door of the public square, confined to what Justice Rutledge once called "the kingdom of the individual man and his God" or, at most, to the hushed confines of the sacristy.[101] Public religion—religion that in Jose Casanova's words "has, assumes, or tries to assume a public character, function, or role"[102]—is incompatible with the nature of authentic religion, the demands of justice, and the personal autonomy of others.

A New Orthodoxy

As Robert P. Hunt points out, while theories of religious liberty informed by Enlightenment Liberalism may speak the language of diversity, toleration, inclusion, and respect and hold the very idea of an orthodoxy to be anathema, these theories ultimately represent "not an alternative to orthodoxy but an alternative orthodoxy."[103] In a public order informed by these theories—namely,

99. Gerard V. Bradley, "Dogmatomachy: A Privatization Theory of the Religion Cases," *St. Louis Law Journal* 30 (1986): 275–330.

100. Richard John Neuhaus, *The Naked Public Square: Religion and American Democracy* (Grand Rapids, MI: Eerdmans, 1984), 89.

101. Everson v. Board of Education, 330 U.S. 1, 57–58 (1947).

102. Jose Casanova, "What Is Public Religion?," in *Religion Returns to the Public Square*, ed. Hugh Heclo and Wilfred McClay (Washington, DC: Woodrow Wilson Center Press, 2003), 32.

103. Robert P. Hunt, "Moral Orthodoxy and the Procedural Republic," in *John Courtney Murray and the American Civil Conversation*, 270.

the ethic of the sovereign self and the vision of man and society, the universe, the nature and scope of human knowledge, and the like—occupies a privileged (a quasi-established) position: it alone orders the community's common life; it alone superintends the making of law and public policy; and it alone supplies both the idiom and conceptual framework informing the community's public argument. In such a public order, Enlightenment Liberalism enjoys the status of an established doctrine, a public orthodoxy.

This in turn means that this ethic determines the understanding of the nature of religion and religious liberty—and hence the limits of religious liberty—operative in the public square. It determines, in other words, what other goods—such as nondiscrimination, equal concern and respect, and individual autonomy—trump the free exercise of religion, when the state is authorized to use force to prevent people from acting in accordance with their religious convictions or to compel them to act in a manner contrary to those convictions. Given its understanding of the nature of religious liberty (as extending only to worship and belief), the scope afforded for the free exercise of religion will be narrow indeed. One thinks here both of the Obama administration's infamous HHS mandate and the US Civil Rights Commission's 2016 insistence that "religious exemptions to the protections of civil rights based upon classifications such as race, color, national origin, sex, disability status, sexual orientation, and gender identity ... significantly infringe upon" the civil rights of other citizens.[104] One also thinks here of the increasing legal pressures being brought to bear on Catholic adoption agencies, foster care providers, hospitals, and more, and of the financial pressures that governmental funding allows it to bring on private institutions.

Orthodoxies, of course, are not only enforced by state coercion, but by social and economic pressure as well. As Megan McCardle notes, orthodoxies are usually "largely self-enforcing, transmitted by a million little social signals you absorb without noticing, and enforced by the ubiquitous fear of what the neighbors will think."[105]

This orthodoxy, furthermore, extends not merely to actions but also to beliefs. Insisting that people are "harmed not just by discriminatory *actions*,

104. US Commission on Civil Rights, *Peaceful Coexistence: Reconciling Nondiscrimination Principles with Civil Liberties. Briefing Report* (Washington, DC: US Commission on Civil Rights, 2016), 25.

105. Megan McCardle, "Meet Your New Woke Inquisitors, Same as the Old Ones," *Washington Post*, April 25, 2019, https://www.washingtonpost.com/opinions/2019/04/25/wokeness-isnt-cultural-socialism-or-religious-zealotry-it-sure-is-an-orthodoxy/.

or even by *words*, but by *beliefs*." As Smith notes, this ideology "is not content to regulate outward conduct but instead seeks to penetrate into hearts and minds."[106] What is demanded here is not an ethos of live and let live, but an ethic of affirmation in which the choices, values, and lifestyles of individuals are affirmed and celebrated. In this view, strong disapproval of someone's self-chosen lifestyle—the view that it is a violation of the moral law, contrary to the will of God, and so on—constitutes an injury and an injustice. One thinks here of Hillary Clinton's famous insistence that the political morality of the sovereign self demands that "deep-seated cultural codes, [and] religious beliefs" be "changed."[107]

In a society that embraces it, the ethic of the sovereign self functions as what Sandoz once described as a "compulsory minimum dogma."[108] To be in good standing, to be accepted as legitimate participants in public life, belief systems must embrace this ethic and undergo the reformation that this ethic prescribes. They must not only embrace the political morality issuing from the ethic of the sovereign self and accept the privatization of their beliefs that this entails, but they must also reinterpret their distinctive beliefs as embodying not universally valid and obligatory truths, but mere subjective preferences, mere lifestyle preferences. They must internalize, in other words, the ethic of the sovereign self's understanding of the epistemological status of their beliefs viewing them as matters of choice, not conscience or obligation; as *our* truth rather than as *the* truth.

Belief systems incompatible with it must be excluded from the making of law and public policy, delegitimized, and driven from the public square; their adherents must be excluded from polite society and relegated to a cultural and legal status that might not unfairly be described as "dhimmitude of a sort."[109] While those who adhere to views incompatible with this orthodoxy may be free to hold their views and discuss them in the privacy of their homes, such views—and much less actions predicated on these views—are not welcome in the public square. Indeed, they are to be stigmatized as bigotry and through

106. Smith, *Rise and Decline of American Religious Freedom*, 154–55.

107. Marc A. Thiessen, "Hillary Clinton Is a Threat to Religious Liberty," *Washington Post*, October 13, 2016, https://www.washingtonpost.com/opinions/hillary-clinton-is-a-threat-to-religious-liberty/2016/10/13/878cdc36-9150.

108. Ellis Sandoz, "The Civil Theology of Liberal Democracy," *Journal of Politics* 34 (1974): 35.

109. R. R. Reno, "A Dhimmitude of a Sorts," *First Thoughts* (blog), February 5, 2013, http://www.firstthings.com/blogs/firstthoughts/2013/02/05/a-dhimmitude-of-sorts/.

a mix of legal, social, and economic sanctions systematically excluded from public life.

Behind the rhetoric of toleration, inclusivity, and diversity employed by the ethic of the sovereign self, in short, lies the reality of a confessional state, which confers on the ethic of the sovereign self the status and privileges of an established doctrine, a public orthodoxy.[110] American Catholics thus confront the spectre of a public order animated by a doctrine incompatible with Catholicism and operating and informed by an understanding of religious liberty incompatible with either the freedom of the Church or the freedom of believers to live in accordance with the faith. As Ryan Barilleaux has noted, this new public order is one in which Catholics are going to "have difficulty finding a comfortable place."[111]

Conclusion

The conclusion toward which this analysis points is simple: over the long haul, it's unlikely that our current strategy of simply appealing to religious liberty will succeed in securing the Church and believers the space they need to live out the faith. As *The Federalist* pointed out, the efficacy of mere "parchment barriers" is limited, and the security of our rights in a democratic polity ultimately depends "on public opinion, and on the general spirit of the people."[112]

While Americans may celebrate the idea of religious freedom, the truly decisive question facing us is how religious liberty is to be understood and what it is thought to encompass. The simple fact is that religious liberty is not self-defining and is of its very nature limited in its scope. How it is understood and what these limits will consist of, in turn, will depend upon the background assumptions about the constitution of being, human nature, the nature of religion and the epistemological status of religious truth, the char-

110. On this point, see J. Budziszewski, "The Strange Second Life of Confessional States," in *Reason, Revelation, and the Civic Order*, ed. Paul R. DeHart and Carson Holloway (DeKalb: Northern Illinois University Press, 2014), 79–98. Since "the constitution and laws of every state are based on certain fundamental commitments," Budziszewski writes, "there is "no such thing as a non-confessional state." It follows that "the fact that a state does not solemnly avow its convictional foundations does not mean that it has none." Such a state, he continues, would be non-declaratory confessional state (84, 85).

111. Ryan Barilleaux, "Put Not Your Trust in Princes: Catholics in the American Administrative State," *Catholic Social Science Review* 22 (2017): 119.

112. Alexander Hamilton, James Madison, and John Jay, *The Federalist*, ed. George W. Carey and James McClellan (Indianapolis: Liberty Fund, 2001), no. 48, p. 256, and no. 84, p. 446.

acter of the human good, the proper organization of man's spiritual life, and the role of the state that inform our thinking.[113] To paraphrase MacIntyre, the politically decisive questions confronting us are, Whose religious freedom? And which intellectual horizon?[114]

This new ethos that is in the process of colonizing our public life propels us toward the desiccated vision of religious liberty—an understanding that tends to reduce religious freedom to a mere freedom of individual belief and worship; that excludes from its scope institutions that exist to do more than worship or to express shared beliefs; that is deeply suspicious of religious institutions and implacably hostile to what we have called strong religion; that fails to take religion and its place in the overall scheme of human life seriously; and that seeks to exclude religious beliefs and institutions from public life—incapable of safeguarding either the freedom of the Church or the freedom of Catholics (and other believers) to live in accordance with their faith. Any doubts of this score can be dispelled by reflecting on the statement by Mark Tushnet, with which we began. If this ethos comes to be embraced by the bulk of Americans, appeals to religious freedom will not suffice to stave off the new intolerance.

Defeating the new intolerance and securing Catholics the freedom we need to live out the faith will necessarily involve something more than appeals to freedom and diversity. It will require rallying public opinion around a better and richer vision of man, society, and the world than that which drives the new intolerance.

113. To suggest that there are competing theories of religious freedom is not to suggest that there is no such thing as a true account. It's simply to acknowledge that, from the point of view of the future of the Church in contemporary America, the politically decisive question is, Which understanding of religious liberty is going to be operative in our public life?

114. MacIntrye, *Whose Justice?*

CHAPTER 4

Liberal Individualist Monism and the Future of Religious Freedom

ROBERT P. HUNT

About thirty years ago, as a lowly untenured assistant professor, I had the distinct misfortune of being expected to participate in one of my college's Diversity Training Workshops. Expecting the worst from the experience, I dutifully attended and, rather quickly, ran afoul of one of the diversity trainers. The topic under consideration was a proposed college diversity mission statement. Among other things, the statement included the imperative that members of the campus community neither discriminate against anyone on the basis of race, sex, religion, or sexual orientation, nor belong to any organization that did so. Suspecting that faculty members were being asked to do more than merely follow a grading policy that would grade students on the basis of relevant criteria (i.e., how well they knew the course material) rather than illegitimate factors such as those mentioned in the proposed mission statement, I inquired about the nature and scope of the substantive commitments that we were being asked to make. The conversation went something like this:

QUESTION: "Suppose my Church tells me that the ordination of female priests is not consistent with Church teaching and that homosexual activity is immoral. Am I violating the proposed college mission statement by being a member of that religious organization?"

ANSWER: "Well, you don't necessarily have to agree with everything that your church tells you."

QUESTION: "Suppose that I do agree with my Church on these matters. What then?"

ANSWER: "Maybe you shouldn't be teaching here at this college."

I have cited this snippet of conversation at numerous college events and academic panels over the course of the past thirty years, primarily to point out the irony of the procrustean limits that my "diversity trainer" would place, in the name of diversity, on the substantive intellectual and religious commitments of members of my college community. In most instances, my captive listeners responded with either a sharp intake of breath or a shake of the head, indicating that they were properly surprised and appalled by my trainer's illiberal willingness to impose on others her comprehensive substantive worldview. But recently, when I related the story to a class of undergraduate students, I did not observe a shake of the head or hear an intake of breath but rather unmoved silence and seeming incomprehension. I cannot say that I was completely surprised. The silence does not bode well for the future of American constitutional democracy, religious freedom, or the Catholic Church in America.

The New Monism

In a series of groundbreaking articles for the journal *Theological Studies* in the late 1940s and early 1950s, Rev. John Courtney Murray attempted to lay out an explicitly moral realist and recognizably Catholic defense of constitutional democracy in general. In particular, he defended the American Constitution, the principles of limited government, and the religion clauses of the First Amendment. His primary rhetorical opponents in those articles were neither secularists nor legal positivists. Rather, they were his Catholic brethren who believed that Catholics could accept the constitutional legitimacy of the religion clauses of the First Amendment, at best, as a practical concession to religious diversity rather than as a principled statement of the proper ordering of society and state, of religion and politics. Murray's goal was to convince his fellow Catholics that the necessary substantive moral and political consensus upon which the unity of the American commonwealth depended should not extend, in principle, to matters of religious doctrine.[1] A true statesman

1. The following articles by Murray are representative of his effort to lay out a principled Catholic

should understand his role to be as "neither *episcopus externus* nor amoral policeman. His role is high indeed but not messianic."[2]

In 1960—a year that now seems to have been moral eons ago—Murray's *We Hold These Truths: Catholic Reflections on the American Proposition* was published.[3] If Murray's objective in his *Theological Studies* articles had been to persuade his fellow religionists that they would benefit, in principle, from the way in which the American constitutional order secured religious freedom, his goal in *We Hold These Truths* was to convince his fellow Americans that they could learn something from the great tradition of Catholic social thought. He argued that faithful and committed Catholics could and should bring the full weight of their faith tradition to bear upon the American experiment in self-government. The American experiment, he argued, needed to be reexamined and reappropriated by each generation of Americans. Catholics were particularly well suited to contribute to this effort because they were able to set the truths of democratic, constitutional government in their proper setting—the natural moral law and human personalism. Murray described what he called the "political substance of democracy" in the following way:

> I take it that the political substance of democracy consists in the admission of an order of rights antecedent to the state, the political form of society. These are the rights of the person, the church, the associations men freely form for economic, cultural, social and religious ends. In the admission of this prior order of rights—inviolable as well by democratic majorities as by absolute monarchs—consists the most distinctive assertion of the service-character of the democratic state. And this service-character is still further enforced by the affirmation, implicit in the admission of the order of human rights, of another order of right also antecedent to the state and regulative of its public action as a state; I mean the order of justice. In other

defense of religious freedom and constitutional democracy: "St. Robert Bellarmine on the Indirect Power," *Theological Studies* 9, no. 4 (December 1948): 491–535; "Contemporary Orientations of Catholic Thought on Church and State in the Light of History," *Theological Studies* 10, no. 2 (June 1949) 177–234; "The Church and Totalitarian Democracy," *Theological Studies* 13, no. 4 (December 1952): 525–63. See also Robert P. Hunt, "The Quest for the Historical Murray," in *Catholicism, Liberalism, and Communitarianism: The Catholic Intellectual Tradition and the Moral Foundations of Democracy*, ed. Kenneth L. Grasso, Gerard V. Bradley, and Robert P. Hunt (Lanham, MD: Rowman & Littlefield, 1995), 197–218.

2. John Courtney Murray, "Governmental Repression of Heresy," in *Proceedings of the Third Annual Meeting of the Catholic Theological Society of America* (Chicago: Chicago Theological Society of America, 1948), 56.

3. John Courtney Murray, *We Hold These Truths: Catholic Reflections on the American Proposition* (New York: Sheed and Ward, 1960).

> words, the democratic state serves the ends of the human person (in itself and its natural forms of social life) and also the ends of justice. As the servant of these ends, it has only a relative value.[4]

Murray's defense of the American experiment was grounded in a distinctly Christian understanding of human nature, the purpose of politics, and the scope and limits of state power. Christian personalism and its substantive defense of certain "natural forms of social life" provided a better foundation for the truths asserted in the Declaration of Independence than those supplied by modernity.

What has come to be called the Murray Project was indeed a liberal project, at least as Murray used the term when writing about the Western "liberal tradition of politics." The "liberal tradition" was committed to "constitutionalism, the rule of law, the notion of sovereignty as purely political and therefore limited by law, the concept of government as an empire of laws and not of men."[5] Murray's goal was to retheorize the substantive intellectual foundations upon which this tradition of constitutionalism had been built, and to do so by purifying it of a philosophical anthropology that undermined the freedom and dignity of the human person and the natural goods of social life. He believed that the Catholic intellectual tradition, shorn of political triumphalism and practical throne and altar arrangements, could contribute significantly to that retheorization. The "liberal tradition" of politics could be redirected into more personalist, associational channels.

The Murray Project was "liberal" in the purely political sense, but it was most decidedly not liberal in the philosophical or anthropological sense. Murray distinguished between this improved politically liberal tradition and another more comprehensive form of philosophical liberalism. For Murray, rather than providing a defense of the liberal tradition of politics, philosophical and political modernity (e.g., Continental Liberalism or laicism) posed a significant danger to a "personalist" view of the American experiment in democratic self-government.[6] Since it lacks a conception of *ordo iuris*, modernity tends to reduce all connections between and among human persons to "power" relationships. Left to its own devices, it can swing wildly from an

4. Murray, *We Hold These Truths*, 326.

5. Murray, *We Hold These Truths*, 32.

6. John Courtney Murray, "The Problem of State Religion," *Theological Studies*, 12, no. 2 (June 1951): 162, 166.

abstract defense of the isolated individual or sovereign self to a defense of the sovereign *demos*. Worse, it can latch on to both poles at one and the same time, endorsing a form of statist individualism.

Murray described the tendency to subordinate authentic personalism and the "natural forms of social life" to the larger social whole as a form of political monism, a tendency that stands in sharp contrast to Christian dualism. For the monist,

> [T]here is only one Sovereign, one society, one law, one faith. And the cardinal denial is of the Christian dualism of powers, societies, and laws—spiritual and temporal, divine and human. Upon this denial follows the absorption of the Church in the community, the absorption of the community in the state, the absorption of the state in the party, and the assertion that the party-state is the supreme spiritual and moral, as well as political authority and reality. It has its own absolutely autonomous ideological substance and its own absolutely independent purpose: it is the ultimate bearer of human destiny. Outside of this One Sovereign there is nothing. Or rather, what presumes to stand outside is "the enemy."[7]

Murray was quite aware of the dangers of this new kind of political monism, and he warned his fellow Americans (and Catholics) of the danger of subordinating one's faith commitments to the demands of a monist conception of human nature and politics:

> [T]he principles of Catholic faith and morality stand superior to, and in control of, the whole order of civil life. The question is sometimes raised, whether Catholicism is compatible with American democracy. The question is invalid as well as impertinent; for the manner of its position inverts the order of values, whether American democracy is compatible with Catholicism.[8]

The impertinent inversion of values about which Murray spoke so eloquently almost sixty years ago has now become a conventional truth among polite progressively liberal members of society. To what extent, they ask, is Catholicism—or any religious tradition that has too deep a set of faith commitments—compatible with American democracy? To what extent is the Catholic

7. Murray, "The Church and Totalitarian Democracy," 531.
8. Murray, *We Hold These Truths*, ix–x.

Church's position on a variety of "public issues" compatible with the principles of "liberal democracy" conceived in voluntarist terms? The answers they give, of course, are a resounding "No" and "They're not."

Under the rubrics of "equal concern and respect" (à la Ronald Dworkin) or moral autonomy (à la David Richards), or even "the need for diversity" (à la my diversity training workshop antagonist), all individuals must be emancipated from the arbitrariness of social and political institutions to which they have not voluntarily chosen to be tied.[9] Those individuals who have not accepted this newly ascendant political orthodoxy—an orthodoxy that claims to put an end to all orthodoxies—are free to believe whatever they choose to believe in religious matters. Those religious beliefs are henceforth to be considered matters of private morality. They are irrelevant to matters of public concern except when those views happen to coincide with this overarching set of political commitments. In short, as my diversity trainer implied, the devout religionist has one of two options. (1) He can remain a vibrant contributor to a "diverse" civic culture, or an assistant professor at a public institution of higher education, only if he "doesn't necessarily agree with" his Church's teaching on matters of contestation between the new "non-orthodoxy" and his faith tradition. (2) He can continue to believe what his faith tradition teaches, but the price for maintaining those beliefs is that he must retire to a smaller enclave of fellow sectarians who, my trainer believed, should have little role to play in the formation of public morality or political governance.

Under this "laicized" dispensation, religious freedom would still be constitutionally protected. After all, the mission statement itself refers to the need not to discriminate on the basis of religion, and any such discrimination would run afoul of the protections afforded by the "free exercise" component of the First Amendment's religion clauses. "Free exercise" would be redefined as the "freedom of worship," and that freedom is not coextensive with the right to translate one's religious views into public morality or public law. It must be confined to the private arena (i.e., churches, synagogues, and mosques) where worship takes place, not the public arena where moral norms are proclaimed and seek wider affirmation. Those more extensive societal norms are subordinated to the requirements of the First Amendment's other component: the non-establishment of religion. In a paradoxical manner, but

9. See David A. J. Richards, *Toleration and the Constitution* (New York: Oxford University Press, 1986).

one thoroughly consistent with its secularist anthropology and social ontology, Continental Liberalism reinvigorates the idea of the statesman as a sort of *episcopus externus* that acts under the guise of an amoral policeman.

Liberal Monism: Normlessness as a Norm

One of the more effective rhetorical devices employed by contemporary liberal individualists is their claim that they are asking nothing more than that the government maintain a position of official neutrality on what constitutes the good life for human beings. Moreover, to be anything other than "neutral" on what constitutes the good life is to violate basic constitutional principles in matters of speech, association, religious freedom, and personal autonomy. For example, Ronald Dworkin famously argued that

> Government must be neutral on what might be called the question of the good life.... Each person follows a more-or-less articulate conception of what gives value to life.... Since the citizens of a society differ in their conceptions, the government does not treat them as equals if it prefers one conception to another, either because the officials believe that one is intrinsically superior, or because one is held by the more numerous or powerful group.[10]

Liberalism's "constitutive morality provides that human beings must be treated as equals by their government" (i.e., treated with "equal concern and respect"), and this constitutive political morality must, as a matter of justice, prevail in law and the protection of rights over more substantive moral commitments.

As political philosophers Michael Sandel and Francis Canavan noted, however, this "deontological" conception of justice, which claims not to privilege any substantive understanding of the good life, is anything but neutral. Sandel claims that this form of liberal individualism privileges the claim "that we are separate, individual persons, each with our own aims, interests, and conceptions of the good, and seeks a moral framework of rights that will enable us to realize our capacity as free moral agents, consistent with a similar

10. Ronald Dworkin, "Liberalism," in *Liberalism and Its Critics*, ed. Michael Sandel (New York: New York University Press, 1984), 64.

liberty for others."[11] In other words, deontological liberalism leads to a particularistic and, one might even argue, sectarian view of the "just" society based on the equal recognition of rights and fundamental moral autonomy.

Francis Canavan properly notes that under this deontologically rigorous effort to exclude deeper substantive religious and moral commitments from the public square "normlessness . . . turns out to be itself a norm. It is a steady choice of individual freedom over any other human or social good that conflicts with it, an unrelenting subordination of all allegedly objective goods to the subjective good of individual preference."[12] One might suspect that this substantive normlessness would lead logically to political, economic, and social libertarianism. There are indeed deontological liberals such as Robert Nozick who have argued for a more libertarian view of the state in the economy of social and political life.[13] Viewed from a certain angle, moreover, this form of libertarianism might well commend itself, if only for purposes of a social *modus vivendi* in pluralist society, to Catholic personalists who would like the state to protect their ability to conduct their lives in conformity with their understanding of human dignity and what Murray described as "the natural forms of social life." To be "let alone" to conduct one's (and one's family's or church's) life free from an overweening paternalistic state is no small thing in a society of differing faith commitments.

In an incredibly prescient essay written about a half century ago, Canavan also noted, however, that while one strand of philosophical liberalism moves in the direction of a libertarian, minimalist state, there is another strand of individualism that moves *necessarily* in an entirely different direction. He wrote:

> Recent constitutional law in the United States has limited government by insisting more and more upon individual rights. Still more recently, so has civil rights legislation enacted by Congress or by the several state legislatures. This undoubtedly limits what government may do to individuals, but by the same token, and necessarily, it increases what government may do for individuals and institutions. Consequently, government today is obligated to be, at one and the same time, individualistic and statist. It is individualistic when it serves an expanding array of rights. But insofar as it uses the

11. Michael Sandel, "Introduction," in *Liberalism and Its Critics* (New York: New York University Press, 1984), 4.

12. Francis Canavan, "The Pluralist Game," *Law and Contemporary Problems* 44 (Spring 1981): 34.

13. Robert Nozick, *Anarchy, State, and Utopia*, reprint ed. (New York: Basic Books, 2013).

> power of the state to impose those rights upon institutions, government is statist, and the fingers of the bureaucracy reach more and more into all the institutions of society.[14]

In his masterful *The Quest for Community*, Robert Nisbet similarly called attention to the kind of statist individualism that, like Tocqueville's soft despotism, tends to emerge from a monistic conception of political sovereignty. Under this monistic dispensation, the goal of politics is not to encourage human flourishing through the natural forms of social life, but rather to employ the power of the state to free already sovereign individuals from arbitrarily constituted social authorities:

> Fundamental to the [modern] political community is the belief that the normal plurality of authorities and functions in society must be supplanted by unity of authority and function arising from the monistic State.... Freedom becomes freedom *from* other institutions, freedom *to* participate in Leviathan. Equality is the mechanical equivalence of talents, functions, and ideas engendered by the State's leveling influence upon all other associations and statuses, and enforced by the iron mold of law.[15]

Nisbet contrasts this monist conception of social order (i.e., of the sovereign state and the sovereign individuals of which that state is comprised) with a truly pluralist conception of social order in which the state seeks to maintain "a pluralism of functions and loyalties in the lives of its people," in which a multiplicity of human ends and purposes are met not by the omnicompetent state as the ultimate bearer of human destiny but through "the significant and meaningful relationships of kinship, religion, occupation, profession, and locality."[16]

More recently, Patrick Deneen has, at least in terms partly reminiscent of Canavan and Nisbet, carried on this critique of anthropological liberalism. He has pointed toward the monist statism implicit in anthropological liberalism from its very inception:

14. Francis Canavan, *The Pluralist Game: Pluralism, Liberalism, and the Moral Conscience* (Lanham, MD: Rowman & Littlefield, 1995), 139.

15. Robert Nisbet, *The Quest for Community: A Study in the Ethics of Order and Freedom* (San Francisco: ICS Press, 1990), 139.

16. Nisbet, *Quest for Community*, 251.

> Ironically, the more completely the sphere of autonomy is secured, the more comprehensive the state must become. Liberalism, so defined [i.e., as the freeing of individuals from the bonds of arbitrary religious, social, political, and economic arrangements], requires liberation from all forms of associations and relationships, from family to church, from schools to village and community, that exerted control over behavior through informal and habituated expectations and norms.... With the liberation of individuals from these associations, there is more need to regulate behavior through the imposition of positive law. At the same time, as the authority of social norms dissipates, they are increasingly felt to be residual, arbitrary, and oppressive motivating calls for the state to actively work toward their eradication.[17]

Liberalism, according to Deneen, "culminates in two ontological points: the liberated individual and the controlling state."[18] The liberal state is both *episcopus externus* and amoral policeman. For Deneen, the classical liberal state of philosophers such as John Locke and Adam Smith was prone from its very inception to the progressive liberal statism of Dworkin and Rawls in its emphasis upon freeing individuals from the arbitrary bonds of constituted social and religious authorities. Whether this was the precise or general intent of classical liberals is where Deneen seems to part company with both Murray and Canavan.

Neither classical nor progressive liberalism can provide a proper foundation for limited constitutional government, the protection of the dignity of the human person, and "the natural forms of social life." In contrast, Murray's neo-Thomist personalism allows him to speak comfortably about the "natural forms of social life" that make for human flourishing, and Nisbet's sociological imagination finds comfort in "the significant and meaningful relationships" mentioned above. But as Stanley Hauerwas has ably pointed out, many liberal individualists, in their desire to emphasize what they assume to be commitment to the institutions of civil society, have reimagined them as "voluntary associations" that are themselves the mere product of the choices of autonomous individuals:

> [T]he very language of "intermediate associations" already betrays liberal presuppositions which distort the moral reality of such institutions as the

17. Patrick Deneen, *Why Liberalism Failed* (New Haven, CT: Yale University Press, 2018), 38.
18. Deneen, *Why Liberalism Failed*, 38.

> family. Whatever the family is, it is not but another voluntary association. The very means used to insure [*sic*] that the democratic state be a limited state—namely, the rights of the individual—turn out to be no less destructive for intermediate institutions than the monistic state of Marxism. For it is the strategy of liberalism to insure the existence of the "autonomy of cultural and economic life" by insuring the freedom of the individual. Ironically, that strategy results in the undermining of intermediate associations because they are now understood only as those arbitrary institutions sustained by the private desires of individuals.[19]

A first necessary step on the road toward a recovery of the type of "personalist" limited form of constitutional government that both Murray and Canavan ably defended is to demonstrate that normlessness is not normless. Rather, it establishes a set of norms and expectations for all members of society. The second essential step is to demonstrate that normlessness is not anti-statist. It cannot help but move from defending what Isaiah Berlin described as "negative liberty" (i.e., individual freedom *from* governmental intervention in social, cultural, and economic matters) to "positive liberty" (i.e., individual freedom *for* individuals to carry out their life plans freed from the burdens imposed by all arbitrary social, cultural, and economic institutions).[20]

Nowhere is this transition from a libertarian individualist defense of negative liberty to a statist individualist defense of positive liberty made more clearly than in a 2002 interview with then-Illinois State Senator Barack Obama. Obama paid homage to the US Supreme Court for the manner in which it had, since at least the 1950s and 1960s under the aegis of Chief Justice Earl Warren, advanced the civil rights movement's push for greater liberty and equality for all American citizens. The problem, he argued, was not the Warren Court's admirable commitment to the moral worth and dignity of every human being, but that its very nature as a court of law precluded it from taking a more activist stand in favor of government's moral obligation to do things *for* individuals. The US Constitution construed by the courts was "a charter of negative liberties" that "says what the states can't do to you" and "what the Federal government can't do to you, but doesn't say what the Federal government or State government *must do* on your behalf." Progressive

19. Stanley Hauerwas, "Christianity and Democracy: A Response," *Center Journal* 1 (Summer 1982): 44–45.

20. See Isaiah Berlin, *Four Essays on Liberty* (New York: Oxford University Press, 1969).

political activists today must rely more extensively on the political branches of government rather than the courts at the federal and state levels, because those branches have a greater capacity to ensure the positive liberty that it is every government's obligation to provide.[21]

This comment became campaign fodder in 2008 and 2012, when Senator (and, later, President) Obama was running for president against Senator John McCain and former Massachusetts Governor Mitt Romney. Those who criticized Obama's comment focused primarily on the *economic* implications of his argument, claiming that he clearly adopted a more socialistic or, at the very least, redistributionist view on questions of political economy than was acceptable in a market-oriented society. It was certainly not unfair for those critics to focus on the economic implications, since Obama himself emphasized them, claiming that "we still suffer from a Constitution that does not guarantee its citizens economic rights."[22]

But it is also certainly fair to ask whether Obama's defense of positive liberty can or should be limited to economic rights or whether it might not equally extend to social and cultural rights, particularly when asserted against social and cultural institutions that do not fully accept the social and cultural implications of those rights. As Francis Canavan might frame the issue, couldn't contemporary liberal progressivism require the state to be both "individualistic and statist," "reach[ing] more and more into all the institutions of society" to remake those institutions in light of its own view of human nature and society?

One might further argue that the jurisprudential defense of negative liberty embraced by the courts since at least the Warren Court's tenure, rather than being a defense of legal libertarianism, marked the first step on the road to the type of social and political monism about which Murray warned us in 1960. Contrary to Obama's perception of the limits of the judiciary's ability to remake American society, the court's defense of negative liberty (i.e., freedom *from* governmental coercion) was itself grounded in a more robust and potentially comprehensive conception of positive liberty that threatened true per-

21. Obama cited in Paul Roderick Gregory, "Why the Fuss? Obama Has Long Been on the Record in Favor of Redistribution," *Forbes,* September 23, 2012. Gregory's essay is characteristic of what I describe below as the primary critical focus on Obama's views on political economy (i.e., that he is an economic redistributionist).

22. Gregory, "Why the Fuss?"

sonalism and the "natural forms of social life." In other words, the courts set the paradigmatic stage for what the political branches of government would do once progressive deontological liberals fully assumed the reins of power.

The US Supreme Court's interpretation of the First Amendment's Free Exercise and Establishment Clauses provides ample evidence of this transition from libertarianism to statism—or, more precisely, from libertarian anti-statism to libertarian statism—all in the name of protecting the putative rights of the individual. The most memorable and constitutionally significant words in Justice Hugo Black's majority opinion in *Everson v. Board of Education of Ewing Township* (1947) are those in which he lays out what the court majority believes to be the foundational principles on which the First Amendment's non-establishment component rests: "Neither a state nor the Federal Government can set up a church. Neither can pass laws which aid one religion, aid all religions, or prefer one religion over another. . . . In the words of Jefferson, the clause against establishment of religion by law was intended to erect 'a wall of separation between church and state.'"[23]

Justice Black's opinion supported the constitutionality of a New Jersey program that reimbursed parents of parochial—primarily Catholic—schoolchildren for the costs of bus transportation to and from school, and it did so precisely because it did not violate the principle of governmental *neutrality* that Justice Black found at the heart of the Establishment Clause. The clause, according to Black, requires that "the state . . . be neutral in its relations with groups of religious believers and non-believers" but does not require "the state to be their adversary. State power is no more to be used to handicap religions, than it is to favor them."[24]

There is much to commend in the court majority's effort to decide the case in favor of the program. First, Justice Black's opinion attempts to set juridical limits to the constitutional powers of federal and state authority in religious matters. Second, Black maintains that these limits should in no way be construed as displaying hostility to religion. Third, state public welfare statutes that incidentally treat religionists as eligible for the same benefits as the general population can in no way be said to violate the constitutional prohibition on an establishment of religion. Why then did John Courtney Murray, who

23. Everson v. Board of Education of Ewing Township, N.J., 330 U.S. 1 (1947), 15–16.

24. Black, cited in David M. O'Brien, *Constitutional Law and Politics,* vol. 2, *Civil Liberties,* 3rd ed. (New York: W. W. Norton, 1997), 86.

took an active part in supporting the statute, claim at the time that "we have won on busing, but lost on the First Amendment"?[25]

One could argue that Murray rejected Jeffersonian separationism as an accurate account of the original meaning of the Establishment Clause, but one could also claim that Murray foresaw the larger philosophical problems implicit in Black's formulation of what constituted permissible church-state relations. In other words, perhaps Murray foresaw that Black's formulation could easily be turned from a defense of limits on the powers of the state in matters of religion in the name of judicial interpretation of the Constitution into a defense of empowering the state to free individuals from the baneful effects of religion in the name of legislative and executive construction of that same Constitution.

Consider, for example, what Black wrote a decade and a half later in *Engel v. Vitale* (1962) when he was forced to explain why the optional daily recitation of prayer in public elementary schools is unconstitutional: "The Establishment Clause . . . stands as an expression of principle on the part of the Founders of our Constitution that religion is too personal, too sacred, too holy, to permit its 'unhallowed perversion' by a civil magistrate."[26] Black rejected what he called "natural law jurisprudence" when practiced by fellow Justices Frankfurter and Harlan to determine which "fundamental rights" were protected against state encroachment by the Due Process Clause of the Fourteenth Amendment. Rather than seeing himself as a moral philosopher, he saw himself as a constitutional literalist. Yet when it came to what Black saw as the "literal" meaning of the First Amendment—idiosyncratically incorporated *in toto* against the states through the very same Due Process Clause—Black read an entirely arguable article of faith into it. He saw it not in *neutral* terms at all (since such terms were, as Canavan ably pointed out, logically impossible) but in liberal individualist terms. He was forced to reach the conclusion he did about the meaning of non-establishment (i.e., freedom from religious establishments) because he depended on a notion of freedom that was itself a child of the Enlightenment.

25. Murray, cited in Jo Renee Formicola, "Catholic Jurisprudence on Education," in *Everson Revisited: Religion, Education, and Law at the Crossroads*, ed. Jo Renee Formicola and Hubert Morken (Lanham, MD: Rowman & Littlefield, 1997), 86.

26. Black, in Engel v. Vitale 370 U.S. 421 (1962), cited in Robert S. Alley, ed., *The Supreme Court on Church and State* (New York: Oxford University Press, 1988), 199.

And what became of the free exercise component of the First Amendment in light of this larger, by no means neutral, reading of the Establishment Clause? Several conscientious objector cases, also from the 1960s, provide examples of a movement on the court's part toward a purely formal, individualistic interpretation of what the free exercise component protects. In *U.S. v. Seeger* (1965), for example, the Supreme Court ruled in favor of an individual who had been denied conscientious objector status because he did not believe in a Supreme Being. The Selective Service Act in question had clearly specified that a religious claim to objector status must be grounded in an acknowledgment of "duties superior to those arising from any human relation."[27] The court ruled that any set of beliefs in ultimate reality, whether grounded in religion or a purely ethical creed, might serve as grounds for exemption from facially valid Selective Service laws. The court stated, "A sincere and meaningful belief which occupies in the life of its possessor a place parallel to that fulfilled by the God of those admittedly qualifying for [conscientious objector] status comes within the statutory definition."[28] Justice Black, in *Welsh v. U.S.*, extended the logic of *Seeger*, claiming that "beliefs that are purely ethical in source and content," if held strongly, are sufficient to justify exemption from military service.[29]

Given the court's paradigmatic embrace of the principle of "governmental neutrality" in its reading of the Establishment Clause, the Free Exercise Clause comes to be interpreted as being about something other than religion. As Gerard V. Bradley has noted on the question of free exercise, "the coherent rationale for a 'superneutral' religious liberty is this: it's about liberty, not religion."[30] Thus the "free exercise of religion" must be understood in light of a larger metaethical commitment to the sovereign ability of each individual to live his or her life in conformity with his or her own life plan, consistent with a similar liberty for others. The free exercise of religion for religionists becomes synonymous with the "freedom of worship," defined in almost precisely

27. U.S. v. Seeger, 380 U.S. 163 (1965), 184.

28. *U.S. v. Seeger*, 380 U.S. 163 (1965), 184.

29. Welsh v. U.S., 398 U.S. 333 (1970), 341–43.

30. Gerard V. Bradley, "Déjà Vu, All Over Again: The Supreme Court Revisits Religious Liberty," *Crisis* 13, no. 4 (April 1995): 41. For another treatment of the same theme, see my own "Two Concepts of Religious Liberty: *Dignitatis Humanae* v. the U.S. Supreme Court," in *Catholicism and Religious Freedom: Contemporary Reflections on Vatican II's Declaration on Religious Liberty*, ed. Kenneth L. Grasso and Robert P. Hunt (Lanham, MD: Rowman & Littlefield, 2006), 19–41.

the same substantive terms as those advanced by my "diversity trainer": you are free to believe and worship as you wish within the enclave of your fellow sectarian believers, but you are not free to enter the public square and impose those beliefs on the larger population.

This "superneutral" form of liberty threatens to break the boundaries and limitations ostensibly placed on governmental power by its ostensibly purely "negative" conception of human freedom. If the first step on the road to political and social monism, as undertaken by the courts, is to free autonomous human beings from arbitrary *governmental* restraints (e.g., on abortion, same sex marriage, and so on), the second step must be to use the power of government to free those same autonomous human beings from arbitrary *social, political, and economic* restraints. As Obama had said, while it might be difficult for courts of law to require government, as a matter of moral obligation, to act *on behalf* of human beings, there are no such institutional constraints placed on the political (legislative and executive) branches of government. In fact, those branches have precisely that moral obligation, and once they have acted, the courts must defer to the best judgments of the political branches about how to advance that more capacious (but ironically still "neutral") use of governmental power, even if that means that a variety of social, cultural, and economic institutions must be transformed in the process.

Former President Obama's concern for the implications of what government can and should do *for* individuals has led to an interesting *volte face* among both contemporary conservatives and progressive liberals on the faith placed in the various branches of government within our constitutional system. For many years, conservatives, experiencing defeat after defeat at the hands of activist federal and state judiciaries, decried the judicial activist tendency to elevate liberally construed "substantive due process" rights, especially in the social and cultural realm (e.g., abortion, same-sex marriage), over the norms embodied in democratically enacted statutes. By contrast, progressive liberals, such as Obama himself, lauded the courts' efforts to guarantee a greater level of freedom and equality conceived in progressive liberal individualist terms to each and every member of society. Even though the courts defined our rights primarily in "negative" terms (i.e., as freedom *from* governmental intrusion), this was a small price to pay for the gradual transformation of society that ensued. More recently, progressive liberals have been transformed into apostles of "judicial self-restraint," which essentially entails societal and judicial quiescence in the face of social and cultural changes already effected by the courts. They have turned to rely on the political branches of government to do most of the political heavy lifting from this point forward. Conservatives and libertarians, having witnessed the extent to which progressive political majorities and the administrative state are willing to ride roughshod over what conservatives understand to be the true constitutionally guaranteed rights of the citizenry (e.g., to the free *exercise* of religion, not merely the right to worship), call for a form of "judicial engagement" to secure persons from the statist consequences of progressive liberalism.[31]

Catholicism and Liberalism

Francis Canavan's concerns about the trajectory of the liberal intellectual tradition and the internal logic of its embrace of both individualism and statism are repeated in Etienne Perreau-Saussine's *Catholicism and Democracy: An Essay in the History of Political Thought* (2011).[32] While Perreau-Saussine focuses primarily on the historical effort in France to effect a rapprochement between the Catholic and liberal intellectual traditions, he also displays a remarkable level of prescience about where possible fault lines might develop for anyone attempting to effect a full rapprochement between the Catholic and liberal intellectual traditions. According to Perreau-Saussine, the liberal tradition tends to emphasize the notion of negative liberty while smuggling a highly individualistic notion of personal autonomy into its defense of freedom. The Catholic Church, however, "did not [in *Dignitatis Humanae*] repudiate its traditional teaching: the freedom to choose between good and evil (*liberum arbitrium*, or negative liberty) was subordinate to the freedom to do good (*libertas*, or positive freedom), that is, the proper use of free will."[33]

This conflict between the Catholic and individualistic notion of freedom,

31. See Randy Barnett, *Restoring the Lost Constitution: The Presumption of Liberty*, rev. ed. (Princeton, NJ: Princeton University Press, 2013), and Timothy Sandefur, *The Conscience of the Constitution: The Declaration of Independence and the Right to Liberty* (Washington, DC: Cato Institute, 2014), for two examples of the libertarian constitutionalist reliance on the courts to restore the American constitutional order to its juridical foundations.

32. Emile Perreau-Saussine, *Catholicism and Democracy: An Essay in the History of Political Thought*, trans. Richard Rex (Princeton, NJ: Princeton University Press, 2012). (All further references directly to this book in the body of the text are to this edition.)

33. Perreau-Saussine, *Catholicism and Democracy*, 128.

Perreau-Saussine contends, is precisely what has compelled the Church to reaffirm its teleological understanding of the human good against more statist forms of individualism. This fault line, the author believes, will be widened as the liberal democratic state makes more exhaustive claims on behalf of the autonomous self. Perreau-Saussine asks whether "liberal democracy [can] compel the Catholic Church to be silent or to change its moral teaching." He also contends that "the notion of non-discrimination (originally envisaged in terms of race)" is "undertaking a radical transformation of society by means of law."[34] The properly secular state is becoming a secularist state and attempting to remake society and the Church in its image.

The future of religious freedom in general and of the Catholic Church in America depends largely upon the Church's willingness to articulate, defend, and live out its own distinctive understanding of the nature and purpose of political and social life. In doing so, it must carefully distinguish between what Murray described as the "liberal tradition of politics" and deontological liberalism. The former is properly committed to "constitutionalism, the rule of law, the notion of sovereignty as purely political and therefore limited by law, the concept of government as an empire of laws and not of men," and the Church must reaffirm its commitment, as articulated in conciliar documents such as *Dignitatis Humanae*, to "the political substance of democracy" upon which that tradition can most securely rest. At the same time, it must forthrightly argue that progressive deontological liberalism embraces a form of voluntarism and statism that threatens the dignity of the human person and the natural institutions of social life. As Murray argued in *We Hold These Truths:*

> [W]e see that the modern concept of freedom itself was dangerously inadequate because it neglected the corporate dimension of human freedom. We see too that modernity was wrong in isolating the problem of freedom from its polar terms—responsibility, justice, order, law. . . . We know that the myopic individualism of modernity led it into other errors, even into a false conception of the problem of the state in terms of the unreal dichotomy, individualism vs. collectivism.[35]

The firmness of the Church's commitment to "liberalism" is entirely contingent upon liberalism's remaining committed to political constitutionalism, a

34. Perreau-Saussine, *Catholicism and Democracy*, 136.
35. Murray, *We Hold these Truths*, 200.

commitment rendered problematic by the liberal intellectual tradition's underlying philosophical nominalism and voluntarist social ontology.

Perreau-Saussine follows Murray's lead by distinguishing this undesirable social ontology from the (liberal) political constitutionalism both he and Murray favor, and he does so by defining liberalism in political terms alone. Thus limited constitutional government and religious freedom become essential characteristics of the liberal tradition, while the voluntarist social ontology that underlies it becomes a disposable distortion of that tradition. "The laicist tradition," for example, "is not really liberal" because it places too much confidence in the state as "a force for emancipation . . . from the tyranny of outmoded intermediate institutions, in particular from religious bodies."[36] But some critics of the liberal intellectual tradition, such as John Hallowell and Francis Canavan, have argued that the liberal intellectual tradition is by no means intrinsically supportive of limited constitutional government and intermediate institutions. This is because of its *essential* philosophical and methodological individualism. On this view, laicism is not merely an unintended distortion of the liberal tradition but a working out of its philosophical premises. In other words, the liberal intellectual tradition arguably contains within itself the seeds for the destruction of the political values it originally held.[37]

Murray and Perreau-Saussine want to preserve the essential political validity of the liberal tradition by purifying it of its laicist, monistic tendencies. Canavan argues that the liberal intellectual tradition has been flawed *in its very essence* from its inception and defends a variation on Murray's Project: to defend constitutional democracy and personalism (like Murray), but to describe that understanding of human nature and politics, both in purpose and structure, as something other than liberalism. Both Hallowell and he leave open the question of whether even the more prudent and traditionalist classical liberals *intended* to effect the type of radical social and cultural changes implied by their larger philosophical commitments.

Patrick Deneen seems to be of two minds on the question of whether "classical liberals" such as Locke *intended* for the classically limited, liberal state to become the unclassically unlimited progressive liberal state. On the one hand, he acknowledges the virtues of the liberal tradition's "continuities

36. Perreau-Saussine, *Catholicism and Democracy*, 88.

37. See my own review of Perreau-Saussine's *Catholicism and Democracy* in *Perspectives on Politics* 12, no. 2 (June 2014): 57–58, where I originally made this argument.

with the deepest commitments of the Western political tradition, particularly efforts to secure liberty and human dignity through the constraint of tyranny, arbitrary rule, and oppression."[38] This claim sounds much like Murray in the latter's distinction between the praiseworthy "liberal tradition of politics" and the deformed ontology and anthropology of laicized "liberalism." Moving beyond liberalism, according to Deneen, requires rejecting the philosophical turn that led even classical liberals to impose upon the world an alien, individualist anthropology that is, ultimately, anything but neutral and limiting in its conception of the purposes and scope of political authority.

One could argue, as Murray and Canavan might, that the classical liberal tradition's sense of caution, of not wanting completely to uproot all social and cultural norms but to ground those norms in a surer, individualistic soil, led them to embrace a degree of continuity with the older tradition that they had set about, at least in part, to supplant. But Deneen goes further than even Murray and Canavan, and at times depicts classical liberals as *purposely* destructive of what had come before. He acknowledges that "liberalism's founders tended to take for granted the persistence of social norms," but then adds immediately that they did so "even as they sought to liberate individuals from the constitutive associations and education in self-limitation that sustained these norms."[39] On Deneen's reading of intellectual history and philosophical intent, "a main goal of Locke's philosophy," for example, "is to expand the prospects for our liberty—defined as the capacity to satisfy our appetites—through the auspices of the state."[40] The "new political technology" that flowed from this nascent statism infected even the framers of the US Constitution whose "modern" form of republicanism "was designed to liberate us from partial loyalties to particular people and places, and make us into individuals who, above all, strive to achieve our individual ambitions and desires . . . while making our interpersonal ties and commitments more tenuous."[41]

In short, Deneen's criticism of the liberal intellectual tradition cuts in two directions at the same time. He contends that "in its earliest moments" the liberal tradition assumed "the health and continuity of families, schools, and

38. Deneen, *Why Liberalism Failed*, 19.
39. Deneen, *Why Liberalism Failed*, 40.
40. Deneen, *Why Liberalism Failed*, 48.
41. Deneen, *Why Liberalism Failed*, 102.

communities," implying that the tradition supported those natural forms of social life even if they were grounded in a more voluntarist social ontology. Conversely, his critiques of Locke and of Madisonian republicanism make it clear that these moments must have been brief, succeeded by "a pincer movement" in which "today's classical liberals and progressive liberals remain locked in a battle . . . to destroy the vestiges of the classical practices and virtues that they both despise."[42] As mentioned above, Murray distinguished between the healthy politics of the liberal tradition and the unhealthy anthropology and social ontology of philosophical liberalism. He embraced the former and rejected the latter while recognizing the limitations imposed by the latter on the former. Similarly, Hallowell distinguished between "integral" liberalism and its later incarnations, acknowledging that, at least in part, the former "retained from the Middle Ages [the notion] that law is the embodiment of eternal truths and values discoverable by reason" and that "it is the rational recognition of the rightness of the content of the law that imposes obligation on the individual," not the law's being a sheer product of human willfulness.[43] In his desire to tell the reader "why liberalism failed," Deneen depreciates the extent to which the more traditional component of the liberal synthesis held the more radical individualist, voluntarist component at bay, and he finds that the very structures of liberal constitutionalism are infected by its faulty anthropology, exactly as Deneen believes liberalism intended from its earliest moments.

Thus the counsel that Deneen provides to the Catholic reader of *Why Liberalism Failed* is decidedly different from that provided by earlier critics of the liberal intellectual tradition, such as Murray and Canavan. The Murray Project, of which Canavan could be considered a practical proponent, was to reconceptualize or retheorize the intellectual foundations of constitutional democracy in more personalist, rather than liberal individualist, terms. Deneen acknowledges that we cannot return to a preliberal age, that "we must build upon [the achievements of liberalism] while abandoning the foundational reasons for its failures."[44] A "better theory of politics and society might ultimately emerge" if we were to "focus on developing practices that foster new forms of culture, household economics, and polis life."[45] For Murray and Canavan,

42. Deneen, *Why Liberalism Failed*, 62.
43. John Hallowell, *The Moral Foundation of Democracy* (Indianapolis: Liberty Fund, 2007), 65.
44. Deneen, *Why Liberalism Failed*, 182.
45. Deneen, *Why Liberalism Failed*, 183.

the Catholic solution to the problem of liberal monist statism is for Catholics to engage the political culture and contribute internally to its retheorization in something other than exclusively anthropologically liberal terms. For Deneen, the solution is primarily extra-political. He wants to disengage from an inherently flawed set of liberal norms *and structures* and tend to our smaller personalist, communalist gardens.

Given the more recent trajectory of progressive liberal politics and its greater tendency to subordinate traditional religious truth claims to its monistic conception of social order, one can understand the temptation to abjure political life and retire to smaller enclaves of believing Christians. Deneen's recipe for disengagement is tempting, and that temptation is only heightened to the extent to which we believe, like Deneen, that the very structures of constitutional democracy are irremediably infected by anthropological liberalism and its voluntarist conception of positive freedom. But if Deneen is correct about the voracious nature of both the classical and progressive liberal effort to remake all societal norms through contemporary political and juridical structures, we should not expect to be "let alone" to tend our own gardens. The proper response to the encroachments made by liberal monism might still be through engagement of the sort envisioned by Murray and Canavan. This should be done not in a spirit of naivete about the possibilities of success but in the sober recognition that leaving the rhetorical and practical playing field to one's adversaries is not a recipe for political success. Nor is a rhetorical strategy that paints the American constitutional order itself as inherently liberal (and therefore monist) in both substance and form likely to produce any lasting victories.

The seeds of anthropological liberalism are bearing bitter fruit today as progressive liberals carry out their long march through the institutions of social life, whether it be through health care mandates and executive orders that require religiously affiliated hospitals to accede fully or in part to their capaciously stultifying understanding of what constitutes an individual's health and well-being, or through judicial decisions that redefine how we understand the nature of marital relations. It is indeed a sign of the times in which we live that the Church's fallback position is to ask simply to be "let alone," to be allowed to live according to its own social ontology and not be "imposed upon" by the federal government or the states. As then-State Senator Obama recognized (and as President Obama decreed through his Secretary of Health and Human Services), the negative freedom to be "let alone" must itself give way to the responsibility of both the federal and states' governments to do things *for* individuals.

In the face of this "moral imperative," the long-term future of the Catholic Church and of religious freedom in any meaningful sense of the term is not bright. We can only hope that the Church's continuing pleas on behalf of the dignity of the human person and the natural forms of social life do not meet with the unmoved silence or seeming incomprehension on the part of the larger society that characterized the response of my aforementioned undergraduate class.

CHAPTER 5

Republican Integralism

Its Roots and Deracination in American Politics

JAMES R. STONER JR.

Let me begin with a well-known definition of integralism, as conveyed in three sentences from Fr. Edmund Waldstein:

> Catholic Integralism is a tradition of thought that rejects the liberal separation of politics from concern with the end of human life, holding that political rule must order man to his final goal. Since, however, man has both a temporal and an eternal end, integralism holds that there are two powers that rule him: a temporal power and a spiritual power. And since man's temporal end is subordinated to his eternal end the temporal power must be subordinated to the spiritual power.[1]

Are the two powers, temporal and spiritual, both political? Perhaps so, in the sense that, as St. Augustine taught, the Christian is a citizen of two cities: the City of God and a city of man. In the City of God, the two cities are intermingled: the former consists of the saints in heaven in addition to the true members of the Church militant on earth, while the city of man includes Catholics (at various stages on the road to sanctity) and non-Catholics, in various proportions, and can be legitimately organized in different ways. Accepting that the spiritual power in Fr. Waldstein's formulation refers to the Catholic Church organized hierarchically under the Roman Pontiff as the Vicar of Christ, how can we identify the temporal power?

1. Edmund Waldstein, O. Cist., "Integralism in Three Sentences," *The Josias*, October 17, 2016, https://thejosias.com/2016/10/17/integralism-in-three-sentences/.

As a political scientist, I find this question difficult to answer regarding the United States. The temporal power in our country is not a unified, centralized sovereign state as is familiar in Europe; one can speak abstractly of the temporal power as a singular entity, but concretely the United States is a federal republic with numerous political institutions among whom power is shared. We speak abstractly of the sovereignty of the people, but the people rule through representative institutions, some more and some less directly chosen; political and legal power is famously separated among branches of government; and the people themselves are constituted simultaneously in their states and in the union. Fr. Waldstein's integralism may be relatively easy to understand in a monarchy—which he concedes is his preferred form of government—but monarchy was rejected in the American Revolution, and the Church herself does not present monarchy as a necessary, or even as the most desirable, political form.

The question that I want to raise in this essay, and that I hope to begin to answer, is what integralism would mean in a republic. Although for the most part I will discuss the American republic, I think the question applies to republican government more generally. What is a republic? Here is a definition from political scientist Antony Black:

> I will define *republic* (as an ideal type) to mean: (1) an institutional order in which rulers are elected and subject to law, major decisions are taken by groups, and the people are assigned some part in the polity; and (2) a political ethic according to which citizens have a duty to serve the common good and a right to fair and equal treatment by public authorities.[2]

Even more simply, a republic is a regime where many rule for the sake of the common good; consider it a translation into Latinate English of Aristotle's *politeia*, in its specific rather than generic meaning. The debate over the relative merits of kingship and republicanism is central to the history of political theory, and I suppose that if it could be summarized in a sentence, it would be this: monarchies are more peaceful and more orderly, while republics are more energetic and freer. Even Thomas Aquinas, who in his book *On Kingship, to the King of Cyprus* makes clear the subordination of the temporal to the spiritual power similarly to Fr. Waldstein, writes this of republics in contrast to monarchies:

2. Antony Black, "Christianity and Republicanism: From St. Cyprian to Rousseau," *American Political Science Review* 91 (1997): 647.

> Men living under a king strive more sluggishly for the common good, inasmuch as they consider that what they devote to the common good, they do not confer upon themselves but upon another, under whose power they see the common goods to be. But when they see that the common good is not under the power of one man, they do not attend to it as if it belonged to another, but each one attends to it as if it were his own.[3]

Turning to the United States, I begin with several observations on which American political scientists might generally agree. First, I take note of the subfield of American political development within the discipline of political science, which has emerged in the past three or four decades, coincident with the demise, or at least the diminution, of the study of political history in departments of history. American political development (APD for short) arose to address the question: Why is there no socialism in the United States? Leaving aside whether that question has now become moot, it originally received an answer that APD scholars generally accepted: the Europeans built their states before they became democratic, while the United States was a democracy before building a centralized modern state.[4] Actually, as these scholars note, the United States really has only a partially centralized state to this day, in part because of our federal system—hence our notion of divided sovereignty—and in part because we leave to the private sector many tasks that most modern countries assign to their governments. It is easy enough to attribute to the modern states of Europe, built as they were by the kings of nations, the whole temporal power and thus to endorse their traditional dependence on the Church, at least as a matter of right. But if we Americans lack a centralized state on the European model, it is not obvious that our governments can be superintended by the Church in the European way.

Second, political scientists distinguish politics at two levels: constitutional politics, which include struggles over the form of government and over the rights insulated from government adjustment, and ordinary politics, which include elections, lawmaking, policy making, law enforcement, and matters of war and peace.[5] This reflects the distinction, dating back at least to the

3. St. Thomas Aquinas, *On Kingship to the King of Cyprus* (Toronto: Pontifical Institute for Mediaeval Studies, 1949), book I, chap. 4, p. 19.

4. Karen Orren and Stephen Skowronek, *The Search for American Political Development* (New York: Cambridge University Press, 2004).

5. See, e.g., Sotirios A. Barber and Robert P. George, eds., *Constitutional Politics: Essays on Constitution Making, Maintenance, and Change* (Princeton, NJ: Princeton University Press, 2004).

American Revolution, between constitutions and laws, or between fundamental law and ordinary law. In theory at least, if not always so clearly in practice, constitutions are made by the people, in an exercise of their sovereign power, and are difficult to change, while ordinary law and policy is made and changed by the people's elective representatives. Establishment of the former is by a "solemn and authoritative act,"[6] and by the terms of the federal Constitution all officeholders must take an oath (or affirmation) to support the Constitution, which does not preclude their seeking to amend it, however. The United States is an extensive republic with a wide array of interests and populations—including, in the language of the founding, a variety of "sects"—and political differences have almost always been dramatic and elections hard-fought. Nevertheless, except at a few moments of crisis, Americans have more or less agreed to settle their political differences within the framework of the Constitution and its animating principles, even if they sometimes spar over the meaning of the Constitution itself.

Third, while the American Declaration of Independence—still our most fundamental organic law, expressing those animating principles—lays out a theory of government that begins with rights and describes the end of government as their protection, it is not obvious that the relation of rights and government therein proposed is "liberal" in the modern sense of the term. First, our "unalienable rights" are said to be God given, not simply natural or self-posited, and they are said to be defined by "the laws of nature and of nature's God." While the emphasis in the Declaration is on the primacy of rights, at least for the purpose of explaining a revolution, there is nothing in this formulation that precludes God-given duties as well as rights, indeed nothing that precludes the priority of duties to rights. Second, while one can contrast the Lockean phrase "pursuit of happiness" to Aristotle's observation that happiness itself is the end that all men seek, inferring that a right to pursuit suggests official indifference as to the outcome, while the Aristotelian focus on the good moves seamlessly to a politics of the common good, the language of the Declaration is sufficiently ambiguous to allow the Aristotelian reading. After all, when speaking in the same extended sentence of the right to change the form of government, the people as a whole are said to be entitled to choose a form that they think "most likely to effect their safety and happi-

6. Alexander Hamilton, James Madison, and John Jay, *The Federalist*, ed. George W. Carey and James McClellan (Indianapolis: Liberty Fund, 2001; orig. 1788), no. 78, p. 406.

ness," not merely to protect its pursuit. Third, the long middle section of the Declaration refers not to liberal abstractions but to the concrete practices and institutions of English constitutionalism, which the colonists claimed as their inheritance and the violation of which triggered the Revolution itself. A remedy for every violation appears in the subsequent Constitution and the Bill of Rights, and many of the practices—for example, the right to trial by jury—are anchored deeply in the common law, not innovations of incipient liberalism. Indeed, the common law was claimed by all of the original states as the basis of their jurisprudence, and its provenance is preliberal, however much liberals later adopted its tolerance of individual liberty and insistence on individual responsibility—originally embedded in a legal order that confidently distinguished moral right and wrong.[7]

Now I concede that not all political scientists or historians adopt this reading of the Declaration, which sees the document and the Revolution it defended as concerned primarily with political liberty, that is, with republicanism. I think this reading was standard through the nineteenth century, but the twentieth century saw the Declaration's rights interpreted as essentially private in character, protective of individual autonomy over against the collective will of the state, with liberalism oscillating between an emphasis on the former and on the latter. American political thought in the nineteenth century allowed for the protection of private property, of course, but also for the defense of public morality. The common law circumscribed the use of one's property by forbidding use that was harmful to the public, and it also circumscribed government regulation by limiting it to the prevention of such harm. It typically upheld public morality not by censorship or suppression, but by making people liable for their wrongdoing after the fact.[8] This was not the republicanism of Rousseau or even of the ancient world; it allowed, after all, for religious liberty and thus did not suppose the republic free to shape citizens however the majority willed. Such republicanism could be called liberal since

7. I expand on this reading of the Declaration in several published writings: *Common Law and Liberal Theory: Coke, Hobbes, and the Origins of American Constitutionalism* (Lawrence: University Press of Kansas, 1992), chap. 11; "Is There a Political Philosophy in the Declaration of Independence?," *Intercollegiate Review* 40, no. 20 (Fall/Winter 2005): https://isi.org/intercollegiate-review/is-there-a-political-philosophy-in-the-declaration-of-independence/; "The Declaration of Independence," in *Natural Law, Natural Rights, and American Constitutionalism* (Princeton, NJ: Witherspoon Institute, 2011), http://www.nlnrac.org/american/declaration-of-independence.

8. I discuss these issues further in *Common-Law Liberty: Rethinking American Constitutionalism* (Lawrence: University Press of Kansas, 2003), chap. 8.

it recognized the right of the people to govern themselves under the law. It did not suppose an absolute autonomy of individuals to live as they willed any more than it supposed an absolute sovereignty in the majority. The nineteenth century was also, one might be reminded, an era of explosive growth for the Catholic Church in America, no doubt part of the cause of the anti-Catholic sentiment that surfaced from time to time.

What, then, would integralism require in the liberal (in the sense just explained), democratic, federal American republic of, say, the late nineteenth century? Since the Constitution forbade religious tests at the federal level (a prohibition not extended to the states until 1961),[9] it obviously would not include a requirement of church membership in order to hold political office. This, of course, worked for the benefit of Catholics, a religious minority who, had religious tests been allowed, were likely to have been excluded; indeed, the constitutional prohibition was a repudiation of English law, which had excluded Catholics from office and even from voting at the time. Nor, again at the federal level, could it involve a role for the Church as part of the structure of government, charged, for example, with education or with consecration of government activities, for the federal Constitution also forbade religious establishment (and left education to the states). At the same time, the Free Exercise Clause of the Constitution protected the freedom of the Church to worship publicly, to own property, even to establish a whole system of Catholic schools and universities, as well as hospitals and social service agencies.[10] Whether these institutions could receive state funds to aid in their operation was a battle fought—and often lost—in many states, with some passing so-called Blaine amendments explicitly forbidding the use of tax money for religious schools, though the effort to pass such an amendment at the federal level failed.[11] One might argue that in those states with such amendments, genuine integralism was precluded, but state constitutions could always be amended again to opposite effect, and at any rate, though the question of a candidate's Catholicism was often at issue in political campaigns, the fact that Catholics were equally enfranchised ensured that it sometimes operated in the favor of Catholic candidates, if also sometimes against them.

9. US Constitution, art. VI; Torcaso v. Watkins, 367 U.S. 488 (1961).

10. Pierce v. Society of Sisters, 268 U.S. 510 (1925).

11. See the discussion of "Blaine amendments" in *Espinoza v. Montana Department of Revenue*, 591 U.S. ___ (2020), slip opinion, p. 15*ff.*, where Montana's was adjudged unconstitutional.

I do not suppose that an integralist can expect that Catholic politicians will succeed in every policy they propose, only that they orient their political activity in the right direction—then exercise the virtue of prudence in deciding what to pursue when and where. It is the nature of republican politics that compromise will usually be necessary and that one must sometimes make common cause with people whom one may dislike, or those with whom one often disagrees, even with those whom one finds unsavory if not immoral. Where Catholics are not in the majority, it will rarely be possible to advocate for a cause simply on the ground that the Church supports it; not only must one find other reasons to persuade those of other faiths or orientations, one must sometimes even avoid specifically Catholic arguments. What can be expected of genuine Catholics among republican officeholders is adherence to the teachings of the Church on matters relevant to their office, and perhaps also consultation with their bishops on matters of policy where questions of the common good might suggest their counsel, even though no explicit question of doctrine is at stake. Here the story of the late nineteenth and early twentieth centuries ought to be instructive, for the emerging social teaching of the Church played an important role, through the efforts of Catholic voters and politicians, in forming national policies in support of government provision of social services and in recognition of the rights of labor. Although *Rerum Novarum* had been promulgated in 1891 and the American bishops drafted and promulgated a program for legislative reform in 1919, chiefly through the efforts of Fr. John Ryan, it is far from clear that either had any direct influence on social legislation or that Catholic politicians would have admitted it publicly if that had been the case.[12] The place to look for what I am calling republican integralism is in Catholics who held public office in the era. Let me briefly sketch the careers of three men, whose most prominent service was each in one of the three principal branches of government.

12. John A. Ryan, *Social Reconstruction* (New York: Macmillan, 1920). I discuss this in "Progressivism, Social Science, and Catholic Social Teaching in the Building of the American Welfare State," in *Progressive Challenges to the American Constitution: A New Republic*, ed. Bradley C. S. Watson (New York: Cambridge University Press, 2017), 160–70.

Three Republican (or Democratic) Integralists

Edward Douglass White was born in Thibodaux, Louisiana, in 1845, son of a prominent planter and politician and grandson of an early settler who had been among the founders of St. Mary's parish in Philadelphia.[13] Educated by the Jesuits in New Orleans, he studied at Mount St. Mary's in Emmitsburg, Maryland, and then at Georgetown before returning home to fight for the Confederacy, being captured and released before seeing much action. By 1865 he was studying law in New Orleans, learning civil law as an apprentice and common law at Tulane. A decade later, at the age of 30, he was appointed to the state supreme court, then returned to private practice and served in the state senate and the US Senate. He was appointed to the US Supreme Court by Grover Cleveland in 1894 and elevated to the chief justiceship by William Howard Taft in 1910. On the court, White tended to support a broad reading of government power, as might be expected of a civil lawyer, dissenting in the *Income Tax Case* and in *Lochner v. New York*, though accepting a narrow reading of the Commerce Power, thus joining the Fuller Court majority in confining Congress's capacity to regulate the national economy.[14] He developed the legal principles that allowed the territories acquired in the Spanish-American War to keep their civil law and not be incorporated into common law and constitutional protections if Congress so chose. He wrote the opinion upholding the draft as constitutional during World War I.[15] As might be expected of a former slave owner and a participant in the Battle of Liberty Place in New Orleans in 1876, he joined the majority in *Plessy v. Ferguson*, though in his last years as chief justice he sided with the majority in *Buchanan v. Warley* and wrote the court's opinions striking down "grandfather clauses" in Oklahoma and Maryland.[16] A friend of James Cardinal Gibbons of Baltimore and clearly conservative in disposition and jurisprudence, he might be described as the closest thing to a European integralist that the United States produced.

Quite different was the "Happy Warrior" Al Smith, the popular governor

13. See Robert Baker Highsaw, *Edward Douglass White: Defender of the Conservative Faith* (Baton Rouge: Louisiana State University Press, 1981), for most of the biographical details here recounted.

14. Pollock v. Farmers' Loan & Trust Co., 157 U.S. 429 (1895); Lochner v. New York, 198 U.S. 45 (1905); see, e.g., United States v. E.C. Knight, 156 U.S. 1 (1895).

15. Insular Cases, 182 U.S. 1 (1901); Selective Draft Law Cases, 245 U.S. 366 (1918).

16. Plessy v. Ferguson, 163 U.S. 357 (1896); Buchanan v. Warley, 245 U.S. 60 (1917); Guinn v. United States, 238 U.S. 347 (1915).

of New York in the 1920s and the Democratic Party's nominee for president in 1928.[17] Smith was born on the Lower East Side of Manhattan in 1873. Dropping out of (Catholic) school at age 14 to help support his family after his father's death, Smith worked a series of jobs in Lower Manhattan before getting involved in city politics and being elected to the state legislature. Noticed as a leading member of the state constitutional convention in 1915, he was elected governor on the Democratic ticket in 1918, was swept out in the Harding landslide of 1920, but returned in 1922 and was reelected in 1924 and 1926, an unprecedented feat in New York politics. His governorship was notable for the passage of minimum wage legislation, protection for labor, and the successful reorganization of state government; he was known to make appointments not of political cronies, but of people of recognized merit—Protestant, Catholic, or Jew, Democrat or Republican. His name was placed in nomination for the presidency at the Democratic National Convention in 1924, but he was defeated (it is generally held) by members of the Ku Klux Klan, who were then at the height of their resurgent power. He won the nomination in 1928 but suffered defeat in the general election by Republican Herbert Hoover.

Smith's Catholicism was an issue in the campaign, a matter joined most eruditely in the pages of the *Atlantic Monthly*. In April 1927, the magazine published an article by a prominent New York lawyer, Charles G. Marshall, an Episcopalian, that quoted Leo XIII's *Immortale Dei* and Pius IX's *Syllabus of Errors* to conclude from the subordination of the temporal to the spiritual power that as president Smith would be obliged by his faith to take orders from the pope.[18] When shown the article, Smith apparently exclaimed, "What the hell is an encyclical?" but after consultation with the archbishop, Patrick Cardinal Hayes—also born on the Lower East Side, a few years before and a few blocks away from Smith—he worked with a popular priest, Fr. Francis P. Duffy, a former seminary professor and army chaplain in the First World War, as well as with an advisor, Judge Joseph M. Proskauer, who was Jewish, to draft a response.[19] Smith categorically denied that "there is conflict

17. For biographical details, I have consulted Christopher M. Finan, *Alfred E. Smith: The Happy Warrior* (New York: Hill and Wang, 2002), and Robert A. Slayton, *Empire Statesman: The Rise and Redemption of Al Smith* (New York: Free Press, 2001).

18. Charles C. Marshall, "An Open Letter to the Honorable Alfred E. Smith," *The Atlantic* (April 1927).

19. Alfred E. Smith, "Catholic and Patriot," *The Atlantic* (May 1927). See Thomas J. Shelley, "'What the Hell Is an Encyclical?' Governor Alfred E. Smith, Charles C. Marshall, Esq., and Father Francis P. Duffy," *U.S. Catholic Historian* 15, no. 2 (Spring 1997): 87–107.

between religious loyalty to the Catholic faith and patriotic loyalty to the United States." Noting he was not a theologian nor a lawyer, he asserted that in his nearly thirty years holding office, he had never experienced a conflict. Key to his sense of the harmony of Church membership and citizenship is his confidence in agreement on common morality:

> The essence of my faith is built upon the Commandments of God. The law of the land is built upon the Commandments of God. There can be no conflict between them. Instead of quarreling among ourselves over dogmatic principles, it would be infinitely better if we joined together in inculcating obedience to these Commandments in the hearts and minds of the youth of the country as the surest and best road to happiness on this earth and to peace in the world to come.[20]

He proceeds to mention other Catholics in high office, specifically Chief Justices Roger Taney and Edward Douglass White; to cite Cardinal Newman's conclusion that the *Syllabus* has "no dogmatic force"; to cite Fr. John Ryan and quote leading members of the American hierarchy to explain that Leo XIII was referring to a state with a wholly Catholic population, not one like America, whose constitutional principles of religious freedom are said by these men to be perfectly compatible with Catholic doctrine in our circumstances; and to refute more particular charges of Roman interference in the politics of other nations in recent years. He concludes by expressing his belief in "absolute freedom of conscience for all men" and "the absolute separation of Church and State."[21]

The third Catholic politician I want to quickly profile is John W. McCormack of Massachusetts.[22] First elected to the House in 1928 and reelected for forty years, he was an important supporter of Franklin Roosevelt's New Deal, majority leader after 1940, and Speaker of the House from 1962 to 1971, presiding over the enactment of Lyndon Johnson's Great Society. Born to a poor family on the South End of Boston, having been abandoned by his father, losing several siblings to tuberculosis in tenements, leaving school to support his mother, parlaying a delivery job into a law office clerkship, learning law by ap-

20. Smith, "Catholic and Patriot."

21. Smith, "Catholic and Patriot."

22. I rely entirely on Garrison Nelson's magisterial biography, *John William McCormack: A Political Biography* (New York: Bloomsbury Academic, 2017).

prenticeship and passing the bar, then navigating Boston Irish politics to win a seat in Congress, McCormack was a straight arrow. He did not drink and ate dinner every night with his wife, though he was for years part of a poker circle on Capitol Hill that included the most powerful midcentury Democrats. (His younger brother "Knocko," once an enforcer for James Michael Curley and then a South Boston tavern owner and longtime grand marshal of the St. Patrick's Day Parade, was at once his opposite and his insurance.) He was friends with Richard Cardinal Cushing (in fact, the cardinal was apparently his confessor), also born poor in South Boston, only a few years later and a few blocks away.

McCormack was well known as a faithful son of the Church when it came to promoting the bishops' agenda in Congress; his biographer says his nickname on the Hill was "the Bishop of Boston." The showdown with John F. Kennedy, the first Catholic elected to the nation's highest office, came in the first months of the new administration, over the question of federal aid to religious schools. Kennedy had made federal aid for education a central part of his domestic agenda, but he had also taken the position that federal aid to parochial schools was unconstitutional. The bishops were pushing for Catholic schools to be included in federal assistance, calling for the bill's defeat if parochial schools were excluded. McCormack, majority leader at the time, was strongly supportive of the bishops' position, and he made common cause with Southern Democrats to see that the bill died in the Rules Committee, much to the consternation of the White House. McCormack and the Kennedy family had a chilly relation, dating back at least a generation in Boston politics and coming to a head the following year when Edward Kennedy defeated McCormack's nephew for the Senate seat that the president had held.

From Kennedy to Cuomo

John F. Kennedy's election to the presidency marked a watershed in American Catholic history. Anti-communism was central to Kennedy's campaign, and the Church, not least its American bishops, including the popular television preacher Bishop Fulton Sheen, was staunchly anti-communist. But Kennedy had gone out of his way to distance himself from the institutional Church, insisting in his much-noted speech to the Houston Ministers Conference, "I am not the Catholic candidate for President. I am the Democratic Party's candidate for President who happens also to be a Catholic."[23] He declared himself "against an Ambassador to the Vatican, against unconstitutional aid to parochial schools, and against any boycott of the public schools (which I have attended myself)."[24] Like Al Smith, he declared himself in favor of separation of church and state, and explained his position thus:

> I believe in an America where the separation of church and state is absolute—where no Catholic prelate would tell the president (should he be Catholic) how to act, and no Protestant minister would tell his parishioners for whom to vote—where no church or church school is granted any public funds or political preference—and where no man is denied public office merely because his religion differs from the President who might appoint him or the people who might elect him.
>
> I believe in an America that is officially neither Catholic, Protestant nor Jewish—where no public official either requests or accepts instructions on public policy from the Pope, the National Council of Churches or any other ecclesiastical source—where no religious body seeks to impose its will directly or indirectly upon the general populace or the public acts of its officials—and where religious liberty is so indivisible that an act against one church is treated as an act against all. . . . I believe in a President whose religious views are his own private affair, neither imposed by him on the nation or imposed by the nation upon him as a condition to holding that office.[25]

Noting that those who complained of the candidacy of a Catholic typically "select quotations out of context from the statements of Catholic church leaders usually in other countries, frequently in other centuries," as had Charles Marshall against Al Smith, Kennedy referred instead to "the statement of the American bishops in 1948 which strongly endorsed church-state separation, and which more nearly reflects the views of almost every American Catholic."[26]

This was a curious reference, for the 1948 "Statement by Catholic Bishops Attacking Secularism as an Evil," published in the *New York Times*, was occasioned by the US Supreme Court's decision in *Everson v. Board of Education* the previous year and their decision that year in *Illinois* ex rel. *McCollum v.*

23. "Address to the Greater Houston Ministerial Association," John F. Kennedy Presidential Library and Museum: Historical Speeches, September 12, 1960, https://www.jfklibrary.org/learn/about-jfk/historic-speeches/address-to-the-greater-houston-ministerial-association.

24. "Address to the Greater Houston Ministerial Association."

25. "Address to the Greater Houston Ministerial Association."

26. "Address to the Greater Houston Ministerial Association."

Board of Education, the first endorsing Jefferson's "wall of separation" between church and state while allowing state aid for bus transportation to parochial schoolchildren, the second striking a "released time" program that allowed for optional religious instruction in public schools.[27] In their statement, the bishops discuss the First Amendment prohibition of religious establishment, which they interpret as prohibiting "preferential treatment to one religion as against another," and they juxtapose to Jefferson's metaphor his actual plan for "a system of cooperation between the various religious groups and the university" of Virginia, which he founded. The aim of the statement is not to endorse separation but to address "the delicate problem of cooperation between Church and State in a country of divided religious allegiance," which they trace back to the founding. Acknowledging then-authoritative papal encyclicals on Church-state relations "under ideal conditions," they add that "the Catholic Church can adapt herself to the particular conditions that may obtain in different countries," and then "find that the First Amendment to our Constitution solved that problem in a way that was typically American in its practical recognition of existing conditions and its evident desire to be fair to all citizens of whatever religious faith."[28]

The thrust of the 1948 statement, from its first words—"Human life centers in God"—through its discussion of the Catholic home, Catholic schooling, economic life, and citizenship, is to oppose secularism, which "has in the past century exercised a corrosive influence," especially on the law, as "it has undermined the religious foundations of law in the minds of many men in the legal profession and has predisposed them to accept the legalistic tyranny of the omnipotent state." Without endorsing any particular public policy, even in relation to parochial schools—interestingly, they note the need for graduate education—they do write, "For if we as Christians are to do our part in restoring order to a chaotic world, Christ must be the Master in our classrooms and lecture halls and the Director of our research projects."[29] That senator and presidential candidate Kennedy would cite the 1948 statement in support of the principles he expounds in the Houston address seems disingenuous, if

27. "Statement by Catholic Bishops Attacking Secularism as an Evil," *New York Times*, November 21, 1948. (I can find no other printing of this statement, signed by fourteen bishops, including Cardinal Spellman of New York and the future Cardinal Cushing of Boston.) Everson v. Board of Education, 330 U.S. 1 (1947); Illinois ex rel. McCollum v. Board of Education, 333 U.S. 203 (1948).

28. "Statement by Catholic Bishops Attacking Secularism."

29. "Statement by Catholic Bishops Attacking Secularism."

not Orwellian. While one might be wary of federal aid to Catholic schools as a matter of policy—surely the bishops themselves would have acknowledged the danger of a secularizing state corrupting those who become dependent upon it—Kennedy's relegation of "religious views" to the realm of one's "own private affair" is precisely the mindset of the secularism the bishops decry. Even before Vatican II's *Dignitatis Humanae*'s emphasis on individual conscience, Kennedy might have invoked that term—which of course was long recognized in American discourse on religious liberty—rather than the modern, liberal term "privacy." And of course the conciliar document teaches, in addition to the right of the individual to religious freedom, that "The social nature of man . . . itself requires that he should give external expression to his internal acts of religion: that he should share with others in matters religious; that he should profess his religion in community."[30] Curiously, Kennedy's predecessor in the presidency, Dwight Eisenhower, had been baptized a few weeks after becoming president, into his wife's Presbyterian faith.[31] Even though anti-Catholic prejudice in America surely made Kennedy's Catholicism more delicate politically than Eisenhower's public profession of faith, it could hardly be said that Americans in 1960 expected their presidents to keep their religion to themselves.

Kennedy's election upon his endorsement of the privatization of religion—or in the bishop's terms, the secularization of society—constitutes a watershed moment in the American history of the relation of religion and politics, quickly followed by the Supreme Court's school prayer cases in 1962 and 1963.[32] Even the court's opinion in *Sherbert v. Verner*, upholding a religious exemption from a general statute as commanded by the Free Exercise Clause, might be seen to ratify this change, as it treated religious objection as a private right.[33] Within two years, the court explicitly invoked this right to privacy to make, for the first time, a constitutional right out of what the Church had taught was a moral wrong, the use of contraception, a right that

30. Second Vatican Council, *Dignitatis Humanae*, para. 3, website of the Holy See, accessed February 19, 2021, https://www.vatican.va/archive/hist_councils/ii_vatican_council/documents/vat-ii_decl_19651207_dignitatis-humanae_en.html.

31. William I. Hitchcock, "How Eisenhower Found God in the White House," History Channel website, accessed August 29, 2021, https://www.history.com/news/eisenhower-billy-graham-religion-in-god-we-trust.

32. Engel v. Vitale, 370 U.S. 421(1962); Abington School District v. Schempp, 374 U.S. 203 (1963).

33. Sherbert v. Verner, 374 U.S. 398 (1963).

by 1972 was endorsed by the court's only Catholic member as an individual right and expanded the following year into a right of abortion.[34] *Griswold v. Connecticut*, the contraception case, but even more so *Roe v. Wade*, the abortion one, make it impossible any longer for Catholic politicians to be able to say as confidently as Al Smith that "the law of the land is built upon the Commandments of God," at least with reference to the modern architects taking charge of renovations. It was to address that new situation that Governor Mario Cuomo of New York spoke at Notre Dame in 1984, laying out what has become the dominant view of the matter, at least among members of his political party, to this day.

Cuomo delivered his address, "Religious Belief and Public Morality: A Catholic Governor's Perspective," at the invitation of the Notre Dame Department of Theology, whose chair, Fr. Richard McBrien, apparently had the blessing of Notre Dame's renowned president, Fr. Theodore Hesburgh.[35] Describing himself as a politician and "a Catholic, a lay person baptized and raised in the pre-Vatican II Church, educated in Catholic schools, attached to the Church first by birth, then by choice, now by love," Cuomo puts the issue thus:

> The Catholic who holds political office in a pluralistic democracy—who is elected to serve Jews and Muslims, atheists and Protestants, as well as Catholics—bears special responsibility. He or she undertakes to help create conditions under which all can live with a maximum of dignity and with a reasonable degree of freedom; where everyone who chooses may hold beliefs different from the specifically Catholic ones—sometimes contradictory to them; where the laws protect people's right to divorce, use birth control and even to choose abortion.
>
> In fact, Catholic public officials take an oath to preserve the Constitution that guarantees this freedom. And they do so gladly. Not because they love what others do with their freedom, but because they realize that in guaranteeing freedom for all, they guarantee our right to be Catholics: our right to pray, to use the sacraments, to refuse birth control devices, to reject abortion, not to divorce and remarry if we believe it to be wrong.

34. Griswold v. Connecticut, 381 U.S. 479 (1965); Eisenstadt v. Baird, 405 U.S. 438 (1972); Roe v. Wade, 410 U.S. 113 (1973).

35. Mario Cuomo, "Religious Belief and Public Morality: A Catholic Governor's Perspective," September 13, 1984, University of Notre Dame Archives. See also Wilson D. Miscamble, CSC, *American Priest: The Ambitious Life and Conflicted Legacy of Notre Dame's Father Ted Hesburgh* (New York: Image, 2019), 190.

> The Catholic public official lives the political truth most Catholics through most of American history have accepted and insisted on: the truth that to assure our freedom we must allow others the same freedom, even if occasionally it produces conduct by them which we would hold to be sinful.[36]

Whatever one can say about Cuomo's account of late-century pluralism, as American history it leaves much to be desired. The ability of Catholics to live and let live had, at least until the 1960s, coincided with a generally shared moral consensus, or at least a consensus that did not promote what Catholics believe to be moral wrongs as constitutional rights—if anything, it was Protestants who complained of Catholic laxity on matters such as gambling and drinking, where Catholics favored prudence and moderation while Protestants insisted on prohibition. Cuomo speaks as though one were legislating from scratch, but the law on divorce, birth control, and abortion had changed dramatically only since John Kennedy's election, with no-fault divorce laws sweeping through state legislatures in the 1970s and the court suspending abortion laws in all the states in one fell swoop in 1973. To be sure, Cuomo has the authority of St. Thomas Aquinas behind him when he argues that not all vices can be suppressed by law and that it is a judgment of prudence when to tolerate wrongdoing for fear of increasing evil by state action.[37] Perhaps even this statement, if taken abstractly, might seem mostly unobjectionable:

> The question "whether or not we admit religious values into our public affairs" is too broad to yield a single answer. "Yes," we create our public morality through consensus and in this country that consensus reflects to some extent religious values of a great majority of Americans. But "no," all religiously based values don't have an a priori place in our public morality. The community must decide if what is being proposed would be better left to private decision than public policy; whether it restricts freedoms, and if so, to what end, to whose benefit; whether it will produce a good or bad result; whether overall it will help the community or merely divide it.[38]

But only "mostly": the substitution of the language of "values" for the stable framework of natural law (prominent in the 1948 statement, by the way) and

36. Cuomo, "Religious Belief and Public Morality."
37. Aquinas, *Summa Theologica* I–II, q. 96, a. 2.
38. Cuomo, "Religious Belief and Public Morality."

the consequent supposition that morality is an artifact society "creates" rather than a reality it either acknowledges or betrays undercuts the real basis of consensus, leaving politicians free to cobble together whatever consensus brings them victory at the polls. "The manipulative invoking of religion to advance a politician or a party is frightening and divisive," says Cuomo, but why is the manipulative invention of moral consensus any less so? Cuomo invokes "the American-Catholic tradition of political realism," even citing the silence of most American bishops on the abolition of slavery before the Civil War and advisory character of their recent pastoral letter on nuclear disarmament. But his "realism," in claiming that the Catholic view on the immorality of abortion is a minority position, that even state prohibitions on abortion would not reduce the practice, that denying Medicaid funding for abortion would do nothing other than "impose financial burdens on poor women who want abortions," that "Catholics, statistics show, support the right to abortion in equal proportion to the rest of the population"—all this, I think, makes hollow his eloquent expression of his personal opposition to abortion as a faithful Catholic ring hollow. Does the relegation of religion to the private sphere mean that religious witness has nothing to add to the public conversation?

Cuomo's argument was, to my mind, definitively answered a decade later by Pope John Paul II's encyclical *Evangelium Vitae*. There St. John Paul laid out with precision the true account of Catholic realism and the duty of the Catholic politician in a republic. On matters like abortion, where a serious wrong is allowed by law that could be suppressed with some success by law, one's duty is to work to move the law toward greater justice, within the limits of what is possible.[39] By endorsing the Supreme Court's invention of the right of abortion and other rights to do wrong, a generation of Catholic politicians has not simply beaten an inevitable retreat, I think, but often led society away from the moral consensus that Catholics and Protestants once shared—something that earlier generations of men such as White, Smith, and McCormack did not do. Their "republican integralism," modest though its achievements may have been in our pluralistic democracy, seems clearly more in line with Catholic teaching than the liberal relativism of more recent Catholic politicians, and more in line with the American tradition of republican liberty than

39. John Paul II, *Evangelium Vitae*, para. 73, website of the Holy See, March 25, 1995, https://www.vatican.va/content/john-paul-ii/en/encyclicals/documents/hf_jp-ii_enc_25031995_evangelium-vitae.html.

the monarchical or administrative integralism to which we have been invited in recent years.

Is something like this possible today? It would depend, I think, upon recovery of an earlier American spirit in the Church and among politicians. The bishops who served a growing immigrant Church and who could still write in the aftermath of the Second World War in criticism of secularization saw themselves as architects of Catholicism in America, not managers of its decline. Together with energetic religious orders, they not only literally built churches, schools, and hospitals, but also saw themselves as building a Catholic culture in America, accommodating themselves to Americans' secular virtues while confidently promoting what Protestant Americans overlooked or shoring up what they had begun to neglect. The politicians, meanwhile, represented their vibrant Catholic communities in the tussle for political goods and brought their Catholic wisdom to their work, whether in the form of White's more cosmopolitan perspective on law, or Smith's patronage of the working poor, or McCormack's tough insistence on a fair distribution of government benefits. They certainly did not seek political gain in dissenting from Church teaching or contradicting it in their personal lives. Today's political issues and social circumstances are clearly different from those faced a century ago, for leaders both in the Church and in the state, but their respective duties to build the kingdom of God and to represent Catholic wisdom seem to me to remain intact, even if inspiration and prudence are still needed to translate principles into action, thought into deed.

PART II

Political Institutions, Catholic Minorities, and the Future

CHAPTER 6

Catholics and Political Parties in the United States

THOMAS F. X. VARACALLI

The election of Joseph R. Biden as the second nominally Catholic president of the United States is a notable moment in American history. Biden's election did not have the same historical significance as John F. Kennedy's victory in 1960, but it spurred several debates among Catholics about the role of church and state, the implications of Pope Francis's papacy, and the controversy surrounding pro-choice politicians receiving communion. Catholics, who abide by the teaching of the Magisterium, criticized him for his advocation of abortion, same-sex "marriage," and transgenderism.[1] The secular Left remained largely ambivalent about his religion. Several progressive Catholics used him as a role model for an evolving liberal Catholicism.[2] Biden also benefited from a carefully tailored image about his religion. Biden's faith is largely private, but public enough to ensure that the country is aware of his religious practices. Thus there were several sympathetic pieces about his Mass attendance on Election Day, his affirmation of the presidential oath on his family's

1. Kenneth Craycraft, "Biden's Betrayal," *First Things*, October 20, 2020, https://www.firstthings.com/web-exclusives/2020/10/bidens-betrayal; Alexandra DeSanctis, "Biden Plays the Catholic Card," *National Review*, August 11, 2020, https://www.nationalreview.com/2020/08/biden-plays-the-catholic-card/.

2. The most comprehensive defense of Biden's Catholicism is found in Massimo Faggioli, *Joe Biden and Catholicism in the United States* (New London: Bayard, 2021). See also Fr. James Martin's interview with Ari Shapiro in All Things Considered, "A Jesuit Priest on How Faith Informs Biden's Leadership," NPR, January 20, 2021, https://www.npr.org/2021/01/20/958905644/a-jesuit-priest-on-how-faith-informs-bidens-leadership.

nineteenth-century Bible during Inauguration Day, and his papal audience with Francis later that year.

Biden's story is emblematic of the trajectory of several midcentury Catholic Democrats, who advanced from ethnic conclaves to mainstream middle-class life. Biden was born into a working-class Irish Catholic family in Scantron. His family struggled financially, but his parents were able to send Biden to Catholic school. Biden's first autobiography, *Promises to Keep*, speaks endearingly about the nuns who taught him, his personal devotion to the rosary (which he learned from his grandparents), and the Scranton stores that proudly displayed crucifixes. He attended the University of Delaware and then law school at Syracuse University. Politically ambitious, he returned to Delaware and immersed himself in Democratic politics, where he fostered an image of himself as a pragmatic and moderate Democrat, concerned with both civil rights and the interests of the white middle class. This balancing act enabled Biden to defeat a two-term Republican incumbent and ascend to the US Senate as one of the youngest senators in American history.[3]

There are several stories that show that Biden maintained a nominally Catholic identity, even if he was not faithful to Church teachings. When he married his first wife, Neilia Hunter, he insisted on a Catholic wedding, over the initial objections of his Protestant father-in-law. Likewise, a Catholic priest presided over his second marriage to Jill Jacobs, though the wedding occurred at the United Nations chapel.[4] In his second autobiography, *Promise Me, Dad*, which recounts the death of his eldest son, Beau, in 2015, Biden shares several instances when he prayed the rosary earnestly in times of crisis.[5] Yet the stories about his Catholic devotion are also accompanied by surprising theological ignorance, especially from his second wife. There are at least two instances in which Jill attempted to interrupt the Sacrament of the Anointing of the Sick. When a Catholic priest was administering last rites to her husband after a spinal tap, she tried to interrupt the priest, since she did not want her husband to think of death. Biden, in his retelling, notably refers to the sacrament as a mere "ceremony."[6] Likewise, when a Catholic priest visited Beau to give him last rites, Jill asked the priest to leave "and not to come back," lest it lead Beau

3. Joseph R. Biden, *Promises to Keep* (New York: Random House, 2007), 57–78.
4. Biden, *Promises to Keep*, 37, 117.
5. Joseph R. Biden, *Promise Me, Dad* (New York: Flatiron Books, 2017), 30, 125, 156.
6. Biden, *Promises to Keep*, 219.

to believe that he was going to die.[7] When Beau is dying, Jill does not console Beau with anything religious. Instead, she asks him "to go to a happy place."[8] No mention in the book is made about whether Beau received last rites. Biden recounts both events as the endearing deeds of a loving wife and stepmother. Yet to a devout Catholic, they are offensive acts, in which a theologically illiterate woman battles against the graces of the sacrament.

Biden's faith is lightweight. In a telling soliloquy about his religion in the face of Beau's death, he writes, "My religious faith provided some refuge from the pain. I've always found comfort in the ritual associated with *my* Catholicism. I find the rosary soothing. It's almost like *my* meditation. And mass is a place I go to be by myself, even in the middle of the crowd."[9] Biden's use of therapeutic language is telling. His faith seems to exist to provide comfort, rather than meaning. It alleviates suffering, instead of embracing it. It soothes, but it does not instruct. It is a personal religion because he transforms it to his tastes. He does not speak of the theological importance of the rosary, prayer, or the Mass. Instead, he speaks of these devotions as a personal preference, as if Catholicism is one of many legitimate wisdom beliefs. Hence it is not surprising that Biden and his second (and infamous) son, Hunter, invited several Protestant ministers, a Jewish rabbi, and a Muslim cleric to join Catholic priests at the altar during Beau's funeral.[10]

Biden's Catholicism is not unique. As Steven Brust and others in this volume point out, this self-styled "cultural Catholicism" is common among Catholics of his generation. Even more telling, the midcentury Catholics of Biden's generation look almost conservative compared to younger Catholics. After all, although Biden's views on abortion and sexuality *are* contrary to Church teaching, at least he attends weekly Mass. Many younger Catholics no longer attend church. Many Catholics reject key Church teachings on abortion, contraception, euthanasia, premarital sex, same-sex "marriage," and transgenderism. Additionally, approximately two-thirds of American Catholics do not believe in core Catholic teachings, like transubstantiation.[11] The

7. Biden, *Promise Me, Dad*, 172.

8. Biden, *Promise Me, Dad*, 190.

9. Biden, *Promise Me, Dad*, 199, emphasis added.

10. Biden, *Promise Me, Dad*, 193.

11. For Catholic views on social issues, see "Very Few Americans See Contraception as Morally Wrong," Pew Research Center, September 26, 2016, https://www.pewforum.org/2016/09/28/4-very-few-americans-see-contraception-as-morally-wrong/. For the figure on transubstantiation, see

rift between what Catholics *ought* to believe and what they *really* believe is significant. Neither the Magisterium nor the bishops have the same influence over the faithful as they did seventy years ago.

The "Catholic vote"—the voting bloc of self-identified Catholics—was never a perfect reflection of Catholic social teaching. On the one hand, the Catholic vote was defensive. Catholics voted against those groups that threatened them—Know Nothing candidates, Blaine Amendment supporters, and prohibitionists, among others. On the other hand, the Catholic vote was motivated by genuine collective interests. Some interests were largely secular, such as party patronage or participation in the city machines. Other interests, however, were influenced by Church teaching on economics, immigration, and social teaching. There are, after all, specific moments in American history when Catholics voted clearly to affirm Church teaching, such as when they voted down Massachusetts state referenda to legalize contraception in both 1942 and 1948.[12] The Massachusetts victories, unfortunately, were soon followed by the slow but continuous splintering of a unified Catholic vote. The Democratic Party changed dramatically in the late 1960s and 1970s, and Catholics, such as Biden, were forced to make a choice about policy preferences. Some progressive and liberal Catholics remained loyal to the Democratic Party because of its commitment to civil rights, collective bargaining, and robust government services for the poor. Conservative Catholics turned to the Republican Party because of its staunch anti-socialism, law and order policies, and social conservatism. The splitting of the Catholic vote in the 1960s and the 1970s had another effect. Catholic Democrats began to accept the doctrines of the emerging New Left, which were contrary to Catholic teaching. For example, Biden and members of the Kennedy clan began to take a pro-choice stance on abortion. Likewise, social conservative Catholics, who joined the Republicans under the auspices of Richard Nixon and Ronald Reagan, began to embrace economic ideas in tension (though perhaps not completely contrary) with Catholic social thought's emphasis on the preferential option for the poor.

Therefore the Church faces three problems. First, the Church continues

---

Gregory A. Smith, "Just One-Third of U.S. Catholics Agree with Their Church That Eucharist Is Body, Blood of Christ," Pew Research Center, accessed January 22, 2022, https://www.pewresearch.org/fact-tank/2019/08/05/transubstantiation-eucharist-u-s-catholics/#:~:text=Transubstantiation%20%E2%80%93%20the%20idea%20that%20during,%27%E2%80%9D.

12. Leslie Woodcock Tentler, *Catholics and Contraception: An American History* (Ithaca, NY: Cornell University Press, 2004), 169.

to lack influence over the political choices of Catholics. Although the Church refrains from endorsing candidates, it has a moral responsibility to instruct and guide the consciences of its congregants. Second, the Catholic vote is split. Neither party encapsulates Catholic social teaching perfectly. Therefore individual Catholics, in accordance with prudence, have had to prioritize certain issues as more morally significant than others. Yet in favoring the primary issues, they often ignore the secondary and tertiary issues, leaving them to the policy analyses of secularists and others. Third, both parties are leading Catholics to accept positions that are contrary to Catholic teaching. As a consequence, both Catholic Republicans and Catholic Democrats have legitimate criticisms of each other. Yet as this chapter argues, the Republican Party is currently the only viable party for faithful Catholics.

The political situation for Catholics is a mess. There is no quick and easy solution to re-create the unity of the prewar Catholic voting bloc, especially since it is easy to exaggerate its original coherence. Yet since voting is a moral act, it is incumbent upon Catholics to vote for candidates who, if not embody, at least approximate Catholic social teaching on both social and economic issues. In order to bridge the divergence between Catholic Democrats and Catholic Republicans, it is necessary to outline the history of Catholic political parties and then map out how the two parties both appeal and repulse Catholics.

Catholic Democrats, 1828–1968

Catholic northern immigrants, western settlers, and states' rights advocates consisted of Andrew Jackson's winning coalition in 1828 and 1832. Catholics found a home in the Democratic Party because it was the party of immigration and expansion. The Democrats gave Catholics political incentives, such as patronage and participation in city machine politics. Most importantly, it provided Catholics political protection from the other political parties of the era. The Whigs and many short-lived third parties, such as the Know Nothings and the Free Soilers, had a virulent anti-Catholic nativist streak. The Whigs even blamed their presidential losses in 1844 and 1852 squarely upon the foreign Catholic vote. Catholics, likewise, were not enamored by the Republicans, the successor of the Whigs, for two reasons. First, the Republicans included many former members of the Know Nothing Party. Second, poor Irish Catholics saw the potential or even partial abolition of slavery as an economic threat. They voted overwhelmingly for James Buchanan in 1856, Stephen Douglas in 1860, and George McClellan in 1864.[13]

Catholics voted for the Democratic Party with varying degrees of support during the nineteenth century, as they became firmly entrenched in the local party patronage of the Democrats. The Republicans continued to have a strong nativist streak and remained opposed to any public funding for Catholic schools, as the state Blaine amendments attest. Republicans viewed Democrats disdainfully, in the words of the Presbyterian Rev. Samuel D. Burchard, as the party of "rum, Romanism, and Rebellion."[14] Yet the alliance between the "Romanism" and the "Rebellion" was an uneasy one. The Ku Klux Klan was anti-Catholic, and the Protestant South was wary of Catholic immigrants. Catholic allegiance to the Democrats weakened in 1896, when William Jennings Bryan became the party's presidential nominee. Catholics had little in common with Bryan's brand of populism, agrarianism, and flirtation with socialism. Although Bryan probably carried Catholics in the election, middle-class Catholics began to gravitate to the Republicans. Catholics admired how Theodore Roosevelt and William Howard Taft managed the Spanish Philippines, and it is possible that a majority of Catholics voted for Taft in the presidential election of 1908.

In the early twentieth century, Catholics began to split their ticket. While they remained loyal to the Democrats at the local level, they became something of a swing vote in presidential elections. Woodrow Wilson received tepid support among Catholics in 1912 and 1916, and Warren Harding and Calvin Coolidge benefited from split-ticket voting in 1920 and 1924. The Election of 1928, however, brought Catholics firmly back to the Democratic ranks. For the first time in its history, the Democrats nominated a Catholic for president; Governor Al Smith of New York received, according to Gallup, an estimated 85 to 90 percent of the Catholic vote.[15]

Smith's nomination inaugurated the well-known and significantly ro-

13. George J. Marlin, *The American Catholic Voter: 200 Years of Political Impact* (South Bend, IN: St. Augustine's Press, 2004), 40, 42, 60, 66, 87–88; William B. Prendergast, *The Catholic Voter in American Politics: The Passing of the Democratic Monolith* (Washington, DC: Georgetown University Press, 1999), 24, 44, 66.

14. Marlin, *American Catholic Voter*, 110.

15. Marlin, *American Catholic Voter*, 94, 99, 104, 109, 111, 118, 121, 155, 157, 164, 171, 179; Prendergast, *The Catholic Voter*, 73–75, 80, 90, 96.

manticized era of the loyal Catholic Democrat. Few groups benefited from Franklin Delano Roosevelt's New Deal more than Catholics. The GI Bill, in particular, inaugurated one of the most important moments in American Catholic history. It established the means for legions of Catholics to attend college or vocational school, advance into the middle class, and move from the ethnic city ghetto into the newly constructed suburbs. Moreover, many important Catholic intellectuals, such as Msgr. John A. Ryan, attempted to entwine Catholic social teaching with the policies of the Democratic Party. These Catholics admired how the Democrats integrated social conservatism with moderately liberal economic policies. They believed that there was a reasonable role for the government to assist the less fortunate (e.g., legal protection for collective bargaining rights) and to defend traditional societal norms against debauchery and vice (e.g., the banning of contraception and prostitution).[16] State and local Democratic leaders, however reluctantly, followed the political clout of the Catholic bishops. When the Massachusetts state legislature was considering the establishment of a lottery, Cardinal William O'Connell's public disapproval essentially ended the debate.[17] Likewise, when Massachusetts attempted to overturn the state law banning contraception for married people, the Boston Archdiocese successfully led campaigns in 1942 and 1948 to defeat the statewide referenda.[18] In turn, Catholics rewarded the midcentury Democratic Party's fusion of social conservatism with a strong welfare state. Catholics, with the exception of the Eisenhower years, remained predominately loyal to the Democrats. Harry Truman received 60 percent of the Catholic vote in 1948. Adlai Stevenson and Dwight Eisenhower roughly split the Catholic vote in 1952 and 1956. Kennedy, a fellow Catholic, carried the Catholic vote by 80 percent, while Lyndon Johnson approximated the same percentage in 1964. Even during the radical year of 1968, Hubert Humphrey received 60 percent of the Catholic vote in 1968.[19]

In the literature of this period, there are several defenses of the Catholic

16. Msgr. Ryan wrote several books, but among the most noteworthy for this argument are John A. Ryan, *A Living Wage: Its Ethical and Economic Aspects* (New York: Grosset and Dunlap, 1906); John A. Ryan, *Family Limitation and the Church and Birth Control* (New York: Paulist, 1916).

17. Russell Shaw, *American Church: The Remarkable Rise, Meteoric Fall, and Uncertain Future of Catholicism in America* (San Francisco: Ignatius, 2013), 133–34.

18. John T. McGreevey, "Shifting Allegiances: Catholics, Democrats, and the GOP," *Commonweal*, September 22, 2006, 16; Tentler, *Catholics and Contraception*, 169.

19. Marlin, *American Catholic Voter*, 199, 223, 234, 236, 257; Prendergast, *The Catholic Voter*, 115, 120, 130, 148, 152, 155.

Democrat. David Carlin and Robert Casey provide the most sympathetic and thoughtful defense of the Catholic Democrat, precisely because they remained loyal to magisterial teachings on abortion and sex while serving in public office as Democrats. Sociologist David Carlin, a former Democratic state legislator from Rhode Island, argues for the compatibility of the New Deal and Catholic social thought. He writes:

> The New Deal followed a *via media* that avoided two extremes condemned in [Catholic social thought]: communism on the one hand, and *laissez-faire* capitalism on the other. The New Deal championed the rights of labor, including above all the right to workers to organize themselves in unions; at the same time, it had no intention of abolishing the rights of capital.[20]

Carlin is correct that Catholic social thought rejects both socialism and laissez-faire capitalism. It rejects socialism's inherent materialism, historicism, idealism, nominalism, and its idolization of politics, in which the state subsumes civil society and the church. Catholic social teaching affirms property and natural rights, while also upholding welfare, unions, and government assistance programs for the poor. Catholic social thought emphasizes both subsidiarity and solidarity; it does not impose a standardized or centralized "one-size-fits-all" solution to politics. The New Deal, according to Carlin, avoided the socialist temptation; it kept the rights of capital and property while protecting the vulnerable, especially workers.

According to this narrative, if Democrats reflected the *via media*, Republicans were the immoderate and greedy capitalists who ignored the common good in favor of their own personal or tribal private goods. Thus the pro-life Democratic Governor of Pennsylvania Robert Casey Sr. argued,

> Only government, when all else fails, can safeguard the vulnerable and powerless. When it reneges on that obligation, freedom becomes a hollow word. A hard-working person unable to find work and support his or her family is not free. A person for whom sickness means financial ruin, with no health insurance to soften the blow, is not free. A malnourished child, an uneducated child, a child trapped in foster care—these children are not free. "Without justice, what are kingdoms but great bands of robbers?" Saint Augustine asked. I believe the most important quality a person can bring

20. David Carlin, *Can a Catholic Be a Democrat? How the Party I Loved Became the Enemy of My Religion* (Manchester, NH: Sophia Institute, 2006), 5.

> to political office is a passion for justice and sense of outrage in the face of injustice.[21]

Casey's invocation of St. Augustine was purposive. Casey was a devout and educated Catholic, and he interpreted government inaction as a significant injustice to the most vulnerable. The state, according to Casey, is not a morally neutral agent. It has a responsibility to act in accordance with objective truth and the common good. Casey believed that the common good was best represented by the Democrats' position on welfare and government regulation. Like many midcentury Catholic Democrats, he insisted that his defense of the unborn was part of the New Deal project to protect the most vulnerable. He claimed that the alternative Republican positions—limited government and deregulation—were rooted more in self-interest than in justice. Republicans were too enamored by the secularism of classical liberalism. They failed to uphold the demands, responsibilities, and obligations of the common good—the cornerstone of citizenship.

Both Carlin and Casey provide a reasonable and thoughtful defense of the compatibility of Catholic social thought and the economic policies of midcentury America. Many faithful scholars, priests, and bishops supported these policies. Yet this narrative is inadequate, and in certain circumstances, wrong. Although there was prima facie compatibility between Catholic social thought and New Deal liberalism on certain matters of policy (e.g., defense of unions), many Catholics were blind to key differences that had existed between the two since the 1930s.

First and foremost, there were significant philosophical differences between Catholics and progressivism. Catholic social thought affirmed the existence of a constant and unchanging human nature accessible through natural law. American progressivism, in contrast, believed in a progressive view of human nature and history. Progressivism's faith in progress demanded the centralization and the expansion of state power, the creation of an administrative state, and central planning. Catholic social thought favored subsidiarity and localism, which the New Deal began to weaken. Catholic social thought affirmed that the Church, family, tradition, and local custom should provide a check against state power. Midcentury progressivism, in contrast, rested upon

21. Robert P. Casey, *Fighting for Life: The Story of a Courageous Pro-Life Democrat Whose Own Brush with Death Made Medical History* (Dallas: Word Publishing, 1996), 137.

a robust and ever-expanding understanding of the state. The modern state is not the exact equivalent of Aristotle's *polis* or Aquinas's *civitas*. The modern sovereign state is an entity that is larger, more demanding, less sympathetic, and occasionally hostile to other important aspects of Catholic political thought, such as natural law, limited government, republicanism, subsidiarity, and localism, among others.[22]

The Church believed that there was a *spiritual* foundation to both government and society, whereas progressivism—exemplified by intellectuals such as John Dewey—viewed politics in a purely materialistic fashion. The progressives dismissed appeals to nature (e.g., natural law or natural right), believing nature itself to be either antiquated or a mere fiction. Instead, they appealed to evolution, historical development, and the demand for continuous social change. Progressives gravitated to social planning and the empiricism of social science without any concern for transcendent truth.[23] The crass materialism of New Deal progressivism reveals itself most clearly on matters concerning sex. New Deal progressivism slowly but surely pushed for the legalization of divorce and contraception, planted the seeds for the legalization of abortion, and engaged in monstrous forms of eugenics. Catholics, however, condemned divorce as contrary to the sacrament of matrimony and contrary to the common good. They taught that contraception was contrary to the natural end of life and considered abortion the equivalent of infanticide. They were one of the few voices to condemn eugenics as a gross violation of human dignity.[24]

The materialism of New Deal progressivism was also soft on socialism and the threat of communism. Roosevelt was not a socialist, but some of his advisers were. Vice President Henry Wallace, in a speech before the Congress of American Soviet Friendship, demonstrated dangerous sympathy for the Soviet Union.[25] Roosevelt, despite his leadership during the Second World War, was soft on Joseph Stalin and the larger threat of Soviet communism. American progressivism did not condone the collectivism of communism, but it sig-

22. Many of these themes are fleshed out in Ronald J. Pestritto, *America Transformed: The Rise and Legacy of American Progressivism* (New York: Encounter, 2021), 15–51.

23. James Ceaser, *Nature and History in American Political Development* (Cambridge, MA: Harvard University Press, 2006), 70–81.

24. E.g., in the infamous *Buck v. Bell* case, eight Supreme Court justices upheld the constitutionality of forced sterilization. Only Pierce Butler, the Catholic justice, dissented. See Ryan J. Barilleaux, "Justice Pierce Butler's Catholic Jurisprudence," *Catholic Social Science Review* 25 (2020): 121–39.

25. Henry Wallace, "Address before Congress of American Soviet Friendship," November 8, 1942, http://www.ibiblio.org/pha/policy/1942/421108f.html.

nificantly underestimated its dangers because of its own reliance on expansive federal government, central planning, and the administrative state. Catholics, however, were staunchly anti-communist; every Sunday, they prayed to St. Michael at the end of Mass for the conversion of Russia. The Spanish Civil War provides one of the most illuminating examples of the differences between progressives and Catholics. Catholics, because of their anti-communism, supported Francisco Franco, who protected Catholics from priest-killers, while progressives—from Ernest Hemingway to Rick Blaine in *Casablanca*—supported the "republicans."[26] The consistency and tenacity with which Catholics condemned communism was one of the things that helped to Americanize a church of recent immigrants. It was also one of the reasons why Catholics began to drift to conservatism and the Republican Party.

Catholics Divided, 1972 to Present

During the Progressive Era, liberal progressivism dominated the public square. The noted literary critic Lionel Trilling, in his classic *The Liberal Imagination*, asserted that "in the United States at this time liberalism is not only the dominant but even the sole intellectual tradition."[27] Yet by the time of its publishing, the intellectual world was changing. Some were beginning to doubt that liberalism and progressivism led to progress; in fact, the conservative position was that progressivism was regressive. Conservatism was more of a "big tent" than a blanket ideology, and conservatives disagreed (and still disagree) about what constitutes the problems of progressivism. Social conservatives argued that societal problems were cultural. Richard Weaver lamented that modernity created "moral idiots," while Russell Kirk championed the preservation of the "permanent things."[28] Economic conservatives, in contrast, criticized the expansion of state power as contrary to liberty. F. A. Hayek decried the "road to serfdom" paved by an expansive administrative state.[29] For many, conservatism was the fruit of long intellectual struggle; several postwar conservatives

26. James Chappel, *Catholic Modern: The Challenge of Totalitarianism and the Remaking of the Church* (Cambridge, MA: Harvard University Press, 2018), 99–100.

27. Lionel Trilling, *The Liberal Imagination* (New York: New York Review of Books, 1950), xv.

28. Richard Weaver, *Ideas Have Consequences* (Chicago: University of Chicago Press, 1984), 1; Russell Kirk, *Enemies of the Permanent Things: Observations of Abnormity in Literature and Politics* (Providence, RI: Cluny, 2016)

29. F. A. Hayek, *The Road to Serfdom* (Chicago: University of Chicago Press, 2007).

were former Marxists, socialists, and radicals, such as James Burnham, Whittaker Chambers, Max Eastman, and Frank Meyer.[30] Several conservatives converted to Catholicism: Willmore Kendall, L. Brent Bozell, Russell Kirk, Frank Meyer, and Jeffrey Hart, among many others.[31]

The most important Catholic conservative intellectual was William F. Buckley. In 1951, he published his first book, *God and Man at Yale*, a scathing criticism of Yale's anti-Christian secularism and anti-capitalist collectivism. Although the book is mostly a criticism of various professors at Yale, its historical importance lies in foreshadowing and sketching the basic American Catholic conservative position: economic collectivism and socialism lead inevitably to hostile secularism. The more the state controls the individual, the more it plays God and aims to mold the individual into the image of the state. Its collectivism leads to materialism. A collectivist state is opposed to the transcendent truths of Christianity because the state does not want a check against its sovereignty and authority. Therefore, to combat collectivism, America needs strong, virtuous, and entrepreneurial individuals; healthy families; and a limited government that does not infringe upon liberty.[32] Catholic conservatism became more mainstream with the creation of the secular, but Catholic-friendly, *National Review*.

The political impact of Catholic conservatism was, at first, rocky. The most significant conservative Catholic Republican in the 1950s was Joseph McCarthy, whose legacy is now remembered as "McCarthyism." Catholics in the 1950s had an overall positive view of McCarthy, and Buckley defended him in *McCarthy and His Enemies*.[33] McCarthy eventually fell into disgrace, but recent work suggests that more of his original claims had merit than were previously thought.[34] Catholic conservatism took a significant hit in 1960, when Kennedy swept the Catholic vote. Yet in 1964, a notable minority of Catholics pulled for Barry Goldwater. L. Brent Bozell ghost-wrote *The Con-*

30. George Nash, *The Conservative Intellectual Movement in America since 1945* (Wilmington: Intercollegiate Studies Institute, 2017), xvi.

31. Patrick Allitt, *Catholic Intellectuals and Conservative Politics in America* (Ithaca, NY: Cornell University Press, 1993), 3.

32. William F. Buckley, *God and Man at Yale: The Superstitions of "Academic Freedom"* (Washington, DC: Regnery, 2017), esp. chaps. 1–2.

33. William F. Buckley and L. Brent Bozell, *McCarthy and His Enemies* (Washington, DC: Regnery, 1954).

34. M. Stanton Evans, *Blacklisted by History: The Untold History of Senator Joe McCarthy* (New York: Crown Forum, 2007).

science of a Conservative for Goldwater, and Phyllis Schlafly came to prominence with *A Choice, Not an Echo*.[35]

Catholic Republicanism developed not only because of conservative Catholics activists, but also as a response *against* the Democratic Party. Between 1968 and 1972, the New Left emerged, and it wanted to use the Democratic Party as a vehicle for radical social change. The Democrats became the party of second-wave feminism, the sexual revolution, abortion on-demand, and gay "rights." This change was engineered not simply by the youth, but by several key Democrats with ties to the Kennedy family. One of the most important architects of this cultural shift was Frederick G. Dutton, Kennedy's first cabinet secretary and a core advisor for Robert F. Kennedy's 1968 presidential campaign. Dutton, in his influential *Changing Sources of Power*, argued that the youth vote emerging in the 1970s and 1980s would fundamentally shift American politics in a more progressive direction. Dutton's book is now largely neglected because, as progressives often do, he predicted the future incorrectly. Still, Dutton's book is illuminating. Although Democrats largely championed Catholics for more than a century, the only significant attention Dutton gives to Catholics is negative. He criticizes the Catholic vote for its hostility to the emerging youth culture and Black migration to northern cities.[36] Dutton and other Democrats began to perpetuate the notion that white ethnic Catholics were too conservative, traditional, racist, and patriarchal for the emerging Democratic Party. Therefore the party's coalition shifted. Instead of appealing to Catholics and the working class (who were, for the most part, opposed to social progressivism), the party appealed to young radicals, feminists, and educated suburbanites.[37] The implicit secularism of the Great Society morphed quickly into a radical secularism.

The New Left directly threatened the ancient teachings of the Catholic Church. Catholics viewed marriage sacramentally, whereas the emerging second-wave feminist movement perceived marriage as a mere transactional contract at best and as harshly patriarchal at worst. Catholics condemned divorce, whereas progressives championed no-fault divorce laws. Catholics

35. Allitt, *Catholic Intellectuals*, 142; Phyllis Schlafly, *A Choice, Not an Echo* (Washington, DC: Regnery, 2014).

36. Frederick G. Dutton, *Changing Sources of Power: American Politics in the 1970s* (New York: McGraw Hill, 1971), 117–19.

37. Mark Stricherz, "Goodbye, Catholics: How One Man Reshaped the Democratic Party," *Commonweal*, November 4, 2005, 10–13.

asserted that abortion was infanticide, whereas the New Left made abortion and contraception the foundations of women's rights. As the New Left began to make inroads among the Democrats, Catholics were not fully aware of the dangers of this shift. Local and state legislators were often more conservative than the national leaders. Plus millions of Catholics continued to vote for their economic interests, such as their support for unions and government-sponsored programs. This shortsightedness allowed some Democrats to believe that they could sweep social conservatism under the rug if they prioritized economic progressivism. It somewhat worked, insofar as it paved the way for men like Joe Biden, Mario Cuomo, and countless Democrats to shift further leftward. It somewhat failed in that it split the Catholic vote.

By 1972, the Catholic vote was no longer safe for Democrats. Nixon carried a clear Catholic majority in his reelection campaign. Jimmy Carter received 56 percent of the vote in 1976 but only 39 percent in 1980.[38] Catholics did not become more conservative. They simply affirmed the same political positions that they had held twenty years earlier. After all, in the 1960s and 1970s, the politics of church-attending Catholics centered on their family, the security of the neighborhood, support for unions, good schools, and socially conservative political positions on abortion and school prayer. Unsurprisingly, the majority of Catholics did not approve of the antiauthority social protest movements, the city riots, and the counterculture.[39] Many Catholics, despite mixed feelings about Vietnam, viewed the burning of the American flag as an *infamia*. Frustration with the Democrats intensified. During his transition from liberalism to conservatism, Michael Novak called in vain for an "ethnic Democratic Party" in 1971.[40] Instead, the emerging liberal coalition of white progressives and racial minorities became increasingly unsympathetic to white ethnic Catholics. After all, white ethnic Catholics disliked affirmative action, busing, and the migration of Blacks into their historical neighborhoods. Many Catholics spoke of their historical neighborhoods in religious language; the intrusion of non-Catholics into their neighborhood was a palpable cultural threat. Affirmative action and busing in particular violated the Catholic prin-

38. James M. Penning, "Changing Partisanship and Issue Stands among American Catholics," *Sociological Analysis* 47, no. 1 (Spring 1986): 31.

39. Michael Novak, *The Rise of the Unmeltable Ethnics: Politics and Culture in the Seventies* (New York: MacMillan, 1972), 6–9, 64–65, 206–7, 237–66.

40. Novak, *Rise of the Unmeltable Ethnics*, 267–91.

ciple of subsidiarity in favor of centralized planning guided by abstract reason, with little regard for preexisting communities.[41]

The middle to late twentieth century also marked increased tension between the laity and the clergy. The United States Conference of Catholic Bishops (USCCB) initially pushed progressive policies that included a staunch anti-war stance, the demand for nuclear deterrence, an end to capital punishment, support for government-funded projects to eliminate poverty, and increased attention to the social ills in the Third World. The dominance of progressive American bishops, exemplified by Cardinal Joseph Bernandin, lasted well into the 1990s, until John Paul II reformed some, but not all, the major archdioceses. Thus, in an age when Catholics voted overwhelmingly for Ronald Reagan, Catholic bishops were authoring *The Challenge of Peace: God's Promise and Our Response* (1983) and *Economic Justice for All: Catholic Social Teaching and the United States Economy* (1986).[42] The average Catholic was more conservative than the policies of their bishops. Therefore these documents had little impact upon the laity or the Church. The Catholic bishops found themselves politically stranded. They held several Democratic views, but they were disturbed by the Democrats' increased support for abortion and sexual liberation. Democratic support for second-wave feminism morphed into an embrace of the postmodernism embedded in third-wave feminism.

For the most part, it was the laity, not the clergy, who grasped the existential threat of the New Left. Thus the Catholic laity helped champion the issue that would serve as the powerful wedge between Catholics and Democrats: abortion. Although polls show that Catholics are divided upon the issue, faithful church-attending Catholics—who are also most likely to vote *as Catholics*—are overwhelmingly against abortion. In other words, pro-choice Catholics are, on average, not as religious or committed to the faith as church-attending Catholics.[43] Abortion is one of the key issues that turned Catholic Democrats into Catholic Republicans. Catholics were at the forefront of the pro-life movement, even before *Roe v. Wade* was decided. They continue to be the main leaders of the pro-life cause because of the significant

41. Novak, *Rise of the Unmeltable Ethnics*, 8.

42. Joseph A. Varacalli, *The Catholic Experience in America* (Westport, CT: Greenwood Press, 2006), 172, 186.

43. Dalia Fahmy, "Eight Key Findings about Catholics and Abortion," Pew Research Center, October 20, 2020, https://www.pewresearch.org/fact-tank/2020/10/20/8-key-findings-about-catholics-and-abortion/.

intellectual and spiritual support they receive from the Church's unequivocal condemnation of abortion. In *Humanae Vitae*, Paul VI instructed, "We are obliged once more to declare that the direct interruption of the generative process already begun and, above all, all direct abortion, even for therapeutic reasons, are to be excluded as lawful means of regulating the number of children."[44] It then reaffirmed, in even more stringent terms, the pro-life position in the 1992 edition of *The Catechism of the Catholic Church,* the 2005 edition of *The Compendium*, and a litany of encyclicals by several different popes.[45]

Catholic social thought teaches that abortion is murder. There is no more important political issue than stopping murder. Abortion therefore *has* to be the preeminent issue for faithful Catholics. Faithful Catholics cannot ignore Church teachings on economics, immigration, and social justice, but the moral severity of abortion is paramount and cannot be reasonably compared to injustices in which people still live. Therefore abortion is *the* sign of how the Democrats betrayed their own values. Until the mid-1970s, the Democrats were the more pro-life party. Many leading Democrats—Edward Kennedy, Hubert Humphrey, Thomas Eagleton, Dick Gephardt, Al Gore, and Jesse Jackson—were once pro-life. Sargent Shriver, McGovern's vice-presidential nominee, was a stalwart defender of life.[46] Many Republican governors in the 1960s and 1970s, such as Nelson Rockefeller of New York, William Milliken of Michigan, and Ronald Reagan of California, were actively pro-choice. Of the Richard Nixon appointees to the Supreme Court, only William Rehnquist, his fourth and last appointee, dissented in *Roe.* But then, as the New Left successfully integrated into the Democratic Party and as the emerging Religious Right aligned with the Republicans, a series of switches occurred. Senator Edward Kennedy became pro-choice, while Ronald Reagan became pro-life.[47]

The number of vocal pro-life Democrats dwindled throughout the 1980s

44. Paul VI, *Humanae Vitae*, para. 14, website of the Holy See, accessed June 11, 2022, https://www.vatican.va/content/paul-vi/en/encyclicals/documents/hf_p-vi_enc_25071968_humanae-vitae.html.

45. *Catechism of the Catholic Church*, para. 2270–75, United States Conference of Catholic Bishops, accessed June 11, 2022, https://www.usccb.org/sites/default/files/flipbooks/catechism/548/; Pontifical Council for Justice and Peace, *The Compendium of the Social Doctrine of the Church* (Washington, DC: United States Conference of Catholic Bishops, 2005), para. 233. John Paul II, *Evangelium Vitae*, esp. chap. 3, website of the Holy See, accessed May 21, 2022, https://www.vatican.va/content/john-paul-ii/en/encyclicals/documents/hf_jp-ii_enc_25031995_evangelium-vitae.html.

46. John T. McGreevy, "Shifting Allegiances: Catholics, Democrats, and the GOP," *Commonweal,* September 22, 2006, 14–19; David Williams, *Defenders of the Unborn: The Pro-Life Movement before Roe v. Wade* (New York: Oxford University, 2016), 169, 171, 187–88, 246.

47. Williams, *Defenders of the Unborn*, 1, 80–84.

and 1990s. The most notable pro-life Democrat was Pennsylvania Governor Robert Casey. Casey, as mentioned above, believed that the common good was best represented by the Democrats' positions on welfare and government regulation. In embracing the legality of abortion, Democrats became shockingly unfaithful to their once-held ideals. In his autobiography *Fighting for Life*, Casey lamented, "Somehow, for reasons deeply mysterious to me, [the Democrats] cannot or will not see the connection between children's rights and abortion . . . Who expected that we would ever *think* of a mother and a child as having separate interests, as rivals in a dispute over power?"[48] The pro-choice position was simply "raw self-interest."[49] Unlike many Catholic Democrats, Casey maintained his belief in the integrity of the pro-life cause until his death, serving as the most important champion of the unborn during the last two decades of the twentieth century. He consciously chose the then-pro-life state senator Mark Singel as his lieutenant governor. Casey embraced his role in *Casey v. Planned Parenthood* and actively sought to defend the Pennsylvania Abortion Control Act of 1982 against Planned Parenthood's legal challenge. Owing to his role as a pro-life champion, the Democrats banned him from delivering a speech in defense of the unborn at the Democratic National Convention in 1992. Deeply disappointed by Clinton's presidency, he established an exploratory committee for president, only to drop out due to his deteriorating health. He passed away in 1999, as did any hope of a strong pro-life resurgence in the Democratic Party.[50]

Millions of Catholics still think like Casey once did, and they are torn by the current political party makeup. The cultural conservatism of devout Catholics did not lead automatically to a complete embrace of the Republican Party. Many Catholics in the Midwest were union workers willing to vote for Democrats perceived to be moderate, such as Bill Clinton. Moreover, ethnic white Catholics—many of whom were working class—voted Democratic out of the belief that the Democrats were the party of the working man.

The current Republican Party struggles to attract economically minded Catholics who want protections for welfare, unions, immigration, entitlement programs, and government-sponsored health care. One of the most cogent

48. Casey, *Fighting for Life*, 146, 147.

49. Casey, *Fighting for Life*, 147.

50. Casey, *Fighting for Life*, 102, 178–89, 197–213. For his articulate positions on abortion, see esp. chap. 13.

defenses of limited government comes from former Speaker of the House Paul Ryan in his personal manifesto, *The Way Forward.* Ryan argues:

> When we look at America, what's the first thing we see: government or society? For me, the answer is society . . . Society functions through institutions that operate in the space between the individual and the state. They include the family and extend to what academics call "civil society"—our religious organizations, our charitable groups, and the markets that compose our free society. . . . Government is not the ultimate or supreme social institution; rather, it is the enabler of other institutions. It exists to keep us safe, to enforce uniform laws, to enable free and open exchange, to ensure fair competition in the marketplace, to promote economic growth, and to provide some basic protections to the vulnerable from the worst risks of human life. But when government doesn't live up to these responsibilities—or oversteps its proper boundaries—all kinds of problems emerge. Instead of facilitating our way of life, it hollows out that vital space where the things we find most meaningful and rewarding occur.[51]

Ryan acknowledges like Msgr. Ryan, Casey, and Carlin that there is an inherent danger to crass individualism, greed, and vice. Government also has a role in combating them. But the former speaker of the house addresses something that Catholic Democrats often neglect: the government can foster individualism, materialism, greed, and other forms of vice as easily as the free market, corporations, and other private interests. In fact, the centralized power of the government makes it potentially more dangerous than the free market. Speaker Ryan fears that, under the Democrats' paradigm of governance, the state subsumes society. Society is usually more conservative and religious than the state. When the state champions liberal progressive ideals, the state can quash conservative traditions and customs, like prayer in public school, state regulations on abortion, bans on pornography and sodomy, and the defense of traditional marriage, among *many* other examples.

Democrats and progressives often attempt to portray Speaker Ryan as a callous libertarian enamored by the doctrines of Ayn Rand, whom he read in college. Yet Ryan's mature thought is opposed to Randian economics. He neither makes appeals to selfishness nor pushes social Darwinism. Rand herself did not share Ryan's concern for a strong civil society. Ryan wants to help the

51. Paul Ryan, *The Way Forward: Renewing the American Idea* (New York: Twelve Books, 2014), 28–29.

poor, the elderly, the unemployed, and working families. Yet he believes that the vulnerable should be served in accordance with the principle of subsidiarity—through local government and organizations (both private and public) with some assistance from the federal government when needed. For Ryan, the demands of Catholic social thought are met best through subsidiarity and solidarity, not through the administrative state or the federal bureaucracy.[52]

On the one hand, Paul Ryan's argument is in tension with the standard position of midcentury Catholic Democrats, who relied upon the New Deal and, to a lesser extent, the Great Society. On the other hand, Ryan's emphasis on solidarity is more compatible with the pre-New Deal Democratic Party, which emphasized the localism of party machines, regionalism, and cultural pluralism. Ultimately, Ryan is correct that contemporary Democrats ignore the danger of the liberalizing and secularizing effects of the state. Unfortunately, too many Catholic Democrats have either ignored or succumbed to the party's secularizing tendencies.

The Contemporary Democratic Party and Its Future

The Democrats have policies that are contrary to Church teaching on the most important issues to faithful Catholics—abortion, homosexuality, and religious liberty. Millions of Catholics, however, ignore or belittle these issues and are still willing to vote for the party of death. Therefore the Democrats have several ways in which to court Catholics. The first, and perhaps newest, way has been opened by the theology of Pope Francis. Francis has condemned abortion and various forms of gender ideology, but the focus of his pontificate has been to further policy positions closer to the Democrats. Francis speaks often about the necessity of government support for the poor, health care, immigration, and environmental protection. He has called for the abolition of the death penalty. He considered receiving the COVID vaccine "an act of love" and criticized individuals who had concerns about the vaccine's origins.[53] Francis is also the author of some stunning condemnations of capital-

52. Ryan, *The Way Forward*, 233.

53. Devin Watkins, "Pope Francis Urges People to Get Vaccinated against Covid-19," *Vatican News*, August 18, 2021, https://www.vaticannews.va/en/pope/news/2021-08/pope-francis-appeal-covid-19-vaccines-act-of-love.html.

ism. Political scientist Daniel Mahoney, in his important *The Idol of Our Age*, has convincingly argued that Francis personifies "misplaced contemporary humanitarianism."[54] Francis, Mahoney argues, sometimes conflates Christian charity with secular humanitarianism. He does not sufficiently emphasize conversion, redemption, and virtue ethics.[55] His sympathy for dictators (e.g., Castro), his compromises with authoritarian nations (e.g., China), his continual criticisms of the United States, and history of questionable activities (e.g., interviews with journalists who claim that the pope denied the existence of hell) have given the Catholic Left a renewed foothold in arguing that the future of the Catholic Church rests with policies similar to the Democratic Party.

A second way in which Democrats hope to court Catholic votes is through health care. The *Compendium of the Catholic Church* lists health care as an essential human right.[56] Some Catholics in America view this right as one that must be provided by the state. Therefore it is not surprising that the USCCB initially supported the Affordable Care Act, when the bishops had the initial assurance that the law would not require mandatory contraceptive coverage. The Obama administration's Health and Human Services (HHS) mandate, promulgated by executive order in January 2012, was hotly condemned by the Catholic bishops. Yet the condemnation was of the additional mandate only, not of the other provisions of the Affordable Care Act. Few bishops were willing to take the stance that the HHS mandate was so egregious that the law in toto had to be revoked. Republicans therefore did not have strong allies among the bishops on the topic. When they attempted to repeal and replace the Affordable Care Act, the bishops raised significant reservations about their proposed plan. In a letter to the Senate cosigned by Cardinal Timothy Dolan, Archbishop William Lori, Bishop Frank Dewane, and Bishop Joe Vasquez, the bishops claimed that "health care is not a privilege, but a right in keeping with the life and dignity of every person."[57] This right-to-health-care argument provides the Democrats with several opportunities. It allows Democrats to

54. Daniel J. Mahoney, *The Idol of Our Age: How the Religion of Humanity Subverts Christianity* (New York: Encounter, 2018), 91.

55. Mahoney, *Idol of Our Age*, 91–113.

56. *Compendium of the Catholic Church*, para. 166.

57. Timothy Dolan, William Lori, Frank Dewane, and Joe Vasquez, "Dear Senator," United States Conference of Catholic Bishops, July 1, 2017, http://www.usccb.org/issues-and-action/human-life-and-dignity/health-care/upload/Senate-Principles-letter-Health-Care-Reform-2017-06-01.pdf.

push for expansive government programs. It suggests that Republicans who do not adhere to the argument that the right to health care must be provided by the state are themselves unfaithful "cafeteria" Catholics. Moreover, through grandiose but exaggerated rhetoric, they can frame health care as an issue of equal moral gravity to abortion and religious liberty.

Immigration is another issue where Democrats can reclaim some lost ground with Catholics. For the past thirty years, both doctrinally orthodox (Archbishop Charles Chaput, Cardinal Timothy Dolan, Archbishop Jose Gomez) and progressive bishops (Cardinal Roger Mahony, Cardinal Joseph Bernardin, Cardinal Blase Cupich) have provided robust defenses of legal immigration and additional protection for undocumented workers. Some conservatives have dismissed the bishops' support of immigration because Hispanics are overwhelmingly Catholic. The bishops have pushed back against this argument. They point to twentieth-century encyclicals, the writings of the last three popes, and the *Catechism of the Catholic Church*, which frames migration as a "natural right."[58]

As Ashleen Menchaca-Bagnulo argues in her essay in this volume, Hispanic Catholics are overwhelmingly Democratic despite a notable contingent of Hispanic Republicans. Although millions of white Catholics became Republican in the 1980s, Hispanic Catholics (who tend to be more recent immigrants) did not shift as significantly to the party of Ronald Reagan.[59] At the beginning of the Trump administration, it looked like Republicans had not made gains with Hispanic Catholics. Many Hispanic Catholics opposed the border wall, raids by Immigration and Customs Enforcement, and family separations, among others. Cardinal Dolan compared many of Trump's stances on immigration to the anti-Catholic Know Nothing Party.[60] Yet the 2020 election did show that Trump and the Republicans gained significant Hispanic support in southern Texas and Florida. Much of this support seems to be economically minded, perhaps mirroring some reasons why white Catholics gravitated to the Republicans in the 1970s and 1980s. Trump's condemnation

58. "Catholic Church's Position on Immigration Reform," United States Conference of Catholic Bishops, August 2013, https://www.usccb.org/issues-and-action/human-life-and-dignity/immigration/churchteachingonimmigrationreform.

59. Penning, "Changing Partisanship," 38

60. Cardinal Dolan, "Why Donald Trump's Anti-Immigrant Rhetoric Is So Problematic," *Washington Post*, July 31, 2015, https://www.washingtonpost.com/news/acts-of-faith/wp/2015/07/31/cardinal-dolan-why-donald-trumps-anti-immigrant-rhetoric-is-so-problematic/.

of socialism and government regulation resonated with many Hispanics. This anti-socialist stance is compatible with Catholic thought.[61] Still, the Democrats carry the Hispanic vote substantially.

Fourth, Democrats have used dissenters to bolster their appeal to progressive Catholics. For example, Democrats invited dissident Sister Simone Campbell of the Nuns on the Bus to speak at the 2012 Democratic National Convention in Charlotte. The Nuns on the Bus movement was sparked by Pope Benedict XVI's just and fair criticism of liberal nuns who ignored or outrightly questioned core Catholic teaches on abortion and homosexuality. Liberal nuns in America challenged Benedict and in doing so gained media notoriety. Armed with this secular attention, the nuns pivoted to discuss economic inequality and social justice. Sister Campbell, before the Democratic National Convention, condemned the budgetary positions of Paul Ryan. The Charlotte crowd applauded, mostly because a Catholic sister was criticizing Ryan, who prided himself on fidelity to Catholic teachings. Then, Campbell concluded her remarks by doing exactly what Benedict had criticized. Campbell considered her support of the Affordable Care Act to be "part of my pro-life stance," but failed to address the millions killed by abortion.[62] Four years later, during the presidential election campaign between Donald Trump and Hillary Clinton, Campbell, in an interview for *Democracy Now!*, blamed the existence of abortion deterministically on economic inequality and consolingly told a woman who had an abortion that she was against the outlawing of abortion.[63]

During the Trump administration, Democrats became increasingly hostile to Catholicism. Senator Bernie Sanders of Vermont (an Independent who caucuses with the Democrats), in a Senate hearing on the nomination of Russell Vought to be deputy director of the Office of Management and Budget, pressed Vought on his belief in the Christian doctrine of hell. Sanders found

61. Aaron Zitner, "Why Hispanic Voters Are Shifting toward the Republican Party," *Wall Street Journal*, January 12, 2022, https://www.wsj.com/story/why-hispanic-voters-are-shifting-toward-the-republican-party-1addo4ef.

62. Simone Campbell, "Transcript of Simone Campbell Remarks as Prepared for Delivery, Democratic National Convention," Daily Kos, September 5, 2012, https://www.dailykos.com/stories/2012/9/5/1128209/-Transcript-of-Simone-Campbell-remarks-as-prepared-for-delivery-Democratic-National-Convention.

63. "Nuns on the Bus at the DNC: Sister Simone Campbell on Abortion Rights, Wealth Gap, Kaine in Honduras," Democracy Now, July 29, 2016, https://www.democracynow.org/2016/7/29/nuns_on_the_bus_at_the.

the standard Christian doctrine to be Islamophobic and questioned whether he could adequately represent all Americans.[64] Many outlets were quick to condemn Sanders's question as a religious test. His comment, however, was overshadowed months later when Senator Dianne Feinstein of California, in a Senate Judiciary Committee hearing on Amy Coney Barrett's nomination to the Sixth Circuit, complained to Barrett that the "dogma lives loudly within you . . . and that's of concern when you come to big issues that large numbers of people have fought for years in this country."[65] Feinstein doubted that Barrett would be an impartial judge because of her personal pro-life stance. Feinstein was criticized by Republicans and some Democrats. But perhaps the most egregious case of anti-Catholic bias occurred when both Senator Mazie Hirono of Hawaii and then-Senator Kamala Harris of California criticized Brian Buescher, a judicial nominee to the District Court of Nebraska, for being a member of the Knights of Columbus. Hirono stated, "the Knights of Columbus have taken a number of extreme positions."[66] Hirono then attempted to frame opposition to same-sex marriage—a position most Americans held fifteen years ago—as an extreme position. Hirono and Harris were criticized, but the Left was mostly silent. Ultimately, Vought, Barrett, and Buescher were appointed to their posts. Yet if Democrats are willing to criticize an organization as moderate and relatively apolitical as the Knights of Columbus, Catholics will certainly have more fights with Democrats in the near future.

Democratic anti-Catholicism is not simply limited to the federal government. It was also apparent during the COVID-19 pandemic, when Democratic governors and local mayors threatened and intimated all Christian denominations from attending church services. Owing to the sheepishness of the bishops and other religious leaders, these measures were not adequately challenged by the Catholic Church—giving the government some precedent for rolling back religious liberty protections in the future. Governor Andy

64. Camila Domonoske, "Is It Hateful to Believe in Hell? Bernie Sanders' Questions Prompt Backlash," NPR, June 9, 2017, https://www.npr.org/sections/thetwo-way/2017/06/09/532116365/is-it-hateful-to-believe-in-hell-bernie-sanders-questions-prompt-backlash.

65. Dianne Feinstein, "The Dogma Lives Loudly within You," C-SPAN, September 6, 2017, https://www.c-span.org/video/?c4723518/dianne-feinstein-the-dogma-lives-loudly-youand.

66. Valerie Richardson, "Harris, Hirano Accused of Anti-Catholic 'Bigotry' for Targeting Knights of Columbus," *Washington Times*, December 30, 2018, https://www.washingtontimes.com/news/2018/dec/30/kamala-harris-mazie-hirono-target-brian-buescher-k/.

Beshear of Kentucky ordered police to take down car license plate numbers of Easter church attendees in order to impose a two-week quarantine. Mayor Bill de Blasio of New York threatened to send the police and fire departments to check if religious services were held.[67] Even when states began to reopen partially from the lockdown, churches were not deemed "essential services" in some states. On May 13, 2020, Minnesota Tim Walz issued an executive order that allowed malls, shops, and variety of businesses, including pet-grooming services—but not churches—to open. After pressure from Lutherans and Catholics, Walz reluctantly allowed church services to resume at 25 percent building capacity.[68] The Democrats' anti-Catholicism stems from progressivism's inherent crass materialism, which privileges the body over the soul. Thankfully, after new justices were appointed by Donald Trump, the Supreme Court ruled in favor of religious liberty in *Roman Catholic Diocese of Brooklyn v. Cuomo.*

The Biden administration has demonstrated great hostility to Roman Catholics. This hostility is manifested in Biden's appointments and policy positions. Biden has appointed officials openly hostile to the Church. He tapped Xavier Becerra as Secretary of Health and Human Services. During his tenure as attorney general of California, he sued the Little Sisters of the Poor over contraception coverage. He also defended, unsuccessfully, a California law that would have mandated pro-life pregnancy centers to inform patients where they could get an abortion.[69] Biden also appointed a transgender person, Richard "Rachel" Levine, as assistant secretary of Health and Human Services; Levine is an activist who wishes to normalize and push "transitioning" and other procedures contrary to the Catholic Church as "gender-affirming care." Levine's argument that opposition to transgenderism is unscientific is a direct threat to the Church. Moreover, Levine has suggested that the state

67. Matthew Brown, "Fact Check: Did Kentucky Order Police to Record the License Plates of Easter Churchgoers?," *USA Today* April 13, 2020, https://www.minnpost.com/state-government/2020/05/new-order-allows-minnesota-churches-to-hold-in-person-services-at-25-percent-capacity/.

68. Ryan Colby, "Minnesota Churches Tell Governor Walz They Are Resuming In-Person Worship Services," Becket Law, May 20, 2020, https://www.becketlaw.org/media/minnesota-churches-tell-governor-walz-resuming-person-worship-services/; Peter Callaghan and Walter Orenstein, "New Order Allows Minnesota Churches to Hold In-Person Services at 25 Percent," MinnPost, May 23, 2020, https://www.minnpost.com/state-government/2020/05/new-order-allows-minnesota-churches-to-hold-in-person-services-at-25-percent-capacity/.

69. Robert Royal, "Xavier Becerra: Catholic Hitman," The Catholic Thing, February 27, 2021, https://www.thecatholicthing.org/2021/02/27/xavier-becerra-catholic-hitman/.

may be able to ignore the wishes of parents when they do not approve of their children's "gender-affirming care."[70]

Biden has supported positions on abortion, transgenderism, homosexuality, and religious liberty incompatible with the faith. He has showed little sympathy for Catholics who disagree with him. Biden has moved even further leftward on abortion. In 2008, Biden had prided himself for having a perceived "moderate" stance on abortion, where he supported the legalization but not the federal funding of abortion. Now, as president, he supports the repeal of the Hyde Amendment. When a draft of Justice Samuel Alito's *Dobbs* majority opinion was leaked in May 2022, Biden actively beseeched Congress to codify abortion access. In the immediate aftermath of the leak, I'm With Ruth, a radical pro-choice group, threatened to storm and disrupt Catholic services on Mother's Day. Biden did not adequately condemn the threats. Likewise, Biden has continuously placated progressive lies about homosexuality and transgenderism. He now partakes in regressive holidays, such as International Day against Homophobia, Transphobia, and Biphobia and Transgender Day of Visibility.[71] Biden's administration is actively seeking to minimize religious liberty exemptions so that Catholic hospitals and doctors could be forced to perform abortions and gender-transition surgeries. As William Donohue states, "Never has religious liberty been more seriously threatened than it is today."[72] For this reason, Catholics are increasingly putting their political hopes with the Republican Party.

The Contemporary Republican Party and Its Future

The Republican Party, as argued above, is the party that protects the most essential aspects of Catholic social thought. The Republican Party champi-

70. Bryon York, "Biden's Transgender Decree," *Washington Examiner,* May 2, 2022, https://www.washingtonexaminer.com/opinion/bidens-transgender-decree.

71. Joseph Biden, "Statement by President Joe Biden on International Day against Homophobia, Transphobia, and Biphobia," website of the White House, May 17, 2022, https://www.whitehouse.gov/briefing-room/statements-releases/2022/05/17/statement-by-president-joe-biden-on-international-day-against-homophobia-transphobia-and-biphobia/; Joseph Biden, "Fact Sheet: Biden-Harris Administration Advances Equality and Visibility for Transgender Americans," website of the White House, March 31, 2022, https://www.whitehouse.gov/briefing-room/statements-releases/2022/03/31/fact-sheet-biden-harris-administration-advances-equality-and-visibility-for-transgender-americans/.

72. "Biden's War on Religious Liberty Spikes," Catholic League for Religious and Civil Rights, November 18, 2021, https://www.catholicleague.org/bidens-war-on-religious-liberty-spikes/.

ons the unborn, religious liberty, the autonomy of Catholic schools, homeschooling, traditional marriage, and conscientious objections to homosexuality, transgenderism, and progressive trends in education. Yet there is still notable tension between Republicans and Catholics on other issues. Republicans want to help the poor, the needy, and the vulnerable, but they often place the responsibility to help these groups with local organizations, local government, private philanthropy, the free market, and voluntary associations. Conservative Catholics correctly fear that the secularism of the state will use its centralized power to not only help the poor, needy, and vulnerable, but also to further abortion, homosexuality, transgenderism, and secular humanism. Progressive Catholics fail to recognize that the secular Left (so long as it remains secular) will never separate abortion access from gender discrimination, homosexuality from equality, and transgenderism from human rights. Therefore it is in accordance with prudence for Catholic social thought, at least for the next few generations, to deemphasize the state and emphasize society. As Paul Ryan argued, society should trump the state. There are many ways through which the Republican Party can continue to appeal to faithful Catholics.

The first—and most important way—is championing the pro-life cause. The majority of Catholics who attend Sunday Mass consider the protection of the unborn to be the most important moral issue of the time. Despite a consistently pro-choice position throughout his life, Donald Trump, in the words of Sister Deidre Byrne of the Little Workers of the Sacred Heart of Jesus and Mary, became "the most pro-life president."[73] The Trump administration rose to the occasion and delivered the pro-life community significant victories. He reinstated the Mexico City Policy, addressed the March for Life in 2018, and appointed several federal judges with clear pro-life credentials. He chose three pro-life justices to the Supreme Court: Neil Gorsuch, Brett Kavanaugh, and Amy Coney Barrett. He also appointed several pro-life judges to other federal courts, such as Sarah Pitlyk of the Eastern District of Missouri, who had previously served as special counsel to the Thomas More Society; Wendy Vitter of the Eastern District of Louisiana, who had previously served as general counsel to the Archdiocese of New Orleans; and Matthew Walden McFarland of the Southern District of Ohio, who was a member of the Scioto County

73. "At RNC, Nun Lauds Trump for Being Anti-Abortion," PBS News Hour, August 26, 2020, https://www.pbs.org/newshour/politics/watch-at-rnc-nun-lauds-trump-for-being-anti-abortion.

Right for Life.[74] Moreover, Republican governors, such as Greg Abbott of Texas, Brad Little of Idaho, Kevin Stitt of Oklahoma, are leading the way nationally in limiting abortion.[75]

The second way in which Republicans can appeal to Catholics is by upholding religious freedom. Despite thoughtful teachings on marriage, Catholicism, the Christian Right, and conservatism failed to convince the public that marriage is only between one man and one woman. Now, with the legalization of same-sex marriage through *Obergefell v. Hodges* and the progressive interpretation of the Equal Protection Clause, Catholic (and conservative Protestant) businesses are open to lawsuits if they do not cater or provide services for same-sex "marriages." Since faithful Catholics believe work and business cannot be divorced from their vocation, they must increasingly rely upon claims to religious liberty and the importance of rightly formed individual conscience.

Democrats claim to support religious liberty in many circumstances, especially in international affairs. Yet Democrats are unsympathetic to the Christian conception of religious liberty because they view it as a vehicle to support thinly veiled discrimination against homosexuals. They assume that the denial of services to a gay couple because of a religious objection is either inherently irrational or, worse, akin to racial discrimination. The narrow view Democrats have of religious liberty, however, affects more than gay "marriage." It touches upon Christian conscientious objections to gay adoption, gay employees in Catholic schools, newly discovered gender pronouns, "transition" surgery, men in women's bathrooms, abortions in Catholic hospitals, and government-paid contraception. Democrats have, at times, opposed religious exemptions for doctors concerning abortion and contraception and for priests

74. Micaiah Bilger, "Senate Confirms More of Trump's Pro-Life Judges, 13 More Conservative Will Join Federal Courts," Life News, December 18, 2019, https://www.lifenews.com/2019/12/18/senate-confirms-more-of-trumps-pro-life-judges-13-more-conservatives-will-join-federal-courts/.

75. Jacob Gershman, "Texas Governor Signs Fetal-Heartbeat Abortion Ban," *Wall Street Journal*, May 19, 2021, https://www.wsj.com/articles/texas-governor-signs-fetal-heartbeat-abortion-ban-11621452346; Laura Kusisto, "Idaho Governor Signs Six-Week Abortion Ban Based on Texas Model, But Voices Concerns," *Wall Street Journal*, March 23, 2022, https://www.wsj.com/articles/idaho-governor-signs-six-week-abortion-ban-based-on-texas-model-but-voices-concerns-11648071555; Laura Kusisto and Jennifer Calfas, "Oklahoma Lawmakers Pass Near-Total Ban on Abortion," *Wall Street Journal*, May 19, 2022, https://www.wsj.com/articles/oklahoma-lawmakers-pass-near-total-ban-on-abortion-11652984908?mod=politics_featst_pos3.

concerning the seal of confession.[76] Conservative Republicans, in contrast, view it as pivotal to uphold such religious and conscientious exemptions.

The third way in which Republicans can appeal to Catholics is by defending (and by promoting) Catholic schools, private schools (such as Montessori schools and great books academies), and homeschooling. Thanks to decisions in *Engel v. Vitale* and other pivotal cases of the Warren Court, public schools are increasingly secular. This secularization has not made curriculum neutral in content. Rather, it allows liberal and progressive ideas to dominate the school curriculum and ideas. Because the Bible is not taught, public school students possess little command of elementary Christian teachings and history. Public schools are now vehicles to press progressive ideas. Sexual promiscuity is directly tolerated and indirectly encouraged through sexual education. Students are taught ideas about sex that are contrary to Christian teaching, such as the "fluidity" of gender. Some schoolteachers teach sexual education to young children, and other institutions promote "drag queen storybook hours."

Public schools, then, are increasingly at odds with core Catholic teachings. Republicans have an opportunity to capitalize on this discontentment. First, Republicans can seek to reform public education at both the state and federal level by either ending or allowing students to opt out of curricula contrary to Catholic teachings. Second, they can pass legislation to increase funds to Catholic schools. This would allow working-class parents, who could not otherwise afford it, to send their children to Catholic school. Third, it is in the interest of Republicans to provide protections for homeschooling families. Over the past thirty years, Catholics (and some conservative Protestants) increasingly utilize the option to homeschool their children. Consequently, homeschooling networks, such as Regina Caeli, are increasingly sophisticated. As they become more popular and influential, progressive Democrats are more likely to target them.[77] For many Catholics, however, the right to homeschool

76. "Biden's War on Religious Liberty Spikes," Catholic League for Religious and Civil Rights, November 18, 2021, https://www.catholicleague.org/bidens-war-on-religious-liberty-spikes/. For a recent seal of confession controversy, see Pablo Kay, "Dangerous California Bill on Seal of Confession Withdrawn Before Key Hearing," *America,* July 9, 2019, https://www.americamagazine.org/politics-society/2019/07/09/dangerous-california-bill-seal-confession-withdrawn-key-hearing.

77. A good overview is provided in Timothy Carney, "Terrifying Liberal Tyrants Want to Ban Most Homeschooling Because They Hate 'Conservative Christian Beliefs,'" *Washington Examiner,* April 20,

their children is intimately tied with religious liberty and the desire for a more rigorous education.

The fourth, and perhaps most surprising, way in which Republicans can appeal to certain Catholics, especially Reagan Democrats, is to become a workers' party directed by a "common good conservatism."[78] Recently, some conservative political pundits, such as F. H. Buckley and Tucker Carlson, have championed the idea of Republicans abandoning some of its libertarian impulses and embracing tariffs, union workers, a moderate welfare state, and reasonable economic regulations.[79] In this way, Trump's "Make America Great Again" policies can further the state's role in responsible stewardship by advocating socially conservative policies without ballooning bureaucracy. A Republican workers' party may begin to resemble the old pre-New Deal Democratic Party, beloved by Catholics for over one hundred years. Although this prospect may seem promising, there are still several obstacles to this project: an administrative state dominated by progressives, a liberal media, powerful woke corporations, and an oddball minority (but powerful contingent) of libertarians and neoconservatives opposed to anything connected to Trump. Still, recent Republican success with the white working class, Hispanics, and other minorities may be able to make a Republican workers party a possibility.

The Upcoming Political Temptations and the Need for Creative Minorities

Although neither political party is aligned perfectly with the teachings of the Church, the Republicans clearly are more in accord with Catholic social thought than the Democrats. There are too many foundational positions within the Democratic Party that are incompatible with the Catholic understanding of human nature. When Republicans differ from Catholic social thought, it is primarily a matter of *means*, not content. Republicans, after all, want to assist the poor, needy, and vulnerable; they just disagree about the

2020, https://www.aei.org/op-eds/terrifying-liberal-tyrants-want-to-ban-most-homeschooling-because-they-hate-conservative-christian-beliefs/.

78. Alexander William Salter, "Common Good Conservatism's Catholic Roots," *Wall Street Journal*, May 20, 2021, https://www.wsj.com/articles/common-good-conservatisms-catholic-roots-11621527530.

79. F. H. Buckley, *The Republican Workers Party* (New York: Encounter, 2018).

method through which to help them. The policy positions of the Democrats on the most important issues, on the contrary, are untenable. Democrats are launching an assault upon gender, marriage, religious liberty, the unborn, the rights of parents, and family structure.

Still, it is uncertain whether the Republicans will remain the defenders of traditional values. Republicans gave up on the explicit defense of traditional marriage in the immediate aftermath of *Obergefell* and retreated quickly to religious liberty exemptions. Many Republican politicians are not as authentically socially conservative as their constituents. Additionally, there are significant differences between younger and older Republicans. On certain issues, younger Republicans have a secular and libertarian streak. They are in favor of gay "rights," marijuana legalization, and transgenderism.[80] Thus, while the Republicans are more likely to be friendlier to Catholics than Democrats, they may not be the loyal allies that serious Catholics need them to be.

The overarching problem with contemporary America is cultural. There cannot be a *purely* political solution, because if culture declines, so will politics. A political party in a democracy can at best mitigate cultural decline, but it cannot stop it. Democratic politicians are shifting further to the left because they are following the cultural shift of their own progressive base. The cultural conservatism inherent in the Republican Party provided a temporary bulwark against these changes, but it may not last. The Republicans, in order to remain a politically viable party, are slowly moving to the left on certain cultural issues. In 2015, many leading Republicans accepted the *Obergefell* decision. Likewise, when the Supreme Court declared that gender identity is protected by the Civil Rights Act, many leading conservative Republicans, such as Senators John Cornyn and Deb Fischer, accepted the decision. One of the few Republicans to criticize the decision was Josh Hawley, a former law clerk of Chief Justice John Roberts. Hawley is an intellectual who understands the importance of first principles. Most Republican leaders, however, lack Hawley's intellectual bent.[81] Catholics therefore cannot put their full faith in the Republican Party, even if the party remains their temporary option.

80. Kristin Soltis Anderson, "Conservatives Have a Millennial Problem," *Weekly Standard*, May 11, 2018, https://www.washingtonexaminer.com/weekly-standard/how-conservatives-can-find-a-way-to-appeal-to-millennials; Scott Bixby, "Meet the Gay Millennial Republicans Who Want to Transform the GOP," Mic, September 1, 2019, https://www.mic.com/articles/124695/meet-chyrs-kefalas-and-the-gay-millennial-republicans-who-want-to-transform-the-gop.

81. Nicholas Rowan, "Most Senate Republicans Unconcerned by the Supreme Court Transgender

There are certain temptations that Catholics must avoid. First, they cannot fall to the apolitical temptation, which posits the insignificance of politics. On the contrary, politics matters substantially. It affects every Catholic every day. Catholics have political interests, such as ensuring that the Little Sisters of Poor are not forced to pay for their employees' contraception, that laws which limit (if not ban) abortion are passed, and that students are not coerced to participate in things that are contrary to their faith.

The second temptation is for Catholics to retreat into their own political circles, where they only dialogue with themselves. Over the past three years, as the integralist movement has gained ground among conservative Catholics, scholars are beginning to revisit alternative Catholic political movements. As these movements are studied, there may be the temptation to establish a Catholic political party or to create a movement like Charles Maurras's Action Française. Both movements backfired in Europe, for a variety of reasons. Catholic political power was ultimately weakened, not strengthened, by them.

Rather, American Catholics—as genuine conservatives—need to use the framework of their own country. Therefore it is beneficial for Catholics to revisit Madison's *Federalist #10*, which provides guidelines for how a political minority can still govern by participating in a coalitional majority.[82] Catholic social thought is rooted in appeals to reason accessible to all that—if charitably, patiently, and persuasively stated—can perhaps shift both our culture and politics in a more traditional direction. The United States of America needs the Catholic Church, and in this century, it is incumbent upon devout Catholics to thwart this country's cultural and political decline through conscientious, innovative, active, and strategic participation in cultural and political renewal.

Decision" *Washington Examiner*, June 17, 2020, https://www.washingtonexaminer.com/news/most-senate-republicans-unconcerned-by-the-supreme-court-transgender-decision.

82. James Madison, "Federalist #10," in *Federalist Papers*, ed. Charles R. Kesler (New York: Signet, 1961), 71–79.

CHAPTER 7

Trust Not in Princes . . . But What about Bureaucrats?

Catholics in the Administrative State

RYAN J. BARILLEAUX

The year 1960 was a watershed for American Catholics. In that year, John F. Kennedy was elected as the first Catholic president of the United States, putting to rest (it seemed) the anti-Catholicism that had marred the 1928 presidential campaign of New York Governor Al Smith. The December 12 issue of *Time* magazine, a leading light of the journalistic establishment of the day, included a cover story on "U.S. Catholics and the State." This cover featured an illustration of Fr. John Courtney Murray, SJ, superimposed on a treatise by St. Robert Bellarmine. The accompanying article, "To Be Catholic and American," discussed the changing place of Catholics in an America whose culture and politics had long been shaped by a Protestant majority. Murray was featured because that same year he had published *We Hold These Truths: Catholic Reflections on the American Proposition*,[1] in which the Jesuit scholar advanced the thesis that the principles that inspired the American Republic share an "evident coincidence" with the core principles of the Western Chris-

1. John Courtney Murray, SJ, *We Hold These Truths: Catholic Reflections on the American Proposition* (New York: Sheed and Ward, 1960). The most recent edition was John Courtney Murray, SJ, *We Hold These Truths: Catholic Reflections on the American Proposition*, introduction by Peter Augustine Lawler (Lanham, MD: Rowman & Littlefield, 2005). Citations to *We Hold These Truths* in this chapter are from the 2005 edition.

based on traditional Christian morality, which state legislators (as recorded in the legislative history) believed were not "forward thinking" about abortion.[15]

Along with the Obama administration's efforts to impose social change through administrative action, the upshot of these developments is that the status of Catholic institutions today—and of Catholics and other believers in America generally—remains uncertain. People of faith who adhere to traditional standards of sexual morality, particularly but not exclusively Catholics, will find it increasingly difficult to practice their faith in any but the narrowest of domains. In addition to a changing national culture, what has also changed is the way government works in the United States.

In the past, disputes over Catholic schools and other institutions largely had to do with whether government could or should provide aid to these institutions. Such debates are what led to the adoption of the various state Blaine amendments, which prohibited public aid to schools with religious affiliations in the second half of the nineteenth century. Today, government agencies have broad reach into American life and the activities of civil society, creating new threats for Catholics and their institutions that make the old debates about tax credits for parochial schools appear almost quaint. The Catholic Church in America, and the faithful who adhere to its teachings, now face not just the hostility of anti-Catholic bigots, but also the power of the administrative state.

Patterns in the History of Catholics in America

The history of Catholics and of the Church in the United States has been marked by freedom and opportunity, but also suspicion and even hostility.[16] Catholics have lived in America since colonial times and some played key roles in the founding. As the nation grew, Catholics were part of its fabric but at times became the subject of hostility from the Protestant majority, particularly when waves of Catholic immigrants changed several American cities (Boston is an excellent example) from Protestant communities into multi-

15. DiGirolami and Walsh, "Kennedy's Last Term."

16. See, e.g., Russell Shaw, *Catholics in America: Religious Identity and Cultural Assimilation from John Carroll to Flannery O'Connor* (San Francisco: Ignatius Press, 2016); James T. Fisher, *Communion of Immigrants: A History of Catholics in America* (New York: Oxford University Press, 2008); Patrick W. Carey, *Catholics in America: A History* (Lanham, MD: Rowman & Littlefield, 2008).

ethnic domains in which Catholics became influential. As late as the middle of the twentieth century, anti-Catholic prejudice was at times open and pronounced; at other times it was quiet, incidental, or irrelevant.[17]

Even in the twentieth century, as Catholics scored achievements in all sectors of American society, Catholicism continued to be the subject of suspicion and prejudice among both elites and masses. Governor Al Smith's 1928 presidential campaign was marred by open anti-Catholic hostility, and even Kennedy's successful candidacy faced resistance because of his religion.[18] Rev. Martin Luther King Sr., for example, initially opposed Kennedy because of his religion. Norman Vincent Peale and Billy Graham, influential Protestant ministers of the time, openly opposed Kennedy's election as threatening freedom in the United States. Members of Congress even offered proposals to strip US cardinals of their voting rights for participating in a "foreign election." Several presidents were frustrated in their attempts to appoint an ambassador to the Holy See, until Ronald Reagan was able to overcome opposition to naming William Wilson to the position. Public aid to parochial school students provoked a long-standing fight in several jurisdictions.

The history of Catholics in America, and in American politics, is certainly not all negative, but neither is it a record of unconditional acceptance of Catholics. The record is complex, but certain patterns can be discerned in American Catholic history that have shaped the Catholic political experience in the United States.

1. The US constitutional system created an environment that has been congenial to the growth and success of Catholic citizens and Catholic institutions. This system is marked by the religious provisions of the First Amendment, as well as the prohibition against a religious test for office. Constitutional interpretation, however, is subject to change, and that has the potential to threaten religious liberty.

The US Constitution offered Catholics in America a more congenial legal environment in which to flourish than most nations in Europe had done. In Britain, the public practice of Catholicism was no longer outlawed by the time of the American founding, but Catholics were explicitly citizens of a

17. See Michael Schwartz, *The Persistent Prejudice: Anti-Catholicism in America* (Huntington, IN: Our Sunday Visitor, 1986).

18. Harris Wofford, "An Anti-Catholic King?," BeliefNet, accessed September 20, 2016, http://www.beliefnet.com/news/politics/2003/11/an-anti-catholic-king.aspx. See also Harris Wofford, *Of Kennedys and Kings: Making Sense of the Sixties* (Pittsburgh: University of Pittsburgh Press, 1992).

lesser class until the nineteenth century. Although Catholics were only 1 percent of the population during the ratification of the Constitution, Catholics were not prohibited from holding office, as outlined in the No Religious Test Clause of Article VI, Section 3.[19] They were guaranteed, with other religious minorities, the free exercise of religion by the First Amendment.

Baltimore, the first Catholic diocese in the United States, was established in 1789 under Bishop John Carroll. In contrast, the Catholic hierarchy in Britain was not restored by the Holy See after the Reformation until 1850. As George Washington made clear in his letter to American Catholics in 1790, America was a place for people of all faiths. Responding to an address of congratulations from American Catholics on his election as president, he specifically referred to "fellow-citizens of all denominations."[20] Responding to an address of congratulations from American Catholics on his election as president, he wrote that "all those who conduct themselves as worthy members of the Community are equally entitled to the protection of civil Government."[21] Although Catholics in America were objects of suspicion and at times discrimination, they enjoyed constitutional protection.

Instrumental to this protection was the underlying nature of the American Republic and specific constitutional provisions. Murray, quoting the Third Plenary Council of Boston, embraced the idea that America's founders "built better than they knew" in crafting the Constitution.[22] American constitutionalism was built on the foundation of the natural law tradition, holding as its central vision "a free people under a limited government."[23] Murray insists that Thomas Aquinas would have endorsed such a vision. This coincidence of American principles and the natural law tradition was strengthened by the provisions of the First Amendment. Taken together, the constitutional basis of the American Republic offered protection to Catholics.

Murray observed, however, that America's protection of religious freedom is not always properly understood. Speaking of "theologies of the First

19. Thomas Craughwell, "History of the Catholic Vote," *Our Sunday Visitor*, October 24, 2012. https://www.osv.com/OSVNewsweekly/ByIssue/Article/TabId/735/ArtMID/13636/ArticleID/3933/History-of-the-Catholic-Vote.aspx.

20. George Washington, "Letter to Roman Catholics in America," National Archives, March 15, 1790, http://founders.archives.gov/documents/Washington/05-05-02-0193.

21. Washington, "Letter to Roman Catholics."

22. Murray, *We Hold These Truths*, 46.

23. Murray, *We Hold These Truths*, 46.

Amendment," he explained that the First Amendment recognized nothing less than what Pope Pius XII wanted the Church to have in secular society: a stable condition within society and full independence in the fulfillment of her divine mission.[24] But he noted that the American consensus in favor of understanding the United States as a "nation under God" was challenged by a secularist school of thought that "reads into the First Amendment a more or less articulated political theory."[25] In a prescient passage, Murray summarized this secularist reading of the First Amendment:

> Civil society is the highest societal form of human life; even the values that are called spiritual and moral are values by reason of their reference to society. Civil law is the highest form of law and is not subject to judgment by prior ethical canons. Civil rights are the highest form of rights; for the dignity of the person, which grounds these rights, is only his civil dignity. The state is purely the instrument of the popular will, than which there is no higher sovereignty . . . Finally, the ultimate value within society and state does not consist in any substantive ends that these societal forms may pursue; rather it consists in the process of their pursuit. That is to say, the ultimate value resides in the forms of the democratic process itself, because these forms embody the most ultimate of values, freedom.[26]

In his day, he could still characterize this position as dissenting from the American consensus, but he was far-sighted enough to anticipate its growing influence over time. The secularist interpretation of the First Amendment, Murray understood, was not only an innovation but also a threat to religious freedom in general and to Catholicism in particular.

In American Catholicism's "watershed moment" in 1960, it seemed that threats to religious freedom from secularist readings of the Bill of Rights were possible but unlikely. After all, religious freedom had enabled a Catholic to become president, and Catholics were increasingly part of the mainstream of American life. It was an age when some thought that Catholics ought to be concerned instead about the arrogance of "triumphalism." What Murray called the "coincidence" between America's founding principles and natural law seemed an undeniable truth; the age of hostility to the Church was more in the past than in the future—or so it seemed.

24. Murray, *We Hold These Truths*, 79.
25. Murray, *We Hold These Truths*, 65.
26. Murray, *We Hold These Truths*, 65.

This first pattern constitutes a kind of substructure to the American Catholic experience. Catholics in the United States enjoyed freedom because the Constitution guaranteed it. A second pattern would interfere with the first, because non-Catholic influences would shape how Americans live and view the place of Catholics in America.

2. *American culture—and therefore American political culture—has been shaped largely by non-Catholic influences: in the nineteenth and early twentieth centuries, a generic Protestantism served as a kind of civil religion; in the post-World War II era, this generic Christianity has increasingly given way to the secularism of the nation's post-Christian elites.*

Officially, the United States is a country with no established religion, but for much of the nation's history, American culture—including its political culture—had a distinctively Protestant cast. As Joseph Bottum put it succinctly, "Protestantism helped define the nation."[27] Protestant Christianity set the tone for public morality and shaped national values regarding work, family, society, and politics. The presumptively Protestant character of American society led some Protestant ministers such as Graham, Peale, and King to resist John Kennedy's candidacy for president. They regarded his possible election as a threat to the fabric of the nation. Notably, King changed his mind after Kennedy called Coretta Scott King in October 1960, following her husband's arrest in De Kalb County, Georgia.[28]

For many American Protestants, Catholics were more or less alien to American culture. In the nineteenth century, this anti-Catholicism took two main forms: nativism and hostility toward Catholic schools. Nativism came in reaction to waves of immigration, much of it by Catholics from Ireland, Italy, Poland, and other European nations. Nativists saw this influx of Catholics as a threat to the fundamentally Protestant nature of American society, leading to anti-Catholic agitation and violence and pressure for restrictions on immigration.[29]

27. Joseph Bottum, "The Death of Protestant America: A Political Theory of the Protestant Mainline," *First Things* (August 2008): https://www.firstthings.com/article/2008/08/001-the-death-of-protestant-america-a-political-theory-of-the-protestant-mainline.

28. John Goodman, "How Martin Luther King Persuaded John Kennedy to Support the Civil Rights Cause," *New York Times*, June 29, 2017, https://www.nytimes.com/2017/06/29/books/review/kennedy-and-king-steven-levingston.html.

29. Joseph Zeitz, "When America Hated Catholics," *Politico*, September 23, 2015, https://www.politico.com/magazine/story/2015/09/when-america-hated-catholics-213177/.

Schools were a further point of contention. Public schools socialized American children in a generic kind of Christianity, a fact that helped to stimulate the creation of a Catholic parochial school system. Many Protestants feared that tax dollars would be used to support such schools, which for them amounted to subsidizing popery. In the second half of the nineteenth century, legislation at the state level and a proposed constitutional amendment sought to prohibit support for nonpublic schools. In 1875, President Ulysses S. Grant called for a constitutional amendment to bar the use of public funds to support "sectarian schools," a measure that was formally proposed by Representative James G. Blaine. It passed the House but failed in the Senate. Similar provisions (generically known as Blaine amendments) were adopted by more than thirty states.[30]

In the twentieth century, particularly after World War II, American culture became more accepting of Catholics and Jews. This trend was especially noteworthy in the 1950s, when President Eisenhower and others promoted the idea of defining America as a Judeo-Christian nation. The political rise of the Kennedys in the 1950s and 1960s, in that watershed moment, seemed to symbolize a new American openness to Catholics.

The 1960s would not prove to be friendly toward Catholicism—or toward religion in general. The United States was rocked by concurrent social and political upheavals, and the generally Protestant culture of America increasingly gave way to secularism. The sexual revolution of the 1960s and 1970s led to widespread acceptance of abortion, sexual promiscuity, divorce, and pornography. Within a few years, acceptance of homosexuality and same-sex marriage would become "mainstream" positions in American culture. Not long into the new millennium, the notion of "gender identity" disconnected from biology would gain widespread acceptance—at least among secular elites.

By the second decade of the twenty-first century, secularism reigned supreme in American society. In 2010, President Barack Obama and members of his administration attempted to redefine religious freedom as "freedom of worship," positing a narrower field for religion than had historically been accepted.[31] The US Commission on International Religious Freedom noted

30. "Blaine Amendments," Becket Fund for Religious Liberty, accessed September 22, 2018, http://www.becketfund.org/blaineamendments-old/.

31. Sarah Eekhof Zylstra, "'Freedom of Worship' Worries," *Christianity Today*, June 22, 2010. https://www.christianitytoday.com/ct/2010/july/freedom-of-worship-worries.html.

the shift in language and observed in its annual report for 2010: "This change in phraseology could well be viewed by human rights defenders and officials in other countries as having concrete policy implications."[32] Many people of faith saw this new language as an attempt to limit religious freedom to worship inside the sanctuary, thus defining the public square as militantly secular. Although the Obama administration later dropped the proposed language because of negative publicity, this narrower reading of the First Amendment was what Murray had warned about in 1960.

Catholics have just as awkward a place in this secular culture as they did in the formerly Protestant one. Like old-fashioned Protestants, secular elites regard the Catholic Church as more dangerous than any other group to their cause of limiting the influence of religion in public life. As evidence, consider this fact: when the contraception mandate was promulgated by the Department of Health and Human Services in 2012, several groups were exempted from its requirements, including Amish communities and several large corporations (ExxonMobil, Pepsi, Chevron, and Visa),[33] but not the Little Sisters of the Poor or other Catholic groups and dioceses or several other non-Catholic religious institutions. Nevertheless, the Obama administration maintained for years that compliance with the mandate was essential to achieve the goal of promoting women's health.[34]

As R. R. Reno has put it, secular elites abandoned the Protestantism of previous generations, but they have retained the anti-Catholic prejudices of their forbears.[35] Not surprisingly, they tend to regard American Catholics as instrumental to their own political and cultural goals.

3. America's non-Catholic elites have generally treated Catholics and their institutions instrumentally, that is, according to whether those elites view Catholicism as consistent with or an obstacle to their social and political agendas.

This pattern can be seen most clearly in the record of the past half century. During the civil rights era, Protestant and secular elites looked favorably on

32. Zylstra, "'Freedom of Worship' Worries."

33. "Understanding Who Is Exempt from the HHS Mandate," Little Sisters of the Poor, accessed September 25, 2018, http://thelittlesistersofthepoor.com/who-is-exempt-from/.

34. For a discussion of this point, see Edward Whelan, "The HHS Contraception Mandate vs. the Religious Freedom Restoration Act," Ethics and Public Policy Center, accessed September 26, 2018, https://eppc.org/publications/the-hhs-contraception-mandate-vs-the-religious-freedom-restoration-act/.

35. R. R. Reno, interviewed on *Kresta in the Afternoon*, Ave Maria Radio, September 5, 2016, https://avemariaradio.net/audio-archive/kresta-afternoon-august-12-2016-hour-1/.

Catholics and their institutions, which largely supported an end to segregation and promoted greater racial equality. Catholic clergy, religious, and laity were active in the civil rights movement, and religiously motivated involvement in politics was looked upon positively because that participation supported the equality agenda of political and social elites. Within a few years, however, the political dynamics changed, as Catholics (along with many Christians and Jews) became active in the emerging pro-life movement.

The Catholic Church opposes not only abortion, but also contraception, euthanasia, and same-sex marriage. Moreover, the Church was and still is led by a celibate male clergy, which makes Catholicism the most visible "sign of contradiction" against the sexual revolution and radical feminism. Not surprisingly, Catholic involvement in politics—unless it was by Catholics like Joe Biden or Tim Kaine, who have embraced the secular progressive social agenda—is now regarded by elites as a threat to American democracy. Many in the pro-life movement have complained that Republican politicians who embraced pro-life positions during their election campaigns seemed unwilling to spend much political capital promoting a pro-life agenda once in office. Likewise, as the Obama administration demonstrated with the HHS contraception mandate, the nation's elites put their own agendas first. For political and social elites, Catholics serve either as useful companions or obstacles to be overcome.

The behavior of Catholic leaders often unwittingly serves the purposes of these secular elites. Take, for example, the statements and activities of some prominent American Catholic politicians who have publicly dissented from Church teaching. Former Vice President Joe Biden actively promoted a social agenda at odds with Catholic teaching, not only supporting abortion and same-sex marriage, but even presiding at the same-sex civil wedding of two White House staff members in 2016.[36] Senator Tim Kaine, the 2016 Democratic vice presidential nominee, publicly endorsed the ordination of women and also predicted that the Church would one day endorse same-sex marriage.[37] Statements and actions like these, even when corrected by statements from Church leaders, help advance the agenda of secular elites by sowing doubt about Catholic teaching.

36. Amanda Calvo, "Joe Biden Officiates at His First Wedding Ceremony for Two White House Staffers," *Time,* August 2, 2016, http://time.com/4434637/joe-biden-white-house-staffers-wedding/.

37. Brian Fraga, "Tim Kaine: A 'Joe Biden' Catholic," *National Catholic Register,* September 23, 2016, http://www.ncregister.com/daily-news/tim-kaine-a-joe-biden-catholic.

The conduct of Catholic clergy and hierarchy can also contribute to advancing the secular agenda. This fact is apparent in the continuing clerical sexual abuse scandal that has plagued the Church in the past decade. One of the oldest charges against Catholicism made by its critics involves claims of sexual abuse. In nineteenth-century America, a widespread scandal arose after the 1836 publication of *The Awful Disclosures of Maria Monk: The Hidden Secrets of a Nun's Life in a Convent Exposed.*[38] The book, an anti-Catholic hoax, was part of an atmosphere of anti-Catholic unrest, and it contributed to the mythical charge that convents were merely places in which young women were held against their will for immoral purposes. The revelations of clerical sexual abuse in the twenty-first century, many involving cases running back over half a century, contribute to this anti-Catholic image of the Church's clergy, religious communities, and hierarchy as systematic practitioners of sexual abuse. In 2002, following the first eruption of the clerical sexual abuse scandal, a poll conducted by the *Wall Street Journal* and NBC News found that 64 percent of Americans believed that Catholic priests "frequently" abused children.[39] Incidents of abuse, and the American hierarchy's failure to deal appropriately and effectively with charges of abuse, invite state officials to become more intrusive in Church personnel matters.

In a non-confessional state such as the United States, the only authority Catholic clergy and hierarchy have is moral authority. In the watershed moment circa 1960, Church leaders enjoyed growing prestige and respect. In the current environment, they have lost most of their moral authority. Prominent Catholics openly dissent from Church teaching and proclaim that their positions on sexual morality are truer to the faith than what the Magisterium teaches. Bishops and priests, rocked by revelations of Theodore McCarrick's activities and apparent cover-ups of abuse in many dioceses, are portrayed as religious bureaucrats (at best) or even criminals (at worst). This fact only makes it easier for secular elites to dismiss the Catholic Church as an obstacle to their ideas of a more enlightened society.

This brief history highlights some key lessons for Catholics regarding their place in America. First, Catholics have prospered in the United States, al-

38. J. Bernard Delaney, OP, "The Real Maria Monk," *Catholic Answers*, October 1, 1995, https://www.catholic.com/magazine/print-edition/the-real-maria-monk.

39. Joseph Bottum, "Anti-Catholicism, Again," *Weekly Standard*, May 3, 2010, https://www.weeklystandard.com/joseph-bottum/anti-catholicism-again.

though no one could mistake this nation for a Catholic one. Second, Catholics should not expect that American culture and policy will be congruent with their values and beliefs; even when American culture was more explicitly religious in tone, that tone was a Protestant one. Finally, as the Psalmist said, "trust not in princes": political and social elites generally put their own agendas first, and Catholic concerns are not usually given a high priority in shaping these agendas. In a political system that has grown increasingly centered on policies set by the executive and administrative agencies, Catholics must expect the political-legal environment to be one that constrains—and at times threatens—them.

America's Administrative State

Few citizens realize the extent to which government in the United States has been turned over to an administrative state. As Professor Bradley Smith has put it so succinctly, the US Constitution was designed to create a federal government of limited power that would be held in check by the operation of its checks-and-balances system. In the twentieth century, that arrangement changed: the power of the federal government, as interpreted by the Supreme Court, came to be seen as essentially plenary in nature, and a functioning checks-and-balances system based in all three branches of government has given way to a system in which citizens, private institutions, or states and local governments take to the courts to halt or claim exceptions to policies they oppose.[40]

Professor Theodore Lowi characterized the emergence of an administrative state as "the end of liberalism" because it replaced a politics marked by clashes among competing interests influencing the shape of legislation produced by Congress ("interest group liberalism") with a system of government marked by administrative rulemaking. For a variety of reasons, including the technical complexity of many areas of public policy and the desire to avoid political fallout from making unpopular decisions, Congress has delegated to administrative agencies broad powers to make and enforce substantive rules that prescribe government policy. Lowi argued that government by rulemaking only

40. Remarks of Professor Bradley Smith, panel on "The Future of the Constitution," Miami University / Janus Forum Constitution Day Symposium, Miami University, Oxford, Ohio, September 22, 2016.

transferred political power to executive officials, displacing political decisions made in Congress with political decisions made by the president—or, more commonly—unelected administrators.[41]

This new arrangement—government by rulemaking—is rightly termed an "administrative state" because administrative agencies have been given all three types of power: Congress has delegated to them the power to write rules that have the force of law; they then enforce those rules and bring charges against violators; most adjudications of administrative violations are heard before administrative judges. Administrative rules are not only now the fastest-growing body of law in the United States, but are also the means by which some of the most significant and controversial aspects of public policy have been enacted. Two of the governmental actions that most concerned Catholics in the past few years—the HHS mandate to provide contraceptives to employees and the Obama administration's guidance letter on bathrooms—have been activities of the administrative state.

These two examples also highlight a feature of the American administrative as it has developed in the past four decades: it has come under increasing White House control (a situation that Lowi predicted in 1969). The original impetus of administrative government came from the progressives of the early twentieth century, who favored "government by expert" over governance by the traditional elected institutions. Although the federal government grew during the New Deal and World War II, the real metasticization of the administrative state occurred as a result of Lyndon Johnson's Great Society programs and laws passed in the 1970s. In response to the spate of new regulations being promulgated each year by agencies, presidents since Richard Nixon have worked to bring the rulemaking process under greater White House control. Chief executives of both parties worked to govern rulemaking and to make sure that the rules issued during their administrations better reflected the priorities and preferences of the president. This trend of White House control came to greatest fruition in the three most recent presidencies.

Presidents George W. Bush, Barack Obama, and Donald Trump all managed to bring agency rulemaking under de facto presidential control.[42] For example, there is no doubt that the HHS mandate on contraceptives was

41. Theodore Lowi, *The End of Liberalism*, 2nd ed., 40th ann. ed. (New York: W. W. Norton, 2009).

42. See Ryan J. Barilleaux and Jewerl Maxwell, "Has Barack Obama Embraced the Unitary Executive?," *PS: Political Science and Politics* 50, no. 1 (January 2017): 31–34.

created under White House influence. When the initial proposed regulation was published in the *Federal Register* in August 2011,[43] there was a significant backlash against it from Catholics as well as other religious groups. In response, in February 2012, President Obama announced a "compromise" version of the regulation, although it was a unilateral compromise made by the president himself.[44]

The battle over the HHS mandate further illuminates the principle of "trust not in princes." During the congressional debate over passage of the Affordable Care Act, the United States Conference of Catholic Bishops (USCCB) and some Catholic organizations lobbied in favor of the bill. The bishops' conference, while working hard to ensure that the bill included language against abortion funding, nevertheless supported the bill in the House and offered to assist the bill's advocates in promoting it in the Senate.[45] Ultimately, the USCCB opposed the final bill because it did not explicitly prohibit abortion funding and included no clause protecting religious conscience. Nevertheless, the bishops had become associated with support for Obamacare. Up to almost the very end of debate over its passage, the bishops had worked to help pass the Affordable Care Act. The Catholic Health Association, led by Sr. Carol Keehan, was particularly important in building support for it.[46]

The announcement of the HHS mandate in 2011 took the bishops by surprise. Cardinal Timothy Dolan, president of the USCCB at the time, wrote to the people of the Archdiocese of New York that he had been assured by President Obama that the work of the Catholic Church would not be impaired.[47] Many observers focused on Cardinal Dolan's implication that the president had deceived him. Others saw Dolan's surprise as the unfortunate consequence of trusting too much in a political leader. With the Affordable

43. Group Health Plans and Health Insurance Issuers Relating to Coverage of Preventive Services under the Patient Protection and Affordable Care Act, 76 Fed. Reg. 46,621 (August 3, 2011).

44. "Obama Administration Offers False 'Compromise' on Abortion-Drug Mandate," Becket Fund for Religious Liberty, accessed September 23, 2018, http://www.becketfund.org/obama-administration-offers-false-%E2%80%9Ccompromise%E2%80%9D-on-abortion-drug-mandate/.

45. David Rogers, "Bishops Offer Help with Senate," *Politico,* March 5, 2010, http://www.politico.com/story/2010/03/bishops-offer-help-with-senate-033962.

46. Terence P. Jeffrey, "Obama: Without Catholic Nun We Would Not Have Gotten Obamacare Done," *CNSNews,* June 10, 2015, http://www.cnsnews.com/news/article/terence-p-jeffrey/obama-without-catholic-nun-we-would-not-have-gotten-obamacare-done.

47. Timothy Cardinal Dolan, "I Owe You an Update," *Gospel in a Digital Age* (blog), accessed September 23, 2016, Archdiocese of New York, http://blog.archny.org/index.php/i-owe-you-an-update/.

Care Act as law, the Obama administration was now in a position to issue regulations that advanced the president's agenda with impunity, save only the government's ability to defend the rule in court.

Donald Trump's administration saw the further march of presidentially directed administrative government. Some of Trump's most important policy actions, such as a rule limiting immigration from seven Muslim-majority countries and imposition of tariffs against imports from several major American trading partners, were administrative rather than legislative in nature. He also reversed several executive actions taken by President Obama, including withdrawing the Environmental Protection Agency's Clean Power Plan, voiding the penalty for not purchasing health insurance under the Affordable Care Act, and lifting the 2016 "bathroom memo." In 2017, the Trump also issued Executive Order 13771, which mandates that agencies repeal two existing rules for every new rule they promulgate.[48] President Trump, like his two immediate predecessors, was an enthusiastic practitioner of executive government, and he joined them in bringing the American administrative state under greater White House control.

Challenging the Administrative State in Court

The Affordable Care Act provides a significant and useful example of the American administrative state in action. It was a sweeping bill (2,700 pages of text) passed by members of only one party in Congress who possessed only a vague and general understanding of what it would do; it contained thousands of clauses that delegated to the secretary of health and human services discretion to write rules to implement the law; it enacted specific requirements and timetables for implementation of the act; and it created new bureaucratic institutions to make the law's provisions a reality.[49] By its very nature, it stimulated the bureaucracy to promulgate thousands of pages of regulations; many of these rules are technical in nature, while others—especially the mandate for all employers in the nation to provide coverage of contraceptive and abortifacient drugs in their health care plans (the HHS mandate)—reflect substantive

48. E.O. 13771, 82 Fed. Reg. 9339 (January 30, 2017).

49. Tevi Troy, *"The Secretary Shall": How the Implementation of the Affordable Care Act Will Affect Doctors* (Washington, DC: Hudson Institute, May 2012), http://www.hudson.org/content/researchattachments/attachment/1034/secshalltroy--052212web.pdf.

political choices by the Obama administration and are highly controversial.

Implementation of the Affordable Care Act presents a microcosm of the contemporary administrative state. Consider these examples:

- Shortly after passage of the law, President Obama issued an executive order that kept in place previous prohibition of federal funds to pay for abortions, as part of a deal to win votes for the bill from several Catholic Democrats in Congress because the bill contained no explicit restriction on abortion funding.
- In several instances, President Obama unilaterally suspended or delayed enforcement of explicit deadlines (e.g., employer-provided insurance, penalties for citizen failure to purchase insurance) in the act, without legal authority to do so.
- The Internal Revenue Service (IRS) authorized taxpayers residing in states that did not establish health insurance exchanges to receive a subsidy for health insurance bought through a federal exchange, despite language in the law and considerable evidence about the background of the law that restricted these benefits to consumers who bought insurance through state-established exchanges (litigated in 2014 in *King v. Burwell*, whereby the Supreme Court ruled in favor of the Obama administration, and Justice Scalia's dissent said that the act should henceforth be called "SCOTUSCare").
- The HHS mandate required religious employers to provide contraceptive coverage in violation of their conscience, exempting only churches but not religious institutions or companies whose owners had strong religious convictions (litigated twice, in *Burwell v. Hobby Lobby Stores*, 2015,[50] and *Zubik v. Burwell*, 2016).[51]

As implemented since 2010, the Affordable Care Act has moved the nation aggressively toward executive/administrative government, with the courts acting as partial (but more or less accommodating) restraints on the administrative state. As these examples demonstrate, implementation has proceeded according to the dictates of the White House. This fact holds true even as President Trump reversed some of the dictates of the Obama administration. The actual

50. Burwell v. Hobby Lobby Stores, Inc., 573 US _____ (2014).
51. Zubik v. Burwell, 578 US _____ (2016).

language of the law was taken by the Obama administration as a license to regulate in pursuit of its policy goals, and the Trump administration used executive action to tailor the law to its goals.

One of the most contentious aspects of Obamacare has been the HHS contraceptives mandate, which led to a spate of lawsuits. The various suits were consolidated into two major cases, *Burwell v. Hobby Lobby Stores* in 2015, and *Zubik v. Burwell* in 2016. In the first, the Supreme Court ruled that privately held corporations could not be compelled to comply with the mandate if it interfered with the free exercise of the owners' religious convictions. In *Zubik*, the court sought to create a compromise between plaintiffs and the government overachieving the administration's objective of universal access to contraception. The Little Sisters of the Poor and other religiously oriented institutions could not be required to offer contraceptive or abortifacient coverage in their health plans, or to facilitate their insurers offering such coverage, but at the cost of the federal government being able to provide access to these drugs to all employees in the United States covered by employer-provided plans. In short, the court upheld the right of religious employers to avoid involvement in offering such drugs, but it prevented religious nonprofit organizations from insulating their employees from contraceptives.[52]

The Supreme Court's compromise in *Zubik* also highlights how American government has changed. Rather than having a matter such as the nature and extent of health care policy in the United States be determined through the legislative process, health care policy is now set through administrative rules, executive fiat, and "compromises" concocted by a court. The Supreme Court was not willing to go as far as the Obama administration wanted it to on the matter of forcing the Little Sisters of the Poor (and other plaintiffs) to violate their consciences, but the court's compromise also ensured that the administration could create a new kind of right of universal access to contraceptives and a mandate that every insurer in the country provide them.

52. See "Supreme Court Rules Unanimously in Favor of Little Sisters," Becket Fund for Religious Liberty, accessed September 28, 2016, http://thelittlesistersofthepoor.com/#supreme-court-ruling.

The Future of Catholics in the Administrative State

The development of American government in the modern era, particularly in the twenty-first century, ought to give Catholics pause. There is no reason to expect that the administrative state will be accommodating to Catholic beliefs and concerns, nor will the courts provide a firewall of protection for religious believers. While it is not inevitable that the United States will become hostile to Catholics, it is the case that the nation has moved a long way from that moment in the 1950s and early 1960s when it seemed that America had accepted Catholics as part of a larger embrace of Judeo-Christian culture.

The United States has not only developed an administrative state, but also presidents since Nixon have worked to make that arrangement an "executive administrative state." Chief executives of both parties endeavored to bring rulemaking under White House control, either to promote presidential objectives or to thwart policies the president opposed, and the result has been that administrative rulemaking is now largely directed out of the Oval Office. Furthermore, presidents—especially Bush (43), Obama, and Trump—have expanded unilateral presidential powers, so more power to make substantive policy decisions has been taken away from lawmaking and placed on the desk of the president. Administrative governance has become the norm for shaping public policy.

The administrative state, especially as it has evolved into a set of institutions under White House control, makes the outcome of presidential elections all the more consequential for American Catholics. Not only does the president now possess extensive power to shape rulemaking and the interpretation of the statutes by which agencies make rules, but the chief executive also nominates candidates for all vacancies in federal judgeships. To the extent that interpretation of the First Amendment can change with shifting majorities on the Supreme Court, presidential elections can affect both policy and constitutional law.

Once again, Obamacare serves as an excellent example of how contemporary American government works and what it suggests about the future. President Obama issued an executive order to prevent the use of federal funds for abortion under the ACA; another president could reverse that order in minutes. The president suspended enforcement of the law, delayed deadlines, unilaterally rewrote a proposed rule and called it a "compromise," saw to it that the IRS reinterpreted the ACA to meet his policy goals, and used HHS to pressure believers in business and the nonprofit sector to advance a pro-contraception and pro-abortion agenda. Trump reversed some of these actions, but his successor can overturn that reversal. The Supreme Court blunted the direct attack on groups like the Little Sisters, but in doing so it shaped a larger policy of mandatory access to contraceptives.

Catholics are likely to find that they inhabit an increasingly narrow space for practicing their religion outside of the sanctuary. Catholic dioceses and organizations have withdrawn from the business of adoption because of laws that require treating same-sex couples as equivalent to married men and women. Increasing pressure to accept anyone as having the right to define their own "gender identity" will further limit Catholic schools, hospitals, and other institutions. Investigations by local prosecutors and state attorneys general into clerical sexual abuse charges and personnel practices will continue to diminish the already tattered moral authority of the American bishops, making it even harder for them to speak out against intrusions on the freedom of the Church. It is not unrealistic to think that one day federal funds given to aid educational, health, and social service institutions—including Catholic ones—will come with a requirement that recipient institutions accept a range of activities and practices unacceptable to Catholics (same-sex marriage, self-defined gender identity, etc.). These developments will further circumscribe Catholic participation in the larger life of the nation. Religion, at least for Catholics, will likely be restricted to the domain of the strictly personal and liturgical—what the Obama administration referred to as "freedom of worship."

It is not outlandish to suggest that Catholics will one day find themselves limited to practicing their faith almost exclusively within the confines of church buildings. With a clergy and hierarchy damaged by a widespread abuse scandal, Catholics will have even less clerical support than they do today.

Things appear to be moving in that direction. Catholic institutions will still have a place in American society, although they will find themselves without government support and able to participate in the public square only to the extent that their activities (e.g., feeding the hungry) are congruent with the agenda of America's elites. Those activities that do not conform to the elite agenda or the secular mainstream, such as protecting natural marriage and families, will have to be self-supporting or will cease to exist.

In *Democracy in America*, Alexis de Tocqueville warned of problems in democracy, including the tyranny of the majority and the threat of a kind of soft despotism.[53] American Catholics, as a minority in a country dominated by first a Protestant and then a secularist culture, will find it difficult to practice their faith beyond the sanctuary. As for soft despotism, Tocqueville warned that it would advance from democratic government's desire to make citizens happy. In contemporary America, making citizens happy has come to mean satisfying the demands of particular groups and not offending those who claim certain identities. The citizens of the United States have not quite become the "timid and industrious" animals of which Tocqueville wrote, but the executive administrative state has moved the nation away from the kind of democratic republic that the founders created. The "watershed moment" of the early 1960s, with a tepidly Catholic president and growing acceptance in a still largely Protestant culture, now seems almost like a lost golden age. Catholics will have difficulty finding a comfortable place in the new secularist order.

53. Alexis de Tocqueville, "What Sort of Despotism Democratic Nations Have to Fear," in *Democracy in America*, accessed September 28, 2016, http://xroads.virginia.edu/~hyper/detoc/ch4_06.htm.

CHAPTER 8

The Future of Catholic Higher Education in America

GERARD V. BRADLEY

For a full generation now, the rallying point and measure of renewal for Catholic colleges and universities in America has been Pope John Paul's *Apostolic Constitution on Catholic Universities*. Promulgated on the Feast of the Assumption in 1990, *Ex Corde Ecclesiae* (*ECE*) has been the touchstone of orthodox criticism of America's many nominally Catholic institutions. How *ECE* is doing here might therefore tell us a lot about the health of American Catholic higher education. Instantly there is an apparent paradox. In a lecture at Villanova University, former Archbishop Charles Chaput of Philadelphia said that the bishops' implementation of *ECE* "had no teeth."[1] The American bishops as a body, in contrast, have invariably said that things are going great. Which is it?

The most probative piece of evidence is the 2012 decennial review by the United States Conference of Catholic Bishops (USCCB) of how *ECE* has been implemented. The single page of their *Final Report for the Ten Year Review of the Application of Ex Corde Ecclesiae* is not an executive summary. It is the *whole* report. This terse document is based upon a data set limited to conversations between some bishops and some university administrators within their dioceses, undertaken between November 2011 and June 2012. Here are the key findings of the report:

1. Archbishop Chaput, quoted in Massimo Faggioli, "A Wake-up Call to Liberal Theologians," *The Commonweal*, May 16, 2018, https://www.commonwealmagazine.org/wake-call-liberal-theologians.

> [T]he prevailing tone [of these conversations] was positive and the news was good. . . . The relationship between bishops and presidents on the local level can be characterized as positive and engaged, demonstrating progress on courtesy and cooperation in the last ten years.
>
> [O]ur institutions of Catholic higher education have made definite progress in advancing Catholic identity. Clarity about Catholic identity among college and university leadership has fostered substantive dialogues and cultivated greater mission driven practices across the university. In acknowledging that much progress has been made, we recognize there is still work to be done.
>
> [A] working group of bishops and presidents will be formed to continue the dialogue about strategic subjects on a national level.[2]

The report concluded that "the success of the ten-year review provides a clear course for continued dialogue regarding Catholic higher education and its essential contribution to the Church and society."[3]

If *ECE* were a coffee table book, it would be selling well. It has been widely noticed and has stimulated a lot of edifying conversations. Pope John Paul II probably had more than notoriety and dialogue, though, when he included in *ECE* several "General Norms" "to be applied concretely at the local and regional levels by Episcopal Conferences and other Assemblies of Catholic Hierarchy in conformity with the Code of Canon Law and complementary Church legislation."[4] Still, the bishops' eminent satisfaction gives one pause, even where so perceptive an observer as Archbishop Chaput has filed a dissenting opinion. One way of dissolving the paradox would be to hypothesize that enforcement of *ECE* was *meant* to be toothless, because neither the bishops nor the colleges ever *wanted* to implement it. Hypothetically, the bishops would be happy to talk endlessly about implementing *ECE,* without a care to succeed in implementing it. Then Archbishop Chaput would be not so happy.

2. United States Conference of Bishops, Committee on Catholic Education, *Final Report for the Ten Year Review of The Application of Ex Corde Ecclesiae for the United States* (Washington, DC: USCCB, June 11, 2012), https://www.usccb.org/beliefs-and-teachings/how-we-teach/catholic-education/higher-education/upload/Final-Report-for-the-Ten-Year-Review-of-The-Application-of-Ex-Corde-Ecclesiae-for-the-United-States-2012.pdf.

3. United States Conference of Bishops, Committee on Catholic Education, *Final Report.*

4. John Paul II, *Ex Corde Ecclesiae, Apostolic Constitution of the Supreme Pontiff John Paul II on Catholic Universities*, Part 2, a. 1, §2, website of the Holy See, accessed August 16, 2021, https://www.vatican.va/content/john-paul-ii/en/apost_constitutions/documents/hf_jp-ii_apc_15081990_ex-corde-ecclesiae.html.

The Unserious Implementation of *Ex Corde Ecclesiae*

When the Vatican released for comment in 1985 a draft schema on Catholic universities, the American colleges opposed the whole idea as unnecessary and even dangerous. The American responses were collected and published in *Origins* on April 10, 1986. The Catholic academic establishment's resistance to episcopal (including papal) involvement goes back at least all the way to the Curran affair at Catholic University of America and to the *Land O' Lakes Statement*, both in 1967, and to the revolt of the theologians against *Humanae Vitae* the following year. Resistance among America's Catholic educational leaders was manifest throughout the 1970s, as the Vatican began developing what would become *Sapientia Christiana,* the Apostolic Constitution on ecclesiastical universities. The 1983 revised Code of Canon Law includes several regulations (in Canons 807–14) about the Catholic character of universities, including the requirement of the *mandatum*, an episcopal license for those teaching "theological disciplines."

During these restive years, it is most likely true that few of America's bishops welcomed the spread of dissenting opinions and the overall secularization of the Catholic colleges. Many did not acquire, moreover, a clear picture of what was happening on campuses. Almost all of those who were cognizant of the problem lacked a plan for anything like preserving the campuses' Catholicity. In any event, since around 1990, the bishops as a national body and almost all of them in the administration of their specific dioceses and archdioceses began taking their cues in academic matters from the colleges. The best that one could say about most bishops on August 15, 1990, is that they might have gone along with a real application of *ECE* if the colleges would have it. But the colleges were most unwilling.

This episcopal docility is most graphically reflected in the bishops' ratification in November 1996 of an *ECE* "Application," which was so bereft of dentures that it makes the current toothless version look fearsome. The Vatican's Congregation for Catholic Education, then headed by Pio Cardinal Laghi, sent it back to the USCCB as—and here I translate the Vatican diplomatic rhetoric into the vernacular—*unserious* (literally, as no more than a first draft). The bishops had adopted it by a vote of 224 to 6.

The Vatican wanted a "juridical" application; the Americans wanted a "pastoral" approach, where "pastoral" was synonymous with "toothless." At the heart of this disagreement was the nature of theology and its practice in relation to the truths of the faith and thus to the authority of Scripture and of the Magisterium. This dispute ripened over the Canon 812 requirement that "[a]ll Catholics who teach theological disciplines in a Catholic university are required to have a *mandatum*" from the competent ecclesiastical authority, typically the local Ordinary. Only at Cardinal Bevilacqua's insistence was any mention of it made in the ill-fated 1996 "Application," and then only in a footnote promising future study of the matter.

The Vatican insisted. The colleges resisted. The bishops were caught in the middle. They were in the uncomfortable position of being made by their ecclesiastical superiors in Rome to do something that the academics would not permit them to do. In the event, the bishops genuflected to Rome and caved to the academics. The enacted "Application," which underwent its decennial review in 2012, affirms that "Catholics who teach the theological disciplines are required to have the *mandatum*," with various details about making that requirement stick. But the preparatory document sent to all the bishops prior to their conversations—also a one-pager—indicates how wobbly it went. Bishops were asked to ask the college presidents: "How has it been possible to incorporate the norms of the Application . . . within the actual situation of the institution?" Included among five categories of topics was "granting the *mandatum*."

Not a word is said of their answers or of the mandatum itself in the ten-year report! In practice, the *mandatum* "requirement" is widely ignored. In other cases, it is rendered meaningless by bishops granting it on request or even sometimes giving the *mandatum* to theologians who have not even asked for it. It is difficult to say more precisely what has happened and is happening because, when it comes to the *mandatum, omerta* is the code: with few exceptions, neither Catholic colleges nor the local diocesan offices reveal publicly who has the *mandatum* and who does not.

Encouraging Signs of Renewal

The bishops' enforcement of *ECE* has gone from feckless to farce. There are nonetheless many encouraging signs of renewal in Catholic higher education. A large handful of institutions, including Franciscan University, Ave Maria

University, Benedictine College, the University of Mary, and Belmont Abbey, have taken to heart the task of providing a genuine Catholic education. These and other institutions have done so while also offering majors that prepare young men and women to take their places as Catholic laity in the workforce. The sobering fact is that the *total* enrollment in *all* the colleges recommended by the Cardinal Newman Society (to take just one index of committed Catholicity) is several thousand *fewer* than the enrollment just at Saint Leo's in Florida or at DePaul in Chicago, neither of which is likely to crack the Newman list any time soon.

Another welcome development in Catholic higher education over the past two decades is the establishment of many Catholic institutes, study centers, and think tanks on or near secular campuses. These foundations, of which the University of Chicago's Lumen Christi Institute would be a prototype, have brought Catholic education to secular institutions, which is where most of America's Catholics enrolled in college or university can be found. These foundations, along with the intellectually (as well as spiritually) ambitious Newman Centers on secular campuses (at the Universities of Illinois, Kansas, and Virginia, for example), provide some of the Catholic education that is available in more substantial measure at the faithful Catholic colleges mentioned above, and more than is available on nominally Catholic campuses.

Sobering is the fact that the market for genuinely Catholic higher education is now quite limited. There are many reasons why it is so. Secularization of society and the comparative affordability of public colleges are two leading reasons. The first obscures the appeal and value of a genuinely Catholic higher education. The second speaks for itself. Another is the ambient reduction of collegiate education to a combination of *pabulum* and vocational preparation, a development that has taken many Catholic colleges and universities in its maws and shows no sign of letting them go. The challenge here is that, in its basic form, a genuine Catholic higher education is neither *pabulum* nor in itself marketable. The market for Catholic higher education is uniquely limited by the fact that a real Catholic higher education is nearly unintelligible to the teens who shop for colleges by considering curb appeal, sports teams' buzz, amenities worthy of cruise ships, and postgraduation job prospects. This consumerist approach to higher education, and the catering to it by so many colleges, constitutes a market in which the appeal of *any* genuine learning—much more the Catholic kind—is increasingly marginal.

Many seriously Catholic parents do not think that if Jack or Jill wants no part of a real Catholic education, he or she should be made to get one anyway. In truth, the appetite for a real Catholic education is an acquired one. It is developed by the cultivation of a tutored desire for it. It is as if one has to *be properly educated in order to want to be properly educated,* which is probably about as true of liberal education generally as it is about Catholic education. Demand for either has to be stimulated and presented to people as a kind of moral imperative. Catholic higher education is not eye-catching in the showroom. It is nonetheless something one is sorely tempted to think one can live without, but which one is glad later on to have gotten anyway. Anyone who troubles to acquire a real Catholic higher education will say later that it was not a luxury option. It is a necessity. A genuine Catholic education is the pearl of great price. It just so happens to be one that few today want to purchase.

It might be worth recalling here that the robust enrollments at Catholic colleges in yesteryear (often at 50 percent, and occasionally higher, of the total number of Catholics attending college or university), resulted partly from a peculiarly potent stimulus; namely, muscular episcopal salesmanship. Bishops preached in season and out of season the crucial importance of patronizing the Church's institutions. Some bishops even enforced up to the mid-twentieth century a disciplinary requirement that Catholics obtain pastoral permission to attend non-Catholic institutions of higher learning. These bishops were worried about the religious indifferentism at public schools and about outright hostility to Catholics at some private institutions. They worried, too, about the occasions of sin that they believed proliferated outside Catholic auspices. Throughout those decades there was even a lively controversy among bishops over whether Newman Centers should be encouraged, lest they make going to a non-Catholic college appealing and spiritually plausible.

At the heart of the episcopal sales pitch through those decades was this message: Catholic higher education meets the challenges of being an adult layperson in mid-twentieth-century America. Probably it did, up to a point. But that does *not* imply that today's Catholic colleges should try to mimic their ancestor institutions, if only because the prevailing understanding of the lay life was quite different then from now. Besides, nostalgia is no recipe for effective education. Ecclesiastical discipline is not an appropriate guide to college choice. Catholic teens and their parents should choose colleges for themselves. But do they know what they should be looking for?

Pastoral Responsibilities and Failures

Do the Church's pastors today teach the faithful about the moral responsibility of every young Catholic to acquire an *adult* faith, to prepare for the lay apostolate, and to discern one's personal vocation? Are parents and teens instructed about how the whole collegiate experience can aid, or hinder, their discharge of those serious moral duties? If they are so taught, they are prepared to conscientiously select a college, and many more than now would demand a genuinely Catholic one.

America's pastors have not so taught the faithful. The dominant message instead suppresses demand for real Catholic higher education. Its depressing effects fall into two categories. For those parents and highschoolers who are interested in Catholic higher education, this dominant line dilutes attempts by the Cardinal Newman Society, the *National Catholic Register*, and others to help them choose the real deal. We should not judge these parents and kids too harshly for believing what a phalanx of professors, presidents, and prelates all profess to be true: things are fine at all the Catholic colleges and universities! After all, that is what the bishops' ten-year review of how well *ECE* is doing on campus.

Some pastors, but not many, dare speak the truth. Few have been as fearless as the now-retired Charles Chaput. Many bishops know the truth about the dismal state of Catholic higher education today; it is plain enough to see. These men are unwilling to mislead the faithful, but they are unable to change the course of the national bishops' conference. These few pastors are also understandably reluctant to speak *so* forthrightly about the dismal state of Catholic higher education as to implicitly rebuke their brother bishops, and the academic establishment, for slack judgment, roseate optimism, and for straight-out duplicity. These alert pastors therefore remain on the sidelines, muffled if not mute. As a consequence, the dominant episcopal line (exemplified by the decennial report's unfounded optimism) causes good pastors to effectively shirk their duty, to tutor the faithful about the true nature and great value of a genuine Catholic higher education, and how it can promote living up to what morality and the faith require of each one of us.

The episcopal line is a pastoral catastrophe, for which there is no decent excuse. Some bishops seem to think that because they may have no direct role in governing the local Catholic college (which typically is civilly incorporated with a lay board of trustees in charge), they can do no more than occasionally "dialogue" with presidents about Catholic "identity." These bishops seem to think that their competence is limited to playing the role (if the local colleges allow) of an occasional senior advisor on Catholic character. These bishops also seem to think that they can achieve success only by operating behind the scenes, confidentially counseling presidents and trustees as circumstances permit. Public confrontation with the colleges over some matter pertaining to the faith is to be avoided at any cost; such conflict is unseemly and spoils prospects for future "dialogue." To the faithful at large, the bishop conveys the message that all is well, and that he is in regular conversation with those in charge of the Catholic colleges in his jurisdiction.

This way of episcopal involvement in Catholic higher education is fundamentally misconceived. In truth, the bishop's role is not to help govern universities, a matter about which he likely knows little. It is to authoritatively judge whether a college in his diocese is truly Catholic, a matter about which he should know a lot. This duty is made most explicit, and certainly obligatory, by Canon 808: "Even if it is in fact Catholic no university is to bear the title or name of Catholic university without the consent of competent ecclesiastical authority." This is the charge of neither a consultant nor an avuncular senior advisor. It is the role of a spiritual governor. There is no doubt whatsoever that civil law courts in this country would enforce a bishop's decision to delete an institution from the *Catholic Directory* and his decree that thereafter it never identify itself as "Catholic."

Bishops must, in addition to properly judging the colleges' Catholicity, should go over their heads to the faithful. The Church's pastors must jump-start demand for a genuine Catholic higher education by teaching all those in their spiritual care what college is for and what a Catholic college should be doing. Bishops must also go over the colleges' heads to the American Catholic donor class. America's Catholics are certainly capable of making a real Catholic collegiate education affordable for all those who want one. Redirecting the contributions of vain baby boomer donors from underwriting an unnecessary "event space" or boutique gym at a rich university, to supporting fellowships at a genuinely Catholic, financially strapped college will be hard pastoral work. Pastors owe instruction about proper stewardship and Catholic higher education not only to students and colleges, but also to those wealthier Catholics who are called to give to higher education. Launching such an ambitious project calls for a compelling description of Catholic higher education and the moral necessity of patronizing and underwriting it. Unfortunately, *ECE* does not supply it.

The Contemporary Need for *Ex Corde Ecclesiae*

So far, we have barely scratched the surface of the question: What is the state of Catholic higher education in America in 2023? After all, Catholic higher education is much more than those 220 or so colleges and universities listed in the *Official Catholic Directory*. Only a tiny fraction of the Catholics in postsecondary schools are enrolled in them. Somewhere between 90 and 95 percent are enrolled elsewhere, in public and non-Catholic private institutions. Add in that only half of those enrolled in Catholic colleges and universities self-identify as Catholic (a percentage in sharp decline over the past few decades, and almost certain to shrink further), and it is even clearer that any consideration of how Catholic higher education is doing, and where it should go, must venture well beyond the Kennedy Directory.

In *ECE*, Pope John Paul II was almost exclusively concerned with Catholic institutions and so with a tiny percentage of Catholics seeking higher education. *ECE* does not say much about the great majority of Catholic institutions, either. It is principally about the modern Catholic *research university*. The percentage of college-going Catholics who are enrolled in such institutions is a tiny fraction of the whole number. With the partial exception of the bishops' own Catholic University of America, is there a research university in America living up to its Catholic mission? No other is listed in the Newman Guide.

ECE is not about Catholic *education*, anyway. It is principally about the dynamic, creative intellectual life of a research university's faculty, considered individually and as a community of scholars. It is also about the constructive if not vital role that the university should play in its host society and culture. In *ECE*, the pope described the Catholic university as "a community of scholars representing various branches of human knowledge and an academic institution where Catholicism is vitally present and operative," citing the International Federation of Catholic Universities' 1972 document "The Catholic University in the Modern World."[5] IFCU was a partnership between

5. John Paul II, *Ex Corde Ecclesiae*, 14.

the Vatican's department of education and Catholic colleges throughout the world. The pope wrote in *ECE* that the mission of the university is the "continuous quest for truth through its research, and the preservation and communication of knowledge for the good of society. A Catholic university participates in this mission with its own specific characteristics and purposes."[6] *ECE* also identified four characteristics that every Catholic university must possess, and Pope John Paul II took this *verbatim* from the 1972 IFCU document. The American bishops' starting point in thinking about implementing *ECE*, as they found it in that document, was probably this summation: "According to *Ex corde ecclesiae*, 'the objective of a Catholic university is to assure in an institutional manner a Christian presence in a university world confronting the great problems of society and culture.'"[7]

These passages and the many like them in *ECE* locate it firmly within a stream of reflections instigated by Vatican II. It is the document foreshadowed in the Council's treatment of education, *Gravissimum educationis* (*GE*), but not delivered until 1990. *GE* was almost entirely about elementary and secondary education, about pupils, schools, and parents. Only a few paragraphs of it addressed higher education. These brief passages in *GE* are best summarized in this excerpt:

> The Church is concerned also with . . . colleges and universities. In those schools dependent on her she intends that by their very constitution individual subjects be pursued according to their own principles, method, and liberty of scientific inquiry, in such a way that an ever deeper understanding in these fields may be obtained and that, as questions that are new and current are raised and investigations carefully made according to the example of the doctors of the Church and especially of St. Thomas Aquinas, there may be a deeper realization of the harmony of faith and science. Thus there is accomplished a public, enduring and pervasive influence of the Christian mind in the furtherance of culture.[8]

Here in *GE* is *ECE* in utero. It might nonetheless be most fruitful to understand *ECE* as an attempt to implement *Gaudium et Spes* (*GS*), Vatican II's

6. John Paul II, *Ex Corde Ecclesiae*, 30.

7. John Paul II, *Ex Corde Ecclesiae*, 13.

8. Second Vatican Council, *Gravissimum Educationis*, 10, accessed August 16, 2021, https://www.vatican.va/archive/hist_councils/ii_vatican_council/documents/vat-ii_decl_19651028_gravissimum-educationis_en.html.

"Constitution on the Church in the Modern World," by and through the activities of the Catholic university. It is no small irony that the document lately taken to be the alter ego of *ECE*—the *Land O' Lakes Statement* of a couple dozen Catholic educational leaders, organized by Notre Dame President Fr. Ted Hesburgh and including the then-head of the Catholic University in Ponce, Puerto Rico, Theodore McCarrick—is squarely within the same stream of reflections. No doubt its authors thought of their work as applying *GS* to their own institutions. Commemorating in 2017 the fiftieth anniversary of that statement, current Notre Dame President Fr. John Jenkins wrote in *America* magazine that *ECE* "can be viewed as the result of the dialogue begun by the Lakes statement, echoing some of its themes, while providing a corrective to others."[9] How could this be? In the United States, these two visions of the contemporary Catholic university—*Land O' Lakes* and *ECE*—have been sharply opposed, as two battle flags under which antagonistic visions of Catholic higher education have warred for hearts and minds.

Fr. Jenkins is right. These statements have a great deal in common. Each is mainly concerned with the social role of the Catholic scholar and of Catholic research institutions as intellectual forces for social change. They could both be neatly folded into the 1972 treatment of "The Catholic University in the Modern World," with only the limited but important canonical commitments of *ECE* appended. It is also telling that in the walk-up to the "Application" of *ECE* to the United States, there was agreement across the aisle between colleges and prelates that *ECE* was a terrific document—until the pope got to the part about juridical implementation, and there mainly Canon 812. To those operating this train of thought, the *mandatum* would naturally become, as it did for the academic establishment as well as the bishops, the tail wagging the dog. In the great work of conversing with the wider intellectual world and of trying to save the rest of it, the ecclesiastical credentialing of theologians, if indeed "theology" should continue to be thought of in connection with the Church at all, would be a footnote, if not an impediment to achieving those large aims.

It is therefore no mystery why the Americans opposed the *mandatum* all along, or why they considered it to be entirely negotiable even after Rome insisted on it. It is also a bit mysterious why anyone, including the pope,

9. John Jenkins, "The Document That Changed Catholic Education Forever," *America,* July 11, 2017, https://www.americamagazine.org/faith/2017/07/11/document-changed-catholic-education-forever.

would make the *mandatum* requirement somehow indispensable to the Catholic university doing the grand extramural work set before it in *ECE*. After all, theology is not a required course at many Catholic colleges. *ECE* does not plainly require that all students be instructed in it. It says only that "Courses in Catholic doctrine are to be *made available* to all students."[10]

It is even likely as a matter of fact that *ECE*'s rich vision of the Catholic research university and its place in society is practically incompatible with providing a true Catholic education to its undergraduates. The sources of incompatibility are many. One is that the commitment of faculty members to their own scholarly work and reputations indentures them to an ambient secular guild of academic professionals that today harbors little or no sympathy for things Catholic. Professors' commitments to graduate students also pull them away from their duty to undergraduates. Departments competing for the best prospective graduate students—themselves aspiring apprentices in the guild—must double down on their secular prestige. It remains true, moreover, that there is nothing *necessarily* incompatible about being both a profoundly serious Catholic intellectual and being a fully engaged and respected participant in the wider scholarly conversation about, say, worthwhile literature or the origins of the universe or government family policy or the history of religion in America or same-sex "marriage." Anyone who has lately tried to unite these aspirations knows that today, in fact, it is a steep uphill climb with trade-offs all along the way.

The understanding of a Catholic university throughout both *ECE* and *LOL* is heavily mortgaged to the prevailing wider understanding of the modern research university. They all understand the Catholic university as a particular inflection of the modern research university, which makes such an institution Catholic, as species within the genus. The Catholic university is enjoined to stay in tune with, and to be a fully respected member of, the contemporary academic scene. It is also enjoined to help solve the political and cultural problems of its host society. This latter injunction would immerse the Catholic university in myriad shifting contingencies and an occasionally bitter partisan rancor. Whatever might have been the wisdom thirty or forty (or fifty) years ago of a clarion call to heed these two external forces, now it is a perilous injunction to immerse the university's Catholic character in

10. John Paul II, *Ex Corde Ecclesiae*, Part 2, a. 4, §5; my emphasis.

acids of radical secularism. Today, a nearly militant independence of purpose and a cultivated indifference to the prevailing winds of academe are essential features of a genuinely Catholic college or university. Neither *ECE* nor *LOL* counsels those essential features.

The Purpose of Catholic Education

Vatican II *should* have transformed Catholic higher education. It did. But its legacy in fact was compromise, dissent, and secularization. The Council *should* have occasioned documents about colleges with a palpable sense of hopeful renewal. In the event we got *Land O' Lakes.* The Council Fathers' work *should* have been consummated by a papal intervention that deepened and concretized the new foundations for Catholic higher education that they articulated. Instead, we got an inadequate, and too-long delayed, papal response in *ECE.*

The basic goal of a distinctly Catholic collegiate education is indicated in *GE*: "the students of these institutions are molded into men truly outstanding in their training, ready to undertake weighty responsibilities in society and witness to the faith in the world."[11] Plainly, preparation for the lay apostolate is the central aim of Catholic higher education. How should that broad aspiration be operationalized?

In *ECE* the Holy Father spoke of the presence of so many laity in the university as a "sign of hope and as a confirmation of the irreplaceable lay vocation in the Church and in the world."[12] But what are the distinctive elements *of* education for the lay apostolate? These distinctive elements have to *go beyond* (i.e., include but surpass or transcend) technical mastery of a discipline and the development of personal piety; otherwise, it would suffice for a Catholic education to plant a good chapel near a non-Catholic campus. A good spiritual life plus a good engineering degree does not equal a Catholic education. The distinctively Catholic elements of a higher education cannot be entirely supplied by a curricular module or summer seminar, as if the Catholic components were affixed to what would otherwise be the schooling on offer at a secular university. These distinctives are well promoted by discrete projects such as courses, seminars, lectures, service opportunities, extracur-

11. *Gravissimum Educationis,* 10.
12. John Paul II, *Ex Corde Ecclesiae,* 25.

ricular activities: all so many "Catholic" moments during an undergraduate's collegiate career. Still, the distinctively Catholic elements are not reducible to such moments. They surpass all particulars and must suffuse the entire enterprise. An energetic Newman Center or nearby institute such as Lumen Christi can supply much of the distinctive education, if students are willing to commit to more than attending the occasional lecture. Offering the occasional lecture or discussion session is useful. But it is better as an invitation to take up the serious business of educating oneself for the lay apostolate.

It would not be wrong to say that inculcating a "Catholic worldview" is the distinctive purpose of a genuine Catholic higher education. Yet it would be more precise to say that inculcating a Catholic worldview is *included* within the interlocking and reinforcing purposes of a distinctly Catholic higher education. That distinctive purpose is not coming to know the Catholic intellectual tradition, much less is it a deep dive into particular parts of that tradition, such as Thomism or early Church history. Studying the Catholic intellectual tradition consists mainly in studying writers: the Fathers, or Bonaventure, or de Lubac. Scholars make careers out of studying Lonergan or John Courtney Murray. Some of those scholars are not Catholic and may not be believers at all. Requiring students to study, say, Aquinas or von Balthasar is in itself fine, but it is still not a recipe for a real Catholic education.

It is better to identify the core of a distinctively Catholic education as the *faith*, or as *the truths of the faith*. Pope John Paul wrote in *ECE* that the Catholic university's "privileged task" is to "unite existentially by intellectual effort two orders of reality" often thought to be opposed; namely, "the search for truth and the certainty of already knowing the fount of truth."[13] The truths of the faith include those accessible to unaided reason, some of which are confirmed (explicitly or implicitly) by revelation, as well as truths accessible only by faith, through a faith that is itself *reasonable* to hold, truths that can only be understood and developed by use of our reason.

The Second Vatican Council founded the renewal of Catholic higher education upon a triple refraction of this core. That tripod specifying this core was: first, the extraordinary development in the Church's understanding of adult Catholic faith in *Dignitatis Humanae*, as a free decision to adhere to the truth, as a whole turning of the person that is uniquely and deeply personal;

13. John Paul II, *Ex Corde Ecclesiae*, 1.

second, the breathtaking teaching on the lay apostolate in *Apostolicam Actuositatem* (*AA*); and lastly, the rediscovery of the concept of *personal vocation*, which had been neglected for centuries before the Fathers of the Council recovered it, and Pope John Paul II presented it so compellingly.

The first leg of the tripod so deepened and universalized the Gospel truth about *metanoia* that it was tantamount to a development of doctrine. The second was a doctrinal innovation. The third revived a theological corpse. Therefore each was, in its own way, startlingly *new*. Together they constituted a transformative impetus for Catholic higher education; they converge upon that span of life when the teen leaves (if not literally, then practically) home and prepares to take up the responsibilities of an adult member of the lay faithful. Every Catholic, college-bound or not, is obliged to make this transition. Every Catholic needs substantial assistance making it, especially because of the intellectual shoals that a complex secularized culture puts in the way to mature faith, and especially where the young Catholic is going to college. Then it is essential that he or she be accompanied on that journey by a faith-filled Catholic higher education.

Adult Faith

The Council's *Declaration on Religious Freedom* (*DH*) is justly acclaimed for its development of doctrine on the right of non-Catholics to the public manifestation of their religions, even in a polity predominantly populated by Catholics. This welcome change is probably the only (strictly speaking) development of doctrine in the document. But *DH* is powered throughout by its fresh recognition that (as the Council Fathers phrased it) "[t]he truth cannot impose itself except by virtue of its own truth, as it makes its entrance into the mind at once quietly and with power."[14] The Fathers added that it is "in accordance with their dignity as persons—that is, beings endowed with reason and free will and therefore privileged to bear personal responsibility—that all men should be at once impelled by nature and also bound by a moral obligation to seek the truth, especially religious truth. They are also bound to adhere to the truth, once it is known, and to order their whole lives in accord with the

14. Second Vatican Council, *Dignitatis Humanae*, 1, website of the Holy See, accessed August 16, 2021, https://www.vatican.va/archive/hist_councils/ii_vatican_council/documents/vat-ii_decl_19651207_dignitatis-humanae_en.html.

demands of truth."[15] This pairing of existential freedom with abiding moral duty is the challenge of coming to a faith-of-one's-own, both mine and true, indeed *mine-because-true.*

This is *adult* faith. It is adult not only because it is one's own (for even children have a genuinely personal faith), but because it is acquired and held by dint of personal conviction of its truth, and not because of habit, conformity to family ways, social advantage, or parental authority. It is also a more critical and sophisticated and integral grasp of the faith than is possible during childhood. It is an adult *faith* in two senses: that of holding certain propositions as true by dint of faith, as well as enjoyment of that intimate relationship with the Master that we so often call "faith."

The journey to adult faith is personal, interior. A more or less formal education fitted to the challenge is nonetheless almost invariably an essential part of that journey for young people in twenty-first-century America. Yet a college or university education in America today is certain to throw up numerous obstacles, including the student's first serious encounter with cultural relativism, evolution, a suitably critical approach to reading scripture, the problem of evil, and the apparent—or at least reported—sufficiency of a personal "spirituality" as an alternative to religion. Thus the overriding importance of a *Catholic* higher education.

In the "Decree on the Apostolate of the Laity" (*AA*), the Council Fathers provided a theological account faithful to revelation but fresh in its departure from centuries of clericalism, which made sense of what had been practically developing within the Church for several decades; namely, the increased role of the laity in social and political affairs consciously as Catholics. Even in its most celebrated moments, such as Pius XI's christening of Catholic Action in the 1920s, activist laity invariably were described as participating in the apostolate of the hierarchy, and so operating in the temporal sphere at the direction of their pastors. Laypersons were soldiers, commanded by clerical generals. Before the Council, there was much truth to the layman's lament that his job in the Church was to "pay, pray, and obey."

Before the Council, a few creative theologians in America developed a theological understanding of lay action that anticipated *AA*. John Courtney Murray published two fine scholarly articles in *Theological Studies* in 1944 on

15. Second Vatican Council, *Dignitatis Humanae*, 2.

the lay vocation.[16] He also favorably reviewed in those pages *The Layman's Call*, an amazingly prescient 1942 book by Rev. William R. O'Connor. In that work, O'Connor emphasized that all members of Christ's body—lay as well as priestly and religious—are called by God to a particular life's work. Each and every Christian is graced by God with a vocation: "no one is without a definite call of some kind from the Lord."[17] Laypersons are called to engage in an apostolate that contributes to the building up of the Kingdom of God and to strive for the perfection appropriate to their state in life. Written two decades before the Council's opening session, one might think that *The Layman's Call* would have contributed to a flourishing conversation in American Catholic thought on the importance of the lay apostolate. Yet O'Connor's contribution to that discussion seems not to have been much noticed, let alone appreciated.

Yves Congar notably contributed to the development of doctrine about the laity, as did Pius XII in several speeches during the 1950s. Even so, these words from *AA* in 1965 were unprecedented and challenging: "The laity are called by God to exercise their apostolate in the world like leaven with the ardor of the spirit of Christ." In this they "share in the priestly, prophetic, and royal office" of the Master. These shares are not derived from participation in the apostolate of the hierarchy. Rather, the laity "have their own share in the mission of the whole people of God in the Church and in the world." This is their "right and duty," rooted in their union with Christ the head.[18]

This task is a form of faith-filled service. Performing it is possible only with the grace of the sacraments. A fervent prayer life is essential, but one more thing (at least) is needed: understanding, or knowledge. To be sure, a Catholic need not receive the sort of advanced higher education that a bachelor's degree offers in order to acquire this knowledge; were that true, most of the Church's saints would not pass muster, notwithstanding that some (the Little Flower among them) championed their faith as a childlike faith. But the understanding or knowledge typically constitutive of the *adult* faith of which I am speaking nevertheless has to be born out of critical reflection on

16. John Courtney Murray, "Towards a Theology for the Layman: The Problem of Its Finality," *Theological Studies* 5 (1944): 43; John Courtney Murray, "Towards a Theology for the Layman: The Pedagogical Problem," *Theological Studies* 5 (1944): 340.

17. William R. O'Connor, *The Layman's Call* (New York: P. J. Kennedy & Sons, 1942), 18.

18. Second Vatican Council, *Decree on the Apostolate of the Laity, Apostolicam Actuositatem*, 2, website of the Holy See, accessed August 16, 2021, https://www.vatican.va/archive/hist_councils/ii_vatican_council/documents/vat-ii_decree_19651118_apostolicam-actuositatem_en.html.

the reasonableness of faith and, to some extent, has to be able to give a reason for one's faith in response to objections, as St. Peter reminded his flock (1 Pt 3:15). In *this* sense, what is needed to perform this form of faith-filled service is precisely what a genuinely Catholic education can well or even paradigmatically provide: a full-orbed Catholic worldview, wherein the connections and pathways between the Catholic faith and the various autonomous spheres of modern life (science, self, sex, economy, politics, and use of force) are illumined. Indeed, the single concept of being "leaven" within the temporal order reveals that each member of the laity is to integrate the Gospel with all his undertakings: scholarly, professional, social, political, economic, familial. Doing so requires learning, but it depends upon models of such integration. For college students, these models would have to include their professors not only in theology, but also and more importantly in the disciplines related to temporal affairs—business, nursing, psychology, science, teaching, and various preprofessional studies.

Finally, Vatican II rediscovered and revivified the idea of personal vocation, what Cardinal Newman talked about beautifully in words quoted by Pope Benedict in 2010 during Newman's beatification ceremonies: "God has created *me* to do him some definite service. He has committed some work to *me* which he has not committed to another. I have my mission."[19] "My mission" is a distinct and unrepeatable assignment. Pope John Paul II once described, in his book *Love and Responsibility*, personal vocation this way: "'What is *my* vocation' means in what direction should *my* personality develop, considering what *I* have in me, what *I* have to offer, and what others—other people and God—expect of *me*."[20] In *Gaudium et Spes,* the Council Fathers taught that Jesus "assures us that ... the way of love is open to all ... [and that] this love is not something reserved for important matters but must be exercised above all in the ordinary circumstances of daily life."[21] These are all unmistakable references to an individualized way of following Jesus, in sea-

19. Pope Benedict XVI, Homily of September 19, 2010, quoting from Newman's *Meditations and Devotions*, 301–2, accessed August 16, 2021, http://www.newmanreader.org/works/meditations/meditations9.html.

20. Karol Wojtyla, *Love and Responsibility* (New York: Farrar, Straus, Giroux, 1981), 257 (my emphasis).

21. Second Vatican Council, *Gaudium et Spes*, 38, website of the Holy See, accessed August 16, 2021, https://www.vatican.va/archive/hist_councils/ii_vatican_council/documents/vat-ii_const_19651207_gaudium-et-spes_en.html.

son and out of season, in life's choices large and small. John Paul II preached regularly throughout his papacy—perhaps most notably in his 1988 Apostolic Exhortation *Christifideles laici*—that each and every one of us is called to a unique life of service for the sake of the Gospel. He said on the Fortieth World Day of Prayer for Vocations:

> How can one not read in the story of the "servant Jesus" the story of every vocation: the story that the Creator has planned for every human being, the story that inevitably passes through the call to serve and culminates in the discovery of the new name, designed by God for each individual? In these "names," people can grasp their own identity, directing themselves to that self-fulfillment which makes them free and happy.[22]

Most of us will come to know what Jesus wants us to do more subtly, through a process of methodical discernment. John Paul II pointed to what might be called the raw data of discernment: one's gifts, one's opportunities, one's training, and, most importantly, the needs of others within the circle within reach, so that one may act in a helpful way.

These three distinctive purposes of Catholic higher education—this Vatican II tripod—are so tightly related that the meaning of each to some extent bleeds into the others. For example, an adult faith includes seeing to it about personal vocation and how to live as layperson in the real world. Who could discern one's personal vocation without an adult faith? Who could spend a lifetime endeavoring to be leaven in an increasingly godless wider world without the resources provided by an adult faith, and the serenity that is a by-product of conscientious discernment? The synergy is powerful, as each of the three purposes depends upon deepening sense of all three.

Conclusion

What might an operational core Catholic higher education look like? How might the truths of the faith be made foundational to a program that promotes the undergraduate's transition to adult faith, preparation for the lay apostolate, and discernment of his or her personal vocation?

22. John Paul II, *Message of His Holiness Pope John Paul II for the Fortieth World Day of Prayer for Vocations*, 3, website of the Holy See, accessed August 16, 2021, https://www.vatican.va/content/john-paul-ii/en/messages/vocations/documents/hf_jp-ii_mes_20021118_xl-voc-2003.html.

Select documents of Vatican II should constitute a required core. To it Catholic colleges could add additional core requirements, up to the limit case where almost the whole four-year program would be a required liberal arts curriculum. Other Catholic colleges could add a modest additional core and then make ample opportunity for practical majors (nursing, business, physical therapy, education, or architecture), as well as majors in the humanities and social and natural sciences. There is nothing like a one-size-fits-all Catholic higher education in the round. But something like what is sketched below is an invariable core of any genuine Catholic higher education. Catholic institutes and Newman Centers should, in addition to their other activities, try to deliver as much as possible of it, too.

The core would consist of eight three-credit courses, one each semester over four years. The entire reading list for each of the first six semesters would be one or two of the Council documents, with limited additional assignments as needed for explanation and illustration. The point of proceeding in this manner is to let the faith be heard by letting the Council speak. Critical engagement with these documents is the objective. The many legitimate questions about translation from the original Latin, historical derivation of leading themes and propositions, as well as how best to give coherent content to vague parts and *lacunae* in them, should be taken up by the teacher and discussion of them led by him or her. A seminar-sized group of students with ample opportunity for discussion and debate is also essential.

The precise order in which the documents should be taken up is debatable. It would seem best to begin, however, with *Dei Verbum,* the "Dogmatic Constitution on Divine Revelation." That way the student learns immediately that there is *truth* in and about religion, that God has chosen to reveal himself to humankind in a way that has been reliably transmitted from the Apostles to us, and that the Church safeguards and expounds that truth. These realities are foundational to further study. The sooner students learn how to read Scripture in a properly critical way, the better.

The second and third semesters would best be devoted to exploring, in one, the nature of the Church and thus *Lumen Gentium* and, in the other, *DH* along with *Nostra Aetate*, the "Declaration on the Relation of the Church with Non-Christian Religions." The priority of *LG* is probably self-evident. The importance of the other two documents is to engage students as soon as practicable in an exploration of the relationships among natural religion, positive or revealed religion, human freedom, and respect for the conscientious but mistaken religious beliefs of other people. The fourth semester almost certainly then should be devoted to *Sacrosanctum Concilium*, the "Constitution on the Sacred Liturgy." The Mass is the source and summit of the Christian life.

Junior year is the time to take up *GS* and then *AA*. The first situates the student within the Church as it conceptualizes its own relationship to the modern world. The latter brings that engagement home to the individual student, as he or she begins to consider concretely, after nearly three years of college, how to be leaven in the temporal order. The seventh semester should be devoted to a suitably critical study of the leading magisterial documents of what is conventionally called Catholic social thought. The final semester is the time to challenge students to develop their own resolve about how, and how faithfully, they will witness to the faith after they go forth from college. Some capstone course suited exactly to that purpose should be required in the final semester.

Ideally, a Catholic college would require all faculty to rotate in and out of teaching all these classes, on the view that if these are the things that every student at a Catholic college should be immersed in, so too every faculty member. A transitional arrangement might be to have the best and most qualified teachers teach these seminars, with other professors encouraged to sit in, and to have perhaps weekly evening receptions where students and faculty are strongly encouraged to come and discuss the week's readings. Doing so would establish a community of learning and of mutual aid in exploring life's challenges. It would foster one big campus conversation about living the faith in contemporary society.

It is perhaps easy to see by now that *ECE*'s stated norm that Catholics constitute at least a bare majority of faculty at a Catholic college is considerably short of the mark. No doubt a faith-filled theology faculty is essential to the educational project at hand as well. The *mandatum* would be a sign of its presence. It is easy to see too that having faithful Catholics throughout the faculty, in all of the disciplines, is possibly even more important than the theologians are to preparing Catholics to be Gospel leaven in the temporal order.

Renewal of Catholic higher education is not a just noble ideal or a desirable aspiration. It is an important obligation. At its core is the perennial faith. Animating its instantiation in institutions—Catholic colleges and universities; Catholic institutes and Newman Centers—are the moral duties of everyone. These duties include those of the young to fit themselves for the life of active adult laymen and -women. They include the obligations of everyone else, from bishops to donors to parents to educators on down, to make readily available a real Catholic education to all who want one.

CHAPTER 9

Whose America? Which Narrative?

Our Lady of Guadalupe and Natality in the United States of America

ASHLEEN MENCHACA-BAGNULO

"And since within any well-developed tradition of enquiry the question of precisely how its history up to this point ought to be written is characteristically one to which different and conflicting answers may be given within the tradition, the narrative task generally involves participation in conflict."[1]

The Problem

On September 11, 2001, Todd Beamer and companions heroically took down the hijackers of United Airlines Flight 93, preventing a piece of a triptych of symbolic destruction alongside the carnage of the World Trade Center and the Pentagon. On the eve of the 2016 presidential election, Michael Anton, under the pseudonym Publius Decius Mus, made a comparison and a plea in a tremendously influential essay: "2016 is the Flight 93 election: charge the cockpit or you die. You may die anyway. You—or the leader of your party—may make it into the cockpit and not know how to fly or land the plane. There are no guarantees. Except one: if you don't try, death is certain."[2]

1. Alasdair MacIntyre, *Whose Justice? Which Rationality?* (Notre Dame, IN: University of Notre Dame Press, 1988), 11.

2. Publius Decius Mus, "The Flight 93 Election," *Claremont Review of Books,* September 5, 2016, https://www.claremont.org/crb/basicpage/the-flight-93-election/.

Fittingly, from the perspective of philosopher Alasdair MacIntyre, Anton's influential essay enters the American political conflict by way of a narrative. Anton's nation is one seeking a hero, a new Todd Beamer, rather than what he depicts as a coalition of weak American conservatives and leftist cosmopolitans who are contributing to the nation's demise by opening the door to a brown invader. Not noting the extent to which American institutions are already shaped by and composed of non-Europeans since the founding, Anton cites "the ceaseless importation of Third World foreigners with no tradition of, taste for, or experience in liberty." Their presence "means that the electorate grows more left, more Democratic, less Republican, and less traditionally American with every cycle. As does, of course, the U.S. population, which only serves to reinforce the two other causes outlined above."[3]

Much of the accuracy of Anton's diagnosis hinges on appropriately identifying what the American nation is and to whom it belongs. Here I offer in response to the idea of the Anglo-European American nation the conception of the nation rooted in the idea of the "mixed" person, or the "mixed" America, as a way forward: the *mestiza* of Gloria Anzaldúa, modeled on the "mulatta" of Albert Murray, captured in a Catholic encapsulation—the lesson of Our Lady of Guadalupe, who in visiting the Indigenous Juan Diego and sending him to the European Bishop Juan de Zumárraga, united the Indigenous and the European in a peace rooted in mutual recognition of dignity as children of God.[4] Using Arendt's concept of natality to untangle the meaning of the mixed American for our current political situation, I argue that rather than corrupting America, Hispanics have offered, and can continue to offer, the energy and structure needed for political rebirth.[5] But first, it is necessary to

3. Decius Mus, "The Flight 93 Election."

4. Gloria Anzaldúa, *Borderlands/La Frontera: The New Mestiza,* 4th ed. (San Francisco: Aunt Lute Books, 2012).

5. I am focusing primarily on the Latino Catholic experience as an alternative model to Flight 93's conception of the nation and the common good for the sake of brevity, though it is important to acknowledge that figures like Dolores Huerta and Caesar Chavez learned how to fight for the common good through sacrifice from the African American civil rights movement. In this we see another *Guadalupian* insight to guide us: the key of self-gift as a way to build community. In the words of Dolores Huerta, one finds an echo of the spiritual and political philosophy that animated the American civil rights movement's use of self-gift from a position of relative powerlessness to bring unity: "Hispanic women . . . know what fasting is, and that it is part of the culture. We know what relationships are, and we know what sacrifice is." Gloria Inés Loya, "Considering the Sources / Fuentes for a Hispanic Feminist Theology." *Theology Today* 54, no. 4 (January 1998): 491–98.

turn to the work of Alasdair MacIntyre on tradition and narrative to build a narrative to counter Anton's.

In the spirit of MacIntyre's attention to traditions of inquiry, evaluating Anton's narrative is most useful in comparison to another account of the American tradition—Albert Murray's presentation of the racially mixed republic in the *Omni-Americans*. Anton portrayed American conservatism as a victim of a "deck . . . stacked overwhelmingly against" all that was right and good.[6] The Left, committed to the demise of American institutions, held the powers of the Right at bay by controlling opinion-makers such as the press and the universities. The Right honorably restrained itself from committing the kinds of manly, dirty deeds needed to fight such a vicious enemy as the Left.

The success of Anton's argument depends on a particular Anglo-American narrative. At the 2019 National Conservatism Conference, those gathered solidified the direction of Anton's lead, with some notable exceptions. Law professor Amy Wax complained that Latino immigrants are too loud and too dirty.[7] She also proposed immigration reform that privileged European immigrants over nonwhite immigrants because "our country will be better off with more whites and fewer nonwhites."[8] Her remarks align with the work of Tom West, who writes that the founders intended that "future citizens would primarily be European" because, in order for political rights to be secured, there needs to be a composite "of nations and cultures that will become and remain one people."[9] Like Wax, West seeks "cultural balance" and is disturbed that "Policies that seek to preserve [it] are vilified in the most hateful terms." The founders believed that "ex-slaves or immigrant blacks" did not have a right to citizenship, though they should not be kept in slavery.[10] West writes, "the fact that it is 'natural' for blacks (or any other aliens living

6. Decius Mus, "The Flight 93 Election."

7. Zack Beauchamp, "Amy Wax, 'National Conservatism,' and the Dark Dream of a Whiter America," Vox, July 23, 2019, https://www.vox.com/policy-and-politics/2019/7/23/20679172/amy-wax-white-national-conservatism-yoram-hazony-racism.

8. Beauchamp, "Amy Wax."

9. Thomas G. West, "The Founders on Race and the Rational Basis of Natural Law: Reply to Peter Myers," *Starting Points,* June 4, 2018, https://startingpointsjournal.com/founders-race-rational-basis-natural-law-reply-peter-myers/.

10. Thomas G. West, *The Political Theory of the American Founding,* (New York: Cambridge University Press, 2017), 65.

in America) to want to be citizens gives them no right to be citizens. For the founders, the social compact is based on equal consent on both sides. Existing citizens should consent to new citizens, just as new citizens should consent before being admitted to citizenship."[11]

But who are the existing citizens, and what is the existing regime's history? Currently, the United States is 18.9% Latino and 13.6% Black; there is a large nonwhite population.[12] At the time of the 1790 Census, based on family surnames alone, the federal government estimated that 20,000 Latinos inhabited the United States.[13] Though present in the founding era, the early influence of Latinos surpassed (radiated beyond) their numbers. "Their impact—social, cultural, political, and economic—is much more profound because of their concentration in particular states and localities."[14] Moreover, the 1790 Census showed that upward of 20 percent of the population was Black;[15] there were also estimates that millions of Native Americans lived in the United States when it was first discovered, though by 1800 the number dwindled to an estimated 600,000.[16] The modern Southwest and the South, particularly, were socially, economically, and culturally enriched by Blacks, Native Americans, and Latinos. Are these cultural contributions simply "un-American" because they are not simply European? Wax, like West, claims that her critique is not about race, but about culture. But if one scratches the surface of this common defense, it falls apart, revealing demarcations between the "true" and "false" Americans that are explicitly identical to racial lines.

MacIntyre as a Lens for Reading Murray

When asked about American race relations following a 2019 keynote lecture at the University of Notre Dame, MacIntyre deftly gestured to the thought

11. West, "Founders on Race."

12. "U.S. Census Bureau QuickFacts: United States," US Census Bureau, accessed July 25, 2022, https://www.census.gov/quickfacts/fact/table/US/PST045221.

13. Loretto Dennis Szucs and Sandra Hargreaves Luebking, eds., *The Source: A Guidebook of American Genealogy*, 3rd ed. (Provo, UT: Ancestry Publishing, 2006), 361.

14. R. G. Rumbaut, "The Making of a People," in *Hispanics and the Future of America*, ed. Marta Tienda and Faith Mitchell (Washington, DC: National Academies Press, 2006), https://www.ncbi.nlm.nih.gov/books/NBK19896/.

15. "1790 Overview," US Census Bureau, accessed May 18, 2023, https://www.census.gov/history/www/through_the_decades/overview/1790.html.

16. Russell Thornton, *American Indian Holocaust and Survival: A Population History since 1492*, reprint ed. (Norman: University of Oklahoma Press, 1990), 43.

of Albert Murray in *The Omni-Americans* as a place for those who wish to bring racial justice and harmony to begin their reflections.[17] While Albert Murray, an American author, scholar and music critic, is an obvious interlocutor for American political theorists writing about social and political change, MacIntyre is a less obvious interlocutor. Though critical of modernity, he has focused less on the nation-state and more on human vulnerability, interdependence, and localism. He writes less on institutions and citizenship and more on ethics and culture that give rise to practices that habituate the citizen and shape the political.[18] Moreover, there are good reasons to believe that insofar as MacIntyre is a localist, or is adopted by localist populists, that this political arrangement inevitably disadvantages minorities.[19] What, then, is the connection, aside from the fact that MacIntyre himself pointed to Murray as an authority for American racial conflict?

The first and most obvious connection is in MacIntyre's account of human interdependency and practical reasoning in *Dependent Rational Animals*. Insofar as America is "mulatto," as Murray says, the character of the nation is not just a matter of the interdependency of individual humans but of the interdependency of groups of humans who may appear separated from one another for superficial, cultural, or historical reasons. To arrive at the proper object of practical reasoning, people must recognize that the political body is neither only abstractly interdependent and mutual, nor as West and Wax suggest, interdependent in the sense that the Anglo-Saxon tradition is normative and shared. Instead, people possess what Murray calls a "composite" culture, a story of mutual contributions and interdependence between diverse groups who have shaped a nation together.

One of the most important contentions of *Dependent Rational Animals* is the significance of networks of giving and receiving, and the way in which all practical reasoning relies upon these relationships to family, friends, and political and social structures. MacIntyre thinks that if these relationships are

17. Alasdair MacIntyre, "To What End? Narrative, Institutions and Practices," presented at the de Nicola Center for Ethics and Culture at the University of Notre Dame, the Centre for Contemporary Aristotelian Studies in Ethics and Politics (CASEP), London Metropolitan University, South Bend, Indiana, July 25, 2019.

18. Nathan J. Pinkoski, "Manent and Perreau-Saussine on MacIntyre's Aristotelianism," *Perspectives on Political Science* 48, no. 2 (April 3, 2019): 125–35.

19. Phil Parvin, "Against Localism: Does Decentralising Power to Communities Fail Minorities?," *Political Quarterly* 80, no. 3 (2009): 351–60.

vicious, the human animal's capacity for practical rationality is limited. It is for this reason that MacIntyre looks askance at 1124b9-10 of *Nicomachean Ethics*, which praises the *megalopsychos* for his embarrassment at reliance on others and his measured pleasure in benefits granted to others.[20] A more accurate account of the human condition recognizes mutual and natural interdependency.

Two assertions of *Nicomachean Ethics*' Book VI are especially important to keep in mind. First, Aristotle states that "choice is longing marked by deliberation" and that reasoning about this longing must be congruent with what the longing seeks. He claims that this is the sum of "practical thinking and practical truth," which relates to action. He contrasts this with contemplative thinking that is unrelated to action and "consists in the true and false respectively."[21] Practical reasoning is done well when there is an overlap between what is true and what one desires. Yet the findings of practical reasoning are susceptible to distortion by pleasure and pain, whereas the angles of a triangle are not changed through what circumstances we endure. Particularly important for this essay are the pains of fear and material scarcity, real or imagined, and the pleasure that Tocqueville, for example, says people find in that which is like them.[22] In practical reasoning, "the principle immediately fails to appear" if one is not habituated to properly confront the insistent existence of pleasure and pain in daily life. The particular needs for members of a given species—or, in the case of humans, the members of a given species and the members of species in a given role—differ but are "conceptually the same." This is because "what it [the member of a given species] needs to flourish is to develop the distinctive powers that it possesses qua member of that species."[23]

Therefore human rationality is inherently bound up with dependency. Recognition of dependency is an important part of the development of rationality.[24] To become what MacIntyre calls "independent rational agents," people need to develop beyond "our initial animal conditions." Virtues are necessary for this to occur, and these virtues of practical reasoning are intrinsically related to the virtues needed to live in society with others.[25]

20. Alasdair MacIntyre, *Dependent Rational Animals: Why Human Beings Need the Virtues* (Chicago: Open Court, 1999), 127.

21. Aristotle, *Nicomachean Ethics*, VI.2 1139a20-25 and 1140b10-15.

22. Alexis de Tocqueville, *Democracy in America*, ed. Eduardo Nolla, new ed. (Indianapolis: Liberty Fund, 2012), 582.

23. MacIntyre, *Dependent Rational Animals*, 67.

24. MacIntyre, *Dependent Rational Animals*, 20.

25. MacIntyre, *Dependent Rational Animals*, 20.

This capacity, which MacIntyre refers to as "independent practical reasoning," is necessary for human flourishing. It is developed in three stages. First, it is important that humans possess the capacity to judge their reasons for action and deem them good or bad, and adjust their action accordingly. This means that people must be exposed to the aforementioned wider range of goods, and this exposure is reliant upon their relationships and the activities in which they are able to partake.[26] To do this, they must be able to achieve a critical distance from what they desire.[27] Lastly, they must be able to imagine their future and to structure the possibilities of their future through their present action. This last capacity is dependent upon their relationships, psychological development, and their opportunities and resources.[28]

MacIntyre emphasizes the necessity of proper relationships for this three-pronged development. He highlights the limitations of poverty upon children's development and the harm done when their emotional needs are neglected. The very development of rationality therefore relies upon social and political factors and historical events and on other people. Such is the nature of human dependency, and vices inhibit the relationships necessary to help people become independent in their practical reasoning.

To be good at practical reasoning, people must possess both intellectual and moral virtues and depend upon others for the development of both.[29] To error intellectually affects practical reasoning. For example, practical reasoning is inhibited when people do not know necessary information for a given situation, when they misinterpret or foolishly augment the factual information they have, or when they rely on erroneous information. But moral error also affects their ability to reason practically. MacIntyre offers the example of people disliking someone so much that they do not assess their interactions with them properly or fail to be "sensitive" toward the nature of their suffering. He writes, "our intellectual errors are often, although not always, rooted in our moral errors. From both types of mistake the best protections are friendship and congeniality."[30]

26. MacIntyre, *Dependent Rational Animals*, 72–73.
27. MacIntyre, *Dependent Rational Animals*, 74.
28. MacIntyre, *Dependent Rational Animals*, 75-76.
29. MacIntyre, *Dependent Rational Animals*, 96.
30. MacIntyre, *Dependent Rational Animals*, 96.

Tradition and Narrative

When it comes to America's racial history, defects of friendship and congeniality abound, limiting our present and past ability to reason about racial equality—the origins and persistence of American racial injustice are failures of both the moral and intellectual virtues. Yet American racism is also a failure of accountability, which emerges from a failure of narrative unity. In *After Virtue*, MacIntyre writes that the modern American tendency toward individualism results in a kind of bewilderment at the thought that there is any individual or communal responsibility for racism because Americans cannot consciously understand themselves or their societies as composites of a narrative. Many Americans "deny the effects of slavery upon black Americans, saying 'I never owned any slaves.'"[31] More reasonable Americans accept some understanding of responsibility because "they themselves have indirectly received from slavery" as inheritors of a national story that began with the cursed institution and is corrupted by all of the terrible forms of oppression descended from it.[32]

Americans who cannot imagine some social responsibility for institutional racism fail to understand themselves in the fullness of what MacIntyre calls the "narrative self":

> For the story of my life is always embedded in the story of those communities from which I derive my identity. I am born with a past, and to try to cut myself off from that past, in the individualist mode, is to *deform my present relationships*. The possession of an historical identity and the possession of a social identity coincide.[33]

In Homeric culture, the question "What am I to do?" was inherently connected to the question "Who am I?"[34] Social responsibility was conceived of as being determined by one's role as a part of a larger whole.[35] As the diversity of translations of Homer across time demonstrate, it is impossible to avoid

31. Alasdair MacIntyre, *After Virtue: A Study in Moral Theory*, 3rd ed. (Notre Dame, IN: University of Notre Dame Press, 2007), 220.

32. MacIntyre, *After Virtue*, 220. He makes a comparison here to the history of British oppression of the Irish.

33. MacIntyre, *After Virtue*, 221.

34. Alasdair MacIntyre, *Whose Justice? Which Rationality?* (Notre Dame, IN: University of Notre Dame Press, 1988), 19–20.

35. MacIntyre, *Whose Justice?*, 22.

projecting the structure of reasoning in which one is steeped onto an inherited narrative.[36] Yet the persistent lesson of Homeric culture's structure of practical reasoning is that moral choices are always connected to the "social and particular" rather than the universal, and that part of this social particular is composed of the sequence of the conflicts and conclusions of relevant previous cultures.[37] In other words, the possibilities for the content and reception of the virtues in our time are path dependent, determined in some part by predecessor cultures, and the justice of particular social and economic institutions is also dependent upon the underlying, fundamental beliefs embodied in these institutions.[38] These beliefs are often, like the virtues, a process of path dependency and inheritance.

An important aspect of the development of virtues, institutions, and their possibilities is the centrality of conflict in the growth of traditions. These conflicts and their conclusions are most apparent in the forms of narrative. In *Whose Justice, Which Rationality*, MacIntyre offers his most explicit definition of tradition and its implications for practical reasoning and the political. Conflict plays an essential role because traditions are themselves arguments:

> A tradition is an argument extended through time in which certain fundamental arguments are defined and redefined in terms of two kinds of conflict: those with critics and enemies external to the tradition who reject all or at least key parts of those fundamental agreements, and those internal, interpretive debates through which the meaning and rationale of the fundamental agreements come to be expressed and by whose progress a tradition is constituted.[39]

Traditions are only understood if people recognize that they are also embodied in social life and practical reasoning. They "give organized expression to concepts and theories already embodied in forms of practice and types of community."[40] The conflicts internal to traditions are themselves subject to

36. MacIntyre, *Whose Justice?*, 16–17.

37. MacIntyre, *After Virtue*, 126–27.

38. Alasdair MacIntyre, *Ethics in the Conflicts of Modernity: An Essay on Desire, Practical Reasoning, and Narrative* (New York: Cambridge University Press, 2020), 85.

39. MacIntyre, *Ethics in the Conflicts of Modernity*, 12. Also see *After Virtue*, where MacIntyre more succinctly describes a tradition as "an historically extended, socially embodied argument, and an argument precisely in part about the goods which constitute the tradition" (206–7).

40. MacIntyre, *Whose Justice?*, 390.

the practice-and-experience-formed perspective of the actors involved. The important conflicts for each person in a tradition, as well as their articulation of the problem and their suggested solutions, are dependent on both the "historical, social and cultural situation of the persons whose problems these are" and "the history of belief and attitude of each particular person up to the point at which he or she finds these problems inescapable."[41] This becomes markedly clear in addressing racial injustice. The ways that one encounters (or does not encounter) racial prejudice are connected not only to history, society, and culture, but also to the underlying attitudes an actor possesses when confronting racism.

Finally, if the development of traditions is intelligible only in terms of narratives of conflicts embodied and informed by social practices and experience, this means that the development of traditions is related to the presence or absence of necessary virtues, which are themselves dictated by the predecessor culture. MacIntyre pointedly contrasts himself to what he calls "conservative antiquarianism." Those who truly understand tradition understand it at least partly as a "grasp of those future possibilities which the past has made available to the present."[42] Viable traditions are unfinished narratives whose possibilities are disclosed by the past, but they do not contain or hold people against their will.[43] Tradition demands the exercise of the classical virtue of prudence, the art of reasoning well about "that which could be otherwise."[44] But if people are deficient in virtues such as justice, courage, and the ability to grasp truth, traditions and their institutions and practices become corrupted, both in the present and in terms of the possibilities they imagine for themselves.[45]

Murray and the *Omni Americans*

In times where a tradition or way of life becomes corrupt or begins to show corruption, a prudent political actor will attempt to "refound"—that is, to reinterpret and re-lay principles and laws that capture the spirit of the founding,

41. MacIntyre, *Whose Justice?*, 393.

42. MacIntyre, *After Virtue*, 223.

43. MacIntyre, *After Virtue*, 223.

44. Aristotle, *Nicomachean Ethics*, trans. W. D. Ross. (CreateSpace Independent Publishing Platform, 2016), 1139a5-9.

45. MacIntyre, *After Virtue*, 223.

to strengthen it and reset it on an uncorrupt path. But a reformer of necessity has to "retain at least the shadow of its ancient modes . . . for since the new things alter the minds of men, you should contrive that those alterations retain" as possible of the previous structure.[46]

MacIntyre is not a Machiavellian, but together they share the insight that keeping a tradition healthy involves being able to diagnose what is wrong with it while also maintaining its forms. A part of the contemporary national conservative movement has depended greatly on the construction of narratives to re-found, or alter, the politically possible. But as good and virtuous practical reasoners, we should try "to arrive, so far as is possible, at a true account of justice and of practical rationality."[47] MacIntyre points us to Murray's *The Omni-Americans* for one possible source of re-founding.

Murray writes in his introduction that "there are white Americans so to speak and black Americans. But any fool can see that the white people are not really white and that black people are not black. They are all interrelated to one another."[48] Rather than a paean to colorblindness, Murray is offering at the outset of his argument a distinction between ignoring ethnic difference and allowing it to enter into American ways of life in inappropriate ways. Cultures need ethnic difference for "cultural diversity and national creativity," and out of a kind of interdependency. Ethnic difference is an engine of "American greatness," but not in the immature sense of human diversity superficial ways represented, only in differences of dress or appearance, rather in the deeper sense of viewpoint and experience diversity. Murray derides liberalism's conception of diversity as just this kind of pretense, a visible array of culture difference that quietly replicates the belief and character of the white American elite.[49] As Murray quips, "Who the hell needs a brown-skinned Norman Mailer?"[50]

The American who cannot accept the fundamentally mixed character of our nation and the American whose diversity is about physical difference rather than a truer multiculturalism share the same problem. In the American

46. Niccolo Machiavelli, *Discourses on Livy,* trans. Harvey C. Mansfield and Nathan Tarcov (Chicago: University of Chicago Press, 1998), I.25.

47. MacIntyre, *Whose Justice?*, 389.

48. Albert Murray, *The Omni-Americans: Some Alternatives to the Folklore of White Supremacy*, ed. Henry Louis Gates Jr. (New York: Library of America, 2020), 3.

49. Murray, *The Omni-Americans.*

50. Murray, *The Omni-Americans*, 178.

context, the "Negro"[51] and the Black American experience are viewed as deviant from the normative case of American-ness—the universal in the country and in human nature is white.[52] Black American culture is consciously or unconsciously understood as the American experience with an asterisk; when art, society, educational institutions, and political organizations encounter the Black experience, it is distorted by what Murray calls the "folklore of white supremacy and [the] fakelore of black pathology."[53]

Paradoxically to some, Murray argues that the folklore of white supremacy not only damages nonwhite Americans by marginalizing them, but it also makes white people less American because they cannot embrace the whole of their national identity but only a part. As long as folklore and fakelore are maintained, the "inaccuracies and misconceptions" fueled by this framework inevitably offer a fundamental rationalization for injustice.[54]

This folklore and fakelore operate in many of our common American narratives—the benevolent progressive, the ardent white nationalist, the love of "cultural balance," and even the Black separatist share a flawed premise when they fail to understand the country as *mulatto*. Black American history *is* American history, Murray writes, and Black citizenship *is* American citizenship. Even though most Black Americans are born into families that have lived here for generations, like strangers to their own land, they do not "enjoy many of the public services, normal considerations, and common privileges."[55] This is especially striking, because while white Anglo-Saxon Protestants are in control of the nation's "power mechanisms," the real test of identity, Murray writes, is culture, and "the nation over which the White Anglo-Saxon power elite exercises such exclusive political, economic and social control is not all-white, not by any measurement ever devised."[56]

This granting of normativity to whiteness in America has devastating consequences for civic friendship, politics, and ethics. As Americans, both native and immigrant, struggle toward the ambiguous concept of whiteness, "they inevitably acquire basic American characteristics—which is to say—Omni-

51. Murray's self-identification.
52. Murray, *The Omni-Americans*, 4.
53. Murray, *The Omni-Americans*, 7.
54. Murray, *The Omni-Americans*, 4.
55. Murray, *The Omni-Americans*, 23.
56. Murray, *The Omni-Americans*, 22.

American—that are part Negro and part Indian."[57] An alternative direction for the narrative of American civil life is found in the work of Albert Murray, and his argument and instructions about how to reject the folklore/fakelore of white supremacy. In contrast to those who see the nation as an Anglo-American entity, with Murray we can recognize the contributions of nonwhites that safekeep liberty.

Guadalupe: The "Mixed" and the "Nation"

As Americans drawn to nationalism during political realignment cast around for ways to articulate the idea of the nation, the most obvious story is readily at hand. Following the work of Albert Murray, the character of the American nation has always been "mixed." Whether we argue that this mixed character is more evident in culture rather than in institutions, as Murray does, or carefully trace the history of labor and participation of non-white Americans—the Black persons dwelling in the United States since its inception, the network of native tribes and federations preceding and existing among the colonized Americas, or the inhabitants of the acquired southwestern territories from Mexico—there is ample evidence that the story we have is a story of a multiracial republican regime.

Nonwhite Americans, in addition to influencing culture and possessing a rightful claim to our role in the nation's building and expansion, have also taught the nation about the meaning of republican freedom. When the Boston Tea Party took place, it was the Native American that the revolutionary invoked, dressed in "war paint and feathers." Even the white American pioneers on the frontier used the town names, weapons, and occasionally the dress, of the Natives they displaced in their own pursuit of freedom.[58] Similarly, the "slaves who were living in the presence of more human freedom and individual opportunity" than had been seen on earth before became the model of what that freedom meant in its deepest sense. As Murray writes:

> That this conception [of being a free man] was perceived by the black slaves is shown by their history as Americans. The fugitive slave, for instance, was culturally speaking certainly an American, and a magnificent one at that. As

57. Murray, *The Omni-Americans*, 21.
58. Murray, *The Omni-Americans*, 15.

> for the tactics of the fugitive slaves, the Underground Railroad was not only an innovation, it was also an extension of the American quest for democracy brought to its highest level of epic heroism.[59]

As the nation's struggle with racism continued, so did the commitment of many Black Americans to the founding ideals of the nation. Instead of responding to the failure of moral courage in fellow citizens with a turn to force, the civil rights movement offered its own moral courage to uplift the nation and substitute for the weakness of those Americans hostile or apathetic to true racial equality. Nikole Hannah-Jones is not wrong to suggest that Black Americans throughout history have persistently brought us closer and closer to the realization of our founding ideals.[60]

Alongside and not against Murray's *Omni-American,* I would like to introduce the Latino-American experience as resource for the nation. Keeping in mind MacIntyre's identification of narrative as an essential part of approaching conflict within a tradition, my goal is to present a story of the Latino and the American nation, reflecting on how it can contribute to a deepening of the nation's self-knowledge and concept of freedom. It cannot be an exhaustive account, but it is a beginning. The path I want to take is one that meditates on the history and present experience of Latinos through the lens of Guadalupe, empress of the Americas, who chose to come to the *indio* Juan Diego to give her message for the entire American continent. First, we must turn to Hannah Arendt's account of natality.

Guadalupe: Natality and Arendt

Challenging Heidegger's suggestion that mortality plays an essential role in the human experience of life, Arendt offers instead the concept of natality as political philosophy's most integral value because in every political action one finds the human capacity for remaking and initiating.[61] Arendt's invocation of natality as a response to Heideggerian "being-towards-death" emerges from her return to her dissertation on Augustine because Augustine presents

59. Murray, *The Omni-Americans,* 18.

60. Nikole Hannah-Jones, "America Wasn't a Democracy, until Black Americans Made It One," *New York Times,* August 14, 2019, https://www.nytimes.com/interactive/2019/08/14/magazine/black-history-american-democracy.html.

61. Hannah Arendt, *The Human Condition,* 2nd ed. (Chicago: University of Chicago Press, 1998), 9.

the human person as a new beginning (a "natal"), as opposed to the Greek concept of the human as a mortal being.[62] Later in *The Human Condition,* Arendt elaborates upon this insight, observing that "the life span of man running toward death would inevitably carry everything human to ruin and destruction if it were not for the faculty of interrupting it and beginning something new, a faculty which is inherent in action like an ever-present reminder that men, though they must die, are not born in order to die but in order to begin."[63] Our actions and words are also like a birth, making politics the province of natality because it is the human space for words and deeds.[64] The Christian perspective differs from the Greek not only because it presents man as the natal and not the mortal, but also because of its virtues of "faith in and hope for the world."[65]

Fittingly, then, Christianity offers a concept of man as an individual with the potential to change society because "one more person may belong to the given society or fundamentally change it."[66] The birth of a new person always occurs in the context of preexisting social relationships because people are always born from mothers who already inhabit a network of interdependency.[67] Such an account describes a political environment that is malleable yet fixed enough for those born into it to find their place in the world.[68] For this reason, Arendt notes, the French philosopher Montesquieu focused on a law's spirit, even though law had previously been conceived of in terms of boundaries. Unlike previous thinkers, Montesquieu studied "the actions [a law's] spirit would inspire" out of recognition for the kind of dynamism Arendt notes in politics' centering of natality. For Montesquieu, laws are viewed "as rapports subsisting between different beings," dynamic relationships rather than limitations that define relationships.[69] It is in this context that Arendt presents

62. Ann W. Astell, "Mater-Natality: Augustine, Arendt and Levinas," *Analecta Husserliana* 89 (2006): 375–76, citing Hannah Arendt, *Love and Saint Augustine*, ed. Joanna Vecchiarelli Scott and Judith Chelius Stark (Chicago: University of Chicago Press, 1998), 51–52.

63. Arendt, *Human Condition,* 246.

64. Arendt, *Human Condition,* 176.

65. Arendt, *Human Condition,* 247.

66. Arendt, *Human Condition,* 164.

67. Cited in Astell, "Mater-Natality," 375n20: Hannah Arendt, "What Is Existenz Philosophy?," *Partisian Review* 13 (1946): 55–56.

68. Stephan Kampowski, *Arendt, Augustine, and the New Beginning: The Action Theory and Moral Thought of Hannah Arendt in the Light of Her Dissertation on St. Augustine* (Grand Rapids, MI: Eerdmans, 2008), 151.

69. See Arendt, *Human Condition,* 192n17.

natality as a Montesquiean principle of Christian political thought, that is, as a principle understood as a "spring" for politics.[70]

For Arendt, natality endangers the boundaries of laws and institutions by showing their artifice. Nothing in the activity of politics itself makes the dimensions of "the fences inclosing private property and insuring the limitations of each household, the territorial boundaries which protect and make possible the physical identity of a people, and the laws which protect and make possible its political existence" self-evident. Yet natality also reveals the significance of such boundaries for the stability of political life, while consistently challenging said boundaries through the "boundlessness" of political action.[71] "This is why," Arendt writes, "the old virtue of moderation, of keeping within bounds, is indeed one of the political virtues par excellence, just as the political temptation par excellence is indeed hubris (as the Greeks, fully experienced in the potentialities of action, knew so well) and not the will to power, as we are inclined to believe."[72]

Thus while natality belies the artificial nature of boundaries, it is also the antidote to the tension it creates between the necessity and unnaturalness of the limitations that help political institutions and laws flourish.[73] It is in this sense that natality is a miracle:

> The miracle that saves the world, the realm of human affairs, from its normal, "natural" ruin is ultimately the tact of natality, in which the faculty of action is ontologically rooted. It is, in other words, the birth of new men and the new beginning, the action they are capable of by virtue of being born. Only the full experience of this capacity can bestow upon human affairs faith and hope, those two essential characteristics of human existence which Greek antiquity ignored altogether, discounting the keeping of faith as a very uncommon and not too important virtue and counting hope among the evils of illusion in Pandora's box. It is this faith in and hope for the world that found perhaps its most glorious and most succinct expression in the few words with which the Gospels announced their "glad tidings": "A child has been born unto us."

70. Kampowski, *Arendt, Augustine, and the New Beginning,* 151.
71. Arendt, *Human Condition,* 193.
72. Arendt, *Human Condition,* 191.
73. Arendt, *Human Condition,* 247.

In the American context, Jefferson and his companions substitute for the Hebrew God/Creator of time and eternity the quasi-religious replacement of the concept of "founding" as a spring for human action that is nearly divine and straddles time and eternity. In the concept and act of founding, Arendt discovers that founders are attempting to renew a system they believe can no longer function by introducing a new thing—a new birth.[74] This new birth is only conceived of in terms of a preexisting social identity, a "we": "No matter how this 'We' is first experienced and articulated, it seems it always needs a beginning, and nothing seems so shrouded in darkness and mystery as that 'In the beginning.'"[75]

Here Arendt relies on Augustine to develop the concept of natality and its relevance to the American founders. Augustine shows Arendt that physical birth, whether in the earthly city's sense of the birth into generations of humans or in the heavenly city's sacramental birth of baptism, points back to the creation out of nothing that is ordained by God for humans, showing us that men are indeed a new beginning in every possible sense, and in this way by nature meant to be free.[76] Human beings possess the memory of being born and are therefore conscious of their freedom to act. Importantly, Augustine raises the possibility that humans who are conscious of their origin in God and not just their origin in human generations possess a greater capacity for freedom. By contrast, natal beings who forget their origin in God become creatures of habit. Arendt sees a similar truth in the foundings of Rome and of the Hebrews. The Romans and the Hebrews reveal "that in the case of foundation—the supreme act in which the 'We' is constituted as an identifiable entity—the inspiring principle of action is love of freedom, and this both in the negative sense of liberation from oppression and in the positive sense of the establishment of Freedom as a stable, tangible reality."[77] This suggests that insofar as Jefferson was only able to create a "pseudo-religious" founding, he marred the American sense of the "We," and consequently limited the horizons that natality offers to our politics. Perhaps in this we find that the decline of religiosity in modernity has introduced political forms that lead us toward death but under the guise of the freedom of the Greeks and the Hebrews,

74. Astell, "Mater-Natality," 386–87.

75. Arendt, *Life of the Mind*, 2:202, cited in Astell, "Mater-Natality," 386.

76. Astell, "Mater-Natality," 385.

77. Arendt, *Life of the Mind*, 2:203–4 cited in Astell, "Mater-Natality," 386.

who by contrast pointed toward natality in their political origins.[78] Anton's Flight 93 essay and other American attempts that minimize the multiracial character of American freedom fall short, I next argue, because they similarly restrict our political horizons and re-found by pointing toward death rather than toward freedom, to only human habit rather than the natality of speech and deeds.

Guadalupe, the Mestiza, as a New Tradition

Arendt invites us to consider a re-founding that is truly a rebirth, but she notes that a re-founding for authentic freedom has to be like that of the Romans or the Hebrews, with a proper conception of the "We" that are born. The perfect inception of our identity is found in the miraculous natality revealed in Our Lady of Guadalupe's presentation of herself as the Mother of the Americas. Our Lady presents herself to Juan Diego, an *indio*, as a pregnant Indigenous woman. She instructs him to relay a message to the Spanish Bishop Zumárraga, ordering the building of a shrine. The idea that an Indigenous man would be heard by a European member of the Church's hierarchy broke all preceding cultural and political norms, as did la Virgen's self-presentation as a woman of the traditions of America's Indigenous, as opposed to the traditions of the Spanish. For the Nahuatl, the flowers she caused to grow among thorny cactuses in the winter were the pre-Hispanic symbol for Truth. Her clothing showed her charge of the important cultural objects of the stars and the moon, and she becomes the Sun itself, "because She carries in Her womb the Child Sun, the New Sun, giving us His presence."[79]

Before Guadalupe, the Indigenous people of the Americas saw the arrival of the Spanish as heralding the death of their political and religious forms. The priests of the old religion of the New World moaned: "What are we to do then/we who are small men and mortals; if we die, let us die; if we perish, let us perish; the truth is that the gods also died."[80] The new priests of the New World were faced with the problem that the Indigenous could not flourish under the political and religious forms of the Christian God when these new

78. Astell, "Mater-Natality," 387.

79. Eduardo Chávez, *Our Lady of Guadalupe and Saint Juan Diego: The Historical Evidence* (Lanham, MD: Rowman & Littlefield, 2006), 21.

80. Chávez, *Our Lady of Guadalupe*, 2.

forms were executed by men who oppressed the Indigenous. The specter of racism threatened to point the New World toward death at its founding, rather than toward the miracle of new life found in authentic freedom of speech and deed. The enslavement of the Indigenous was predicated on the belief that they were subhuman and consequently possessed no rights: "the indigenous were only objects to use to obtain easy fortunes."[81]

One year before Juan Diego told him of the Apparition, Juan de Zumárraga wrote to Emperor Carlos V to testify to the injustices of the Spanish toward the Indigenous.[82] He told the emperor of the destruction and confiscation of the Natives' property. He noted several instances of the Spanish taking water away from the Natives so that they would die of thirst in the arid land. "And because I think that nothing should be hidden from Your Majesty," he wrote:

> I tell you that the Lords of Tlaltelolco came to me, crying, so that I felt sorry for them. They complained that the President and judges had asked for their daughters, sisters and relatives who were good looking, and other men told me that Pilar had asked for eight young girls who were well-disposed for the President. I told a Guardian Priest, who was my interpreter, to tell them not to give the girls to sin. As a consequence, supposedly, they wanted to hang one of these men.[83]

The president who raped the Indigenous girls and women sent a threat to Zumárraga and disregarded his intervention for the women by taking a group of men on Sunday afternoons "from house to house, calling women and forcing them out of their houses, and there many unlawful things happen."

Where Zumárraga did not effectively intervene, la Virgen did. The ultimate message of her apparition is that the Indigenous "world is not finished, it is transformed."[84] She represents the freedom of new birth for the Americas in contrast to the Spanish, whose politics seemed to introduce rape, death, and oppression. In the words of John Paul II, "America, which has historically been a melting pot for people, has recognized 'in the mestizo countenance of the Virgin of Tepeyec' . . . in Holy Mary of Guadalupe . . . a great example of Evangelization, perfectly enculturated."[85] Returning again to Jefferson's

81. Chávez, *Our Lady of Guadalupe*, 4.
82. Chávez, *Our Lady of Guadalupe*, 4–6.
83. Chávez, *Our Lady of Guadalupe*, 5.
84. Chávez, *Our Lady of Guadalupe*, 21.
85. Chávez, *Our Lady of Guadalupe*, 141.

quasi-religious founding, we confront an important question. Are American politics, as some suggest, the politics of rape, oppression, and death that are embodied perhaps most explicitly in the genocide of the American Indigenous, of the enslavement of persons of African descent, and of the exploitation and dispossession of the Latinos acquired with the southwestern territories? Or are they the politics of the Declaration's acknowledgment of the rights of all men and of Lincoln's "new Birth of Freedom"?

The *mestiza* Guadalupe tells Juan Diego that she will give "Him [Christ] to all people . . . because truly I am your compassionate Mother, yours and that of all the people that live together in this land, and also of all the various lineages of men, those who love me, those who cry to me, those who seek me, those who trust me."[86] She invokes the truth about politics Arendt finds in Augustine. Authentic politics yields the miracle of new birth through action and deeds, but as Augustine argues, action can be discerned by its order of loves. The inheritors of the politics of Guadalupe are those who cry to God, seek him, and trust him. As Richard Rodriguez writes, "The word race encourages me to remember the influence of eroticism on history. For that is what race memorializes."[87] In other words, the demographic transformation of America is fitting with the natality of politics. Instead of requiring the suicide mission of Flight 93, a healthy politics can be founded in the *mestiza* Guadalupe and her political-theological message.

What to Expect: Social Science, Latino Identity, and Cross-Pressures

As Timothy Matovina argues, "The mutual influence of Catholicism and Hispanic peoples in the United States is shaping not just the future of American Catholic life but also the life of the nation."[88] This trend is likely to continue as the face of the American church becomes more *mestizo*. In 2043, if immigration patterns remain at present levels, 35 million more Catholics will be present in America than otherwise projected absent immigration.[89] As it

86. Carl Anderson and Eduardo Chavez, *Our Lady of Guadalupe: Mother of the Civilization of Love* (New York: Doubleday Religion, 2009), 9.

87. Richard Rodriguez, *Brown: The Last Discovery of America.* (New York: Penguin, 2003), xv.

88. Timothy Matovina, *Latino Catholicism: Transformation in America's Largest Church* (Princeton, NJ: Princeton University Press, 2011), viii.

89. Vegard Skirbekk, Eric Kaufmann, and Anne Goujon, "Secularism, Fundamentalism, or

stands, two-thirds of the Latino population in America are Catholic; they are characterized as "highly religious" and comparatively young, with nearly 58 percent of Catholics under the age of 35 identifying as Hispanic.[90] These statistics are unsurprising, given that Latinas share with Muslim women the distinction of having the highest fertility rates in America, at 2.8 children per woman.[91] Young Catholic Hispanics are also particularly active, with Latinos comprising 67 percent of young people who attend mass frequently. The American Catholic Church is becoming more Hispanic in its ethnic composition with every passing year. Some scholars think that without Latinos, the Catholic American Church would be in sharp decline.

The 2013 Hispanic Values Survey by the Public Religion Research Institute showed that 45 percent of Latinos preferred the characterization of their political views as "moderate," although a substantial number of Latinos consider themselves to be Democrats. According to Juhem Navarro-Rivera, Latinos identify themselves as moderates "because most Latinos identify religiously as Catholics ... a group likely to feel cross-pressures between their views on social issues such as same-sex marriage or abortion and their views on economic issues such as government aiding the poor."[92] The influence of Catholicism on Hispanic political identity is extensive, and Hispanic interpretation of American political party platforms occurs particularly through the lens of church teaching.

According to a 2015 study by the Pew Research Center, in America, Hispanic Catholics are less likely than white Catholics to disagree with Church teaching. Twenty seven percent more Latino Catholics than white Catholics think it is a sin to remarry without an annulment (52 percent versus 25 percent), and 22 percent more Latino Catholics than white Catholics think homosexual sex is a sin (59 percent versus 37 percent). Latino American Catholics display similar obedience regarding Church teaching concerning poverty: "roughly half of Latino Catholics (55%) say it is a sin to spend money on

Catholicism? The Religious Composition of the United States to 2043," *Journal for the Scientific Study of Religion* 49, no. 2 (2010): 293–310; 300.

90. Robert D. Putnam and David E. Campbell, *American Grace: How Religion Divides and Unites Us* (New York: Simon & Schuster, 2012), 285, 300.

91. Vegard Skirbekk, Eric Kaufmann, and Anne Goujon, "Secularism, Fundamentalism, or Catholicism? The Religious Composition of the United States to 2043," *Journal for the Scientific Study of Religion* 49, no. 2 (2010): 297.

92. Juhem Navarro-Rivera, *The Diversity of Latino Ideology* (Storrs: University of Connecticut, 2015), 18.

luxuries without also giving to the poor, compared with a third of white Catholics who say this (34%)."[93] Latino Catholics also overwhelmingly support Pope Francis, with 84 percent reporting a favorable view of the pontiff, and 64 percent report high levels of satisfaction with their experience of the liturgy.[94]

Hispanic Catholics also possess a different political profile than white American Catholics. According to a Pew study of American Catholics in 2014, while 76 percent of Catholics who identify as Republican are white, only 19 percent of Republican Catholics are Latino. By contrast, 50 percent of Catholics who identify as Republican are white, and 39 percent of Democratic Catholics identify as Latino. On social issues, however, Latino opinions trend in the direction of Democrats on gay marriage and toward the Republican position on abortion.[95] While a significant percentage identify homosexual behavior as a sin, this opinion about gay sex is separated from the question of the possession of civil rights, with 49 percent of Latino Catholics believing that gay marriage should be legalized. The vast majority of Hispanic Catholics, however, oppose abortion, with 54 percent of Latino Catholics agreeing that abortion should be all or mostly illegal.[96] Put another way, 61 percent of Catholics who say that abortion should be legal in all or most cases identify as white, while 30 percent of Catholics who support legal abortion identify as Latino.[97]

Overall, the political identity of Catholic Latinos is something that our existing partisan categories cannot contain. There is some evidence that religious conservativism leads to an emphasis on the prioritization of equality in minority political behavior, and that the familiar connection between conservatism and religion is unpredictable in its particular effects when it comes to Latino Catholics. This is because the "multiple identities" that put "pressure" on the Latino voter in America do not render nicely into the kinds of ideolog-

93. Jessica Martínez, "Among Catholics, Fewer Latinos Than Whites Seek Changes to the Church," Pew Research Center, September 21, 2015, https://www.pewresearch.org/fact-tank/2015/09/21/latino-catholics-white-catholics-changes-to-church/.

94. "The Shifting Religious Identity of Latinos in the United States," Pew Research Center, May 7, 2014, https://www.pewresearch.org/religion/2014/05/07/the-shifting-religious-identity-of-latinos-in-the-united-states/.

95. "Party Affiliation among Catholics—Religion in America: U.S. Religious Data, Demographics and Statistics," Pew Research Center's Religion and Public Life Project, accessed April 11, 2023, https://www.pewforum.org/religious-landscape-study/.

96. Shifting Religious Identity of Latinos in the United States."

97. "Views about Abortion among Catholics—Religion in America: U.S. Religious Data, Demographics and Statistics," Pew Research Center's Religion and Public Life Project, accessed January 9, 2020, https://www.pewforum.org/religious-landscape-study/.

ical groupings that fit the contemporary American two-party system. While it is certainly the case that Latinos themselves face many cross-pressures, it also seems that they challenge much of the conventional wisdom concerning class, race, religion, and economics that sometimes place those pressures on them.[98] In doing so, they may be bringing Catholic social teaching to bear upon American political categories in a novel way.

The future of Latino Catholics does not only depend upon how they view themselves and their commitments, but also on how other American Catholics view them. Through private correspondence, one white American Catholic related a story of peers' reluctance to donate to their parish community because they felt that the parish and its school were demographically shifting to a Latino profile. Consequently and unenticingly, their financial contributions would subsidize the Latino population and its enjoyment of the church's ministries and particularly its school, because the Latino population was able to contribute considerably less to the finances of the parish.[99] The parishioner's attitude could best be summed up as, "Why should *we* pay for *their* kids?" They did not see the Latino members of their parish as part of their parish family, but as a distinct and discrete entity.

Though the United States' first Catholic church was a Hispanic church and the historical missions of the Southwest are some of the oldest Catholic monuments in the country, Latino Catholics do not always seamlessly integrate into the nation's preexisting parish communities.[100] Brett C. Hoover theorizes that the contemporary experience of Hispanic American Catholics is one of "shared spaces" where Latino and non-Latino Catholics worship in the same physical parish but in ways that reify the parishioners into separate communities based on ethnic lines.[101] Consequently, instead of creating one, unified parish body, the church community becomes two different communities that avoid or seek not to "disrupt" one another. For this reason, "The shared parish can easily become kind of a permanent crucible of grief where resentments and frustrations dominate the scene over time."[102]

98. Angel Saavedra Cisneros, *Latino Identity and Political Attitudes: Why Are Latinos Not Republican?* (New York: Palgrave Macmillan, 2016), 17.

99. Menchaca-Bagnulo, private correspondence, January 9, 2020.

100. Mark Gray, "U.S. Hispanic Catholics in the Pews," *Journal of Prevention and Intervention in the Community* 46, no. 4 (2019): 315.

101. Gray, "U.S. Hispanic Catholics in the Pews," 315.

102. Brett C. Hoover, *The Shared Parish: Latinos, Anglos, and the Future of U.S. Catholicism* (New York: New York University Press, 2014), 222.

These resentments often emerge from the complexity of the interactions between differences in economic wealth, citizenship status, and attitudes toward racial reconciliation, among other conditions that influence how power is brokered within the parish.[103] Hoover suggests that the shared parish model is currently following the pattern of discriminatory negligence that characterizes the experience of Latino students in American schools. The parishioners, like the students, attempt to become "smaller" and to avoid drawing attention to themselves, but this also means that they are unable to benefit from and participate in the myriad kinds of social and spiritual capital that are a part of church life.[104] In one case study, Hoover recalls that Latino leaders in the church sought to prevent conflict by encouraging Hispanic parishioners to minimize interaction with potentially hostile Anglo parishioners. One priest even went so far as to develop a parking plan so that Anglo parishioners would not become aggressive toward the Latino parishioners over parking spaces.[105] In this same case study, many Hispanic members of the church expressed that they were afraid of their fellow Anglo parishioners because they felt their undocumented status made them vulnerable, and some Latino parishioners even expressed the fear that the white parishioners in the shared parish belong to the Ku Klux Klan.

Even though the pews of American Catholic churches are increasingly filled by Hispanics, leadership positions do not represent the change in demographics. In 2012, though 40 percent of Catholics were Hispanic, only 6 percent of lay ministers and 6 percent of priests were Hispanics, making the formation of Hispanic lay and religious vocations imperative.[106] The Hispanic ministers that are present report that the integration of Latinos into parish life is comparatively underwhelming and a subject for concern.[107]

As the review of the literature has shown, the influence of Hispanic culture upon American Catholicism is complex. On the one hand, Latino Ca-

103. Brett C. Hoover, "Power Dynamics in Catholic Parishes Shared by Latinos," *Journal of Prevention and Intervention in the Community* 46, no. 4 (October 2, 2018): 380–92, 382.

104. Hoover, "Power Dynamics," 386–87.

105. Hoover, "Power Dynamics," 386–87.

106. Susan B. Reynolds and Andrew D. Reynolds, "The Integration of Hispanic Parishioners in US Catholic Parishes with Hispanic Ministry: Results from a National Survey," *Journal of Prevention and Intervention in the Community* 46, no. 4 (2018): 355–71, 360–61.

107. Hosffman Ospino, *Hispanic Ministry in Catholic Parishes: A Summary Report of Findings from the National Study of Catholic Parishes with Hispanic Ministry*, Spanish-English ed. (Huntington, IN: Our Sunday Visitor, 2015), 19.

tholicism represents a kind of coming home for American Catholicism, given that the roots of American Catholic life are distinctly Hispanic. In this way, it is not appropriate to ask whether Latino Catholics in America will assimilate into the Church because it is in a way already a product of their culture. On the other hand, the influence of Hispanics upon Catholicism presently seems to be less evident in leadership and more present in the pews and communion lines.

Pressure for assimilation disrupts racial reconciliation.[108] While it is true that the "shared-parish" model is leading to conflicts, what seems to be more problematic is the idea that Latino American Catholics should relinquish their religious and cultural practices in order to become "true" American Catholics.[109] Some scholars argue that Catholicism's theological commitment to the practice of inculturation and hospitality to the outsider will prove extremely significant in the future of American Catholicism, aided by the example and inspiration many Latino Catholics have found in the civil rights movement's Christian articulation of the need for recognition and equality.[110]

It might be better to say that Hispanic American Catholics will supervene upon or enhance American Catholic belief culture rather than assimilate into it. What changes might the twentieth-first century expect to see? In a study conducted by Mark Gray, surveyed Hispanic Catholics shared high appreciation levels for hospitableness, a solid liturgy, and a sense of community belonging with other Catholics. But they ranked the following values higher than other Catholics surveyed: the Church's aesthetic appeal (66 percent to 50 percent), the diversity of the parish population (56 percent to 42 percent), the honoring and practice of ethnic cultural traditions (63 percent to 42 percent), the offering of Mass in one's native language (57 percent compared to 41 percent), and adult faith formation (53 percent to 39 percent).[111] A more Latino American church might result in more ornate physical structures, ceremonies, and liturgies and different ways of disseminating social capital like social, political, and linguistic knowledge to newcomers.

I would like to offer one final caveat. Much of the political future of His-

108. Kathleen Garces-Foley, "Comparing Catholic and Evangelical Integration Efforts," *Journal for the Scientific Study of Religion* 47, no. 1 (2008): 17–22, 22.

109. Garces-Foley, "Comparing Catholic and Evangelical Integration Efforts."

110. Garces-Foley, "Comparing Catholic and Evangelical Integration Efforts," 19.

111. Gray, "U.S. Hispanic Catholics in the Pews," 319–20.

panic American Catholics is likely to be influenced by what Hispanic identity comes to mean and how closely it is situated to the American racial category of Black in contradistinction to the category of American "whiteness."[112] This distinction, which is already embedded in the preexisting Hispanic *casta* system that sets up a hierarchy among Hispanics divided with those more "purely" European and less indigenous or African on top,[113] capitalizes on the fact that to be Latino is to be "mixed" by definition. What is clear is that however American Latinos conceive of themselves, those white non-Hispanic Americans who think of American identity as an Anglo-European endeavor will likely never conceive of Latinos as truly "white."

For better or worse, the fate of Latinos will in large part be influenced by the preexisting narratives surrounding race that are offered most clearly by the binary of current American political parties. As American political realignment occurs, it is these narratives that are already shifting and changing on the right.[114] Ultimately, those who cannot be assimilated into the more European aspects of the capacious umbrella of "Latino" will likely not be welcomed into political parties that are less welcoming to non-European Americans. It is also possible that between Latinos themselves a rehashing of the battles of *casta*

112. David R. Roediger, *Working toward Whiteness: How America's Immigrants Became White: The Strange Journey from Ellis Island to the Suburbs*, reprint ed. (New York: Basic Books, 2018); Noel Ignatiev, *How the Irish Became White* (New York: Routledge, 1995); Jennifer Lee and Frank D. Bean, "Reinventing the Color Line Immigration and America's New Racial/Ethnic Divide," *Social Forces* 86, no. 2 (2007): 561–86; George Yancey, *Who Is White? Latinos, Asians, and the New Black/Nonblack Divide* (Boulder, CO: Lynne Rienner, 2003).

113. Leslie B. Rout Jr., *The African Experience in Spanish America* (Princeton, NJ: Markus Wiener, 2015), 126–41; Stuart B. Schwartz, "Colonial Identities and the Sociedad de Castas," *Colonial Latin American Review* 4, no. 1 (January 1, 1995): 185–201. For more information on the complexity of African descent in Mexico, see Ben Vinson, "Free Colored Voices: Issues of Representation and Racial Identity in the Colonial Mexican Militia," *Journal of Negro History* 80, no. 4 (1995): 170–82, 126–41.

114. See Tom West cited in Ashleen Menchaca-Bagnulo, "Who Is 'Like Us?': American Diversity as Heritage," *Public Discourse*, April 16, 2019; Amy L. Wax, "Debating Immigration Restriction: The Case for Low and Slow," *Georgetown Journal of Law and Public Policy* 16 (2018): 837. Also see Wax quoted in Zack Beauchamp, "Trump and the Dead End of Conservative Nationalism," Vox, July 17, 2019: "She explicitly advocated an immigration policy that would favor immigrants from Western countries over non-Western ones; 'the position,' as she put it, 'that our country will be better off with more whites and fewer nonwhites.' (She claims this is not racist because her problem with nonwhite immigrants is cultural rather than biological.)" In his blog *Unqualified Reservations*, Curtis Yarvin, an author featured in Claremont's American Mind (who sometimes writes under the name Mencius Moldbug), argued that America is currently undergoing a conflict between caste systems, among whom are the "swarthy helots" (Latinos) who are allying with progressives to unseat white American culture. Cf. Curtis Yarvin, "Why I Am Not a White Nationalist," *Unqualified Reservations* (blog), November 22, 2007, https://www.unqualified-reservations.org/2007/11/why-i-am-not-white-nationalist/.

will become another part of the picture of the political destiny of American Latinos. These undercurrents can deeply affect the future of Catholic Latino Americans.

It remains to be seen how the complexities of Hispanic heritage might play out in the United States, though the increasing use of Our Lady of Guadalupe in the pro-life movement[115] and the relatively strong preference against abortion in American Latino Catholics may intimate one direction things might go. The use of Our Lady of Guadalupe in protest imagery and prayer for undocumented persons is also becoming more popular as debates around immigration and the internment of migrant children continue.[116] Thus Our Lady of Guadalupe opens up new possibilities for the American dynamic by bridging Republican and Democratic policy preferences as a symbol of justice that surpasses the stagnant American political divide, offering us perhaps the first steps in the United States' own miracle of natality, the only kind of miracle that "saves the world."[117]

115. Judith Samson, "The Scars of the Madonna: The Struggle over Abortion in the Example of an American Post-Abortion Pilgrimage to Mary," *Journal of Ritual Studies* 28, no. 2 (2014): 37–49; Judith Samson, "EU Criticism in Two Transnational Anti-Abortion Movements," in *Gender, Nation and Religion in European Pilgrimage*, ed. Catrien Notermans and Willy Jansen (Burlington, VT: Routledge, 2012), 71–88.

116. Linda B. Hall, "The Virgin of Guadalupe and the Americas: Migration and Movement," in *Marian Devotions, Political Mobilization, and Nationalism in Europe and America*, ed. Roberto Di Stefano and Francisco Javier Ramón Solans (Cham: Springer International, 2016), 233–52, esp. 244; Jeff Gammage, "The Virgin Mary in Handcuffs: How a Viral Image Humanizes the Immigration Debate," Inquirer, December 12, 2019, https://www.inquirer.com/politics/nation/virgin-mary-unholy-escort-katie-jo-suddaby-20191212.html; Alejandra Molina, "As the Feast of Our Lady of Guadalupe Approaches, the Virgin Mary Inspires Community," National Catholic Reporter, December 12, 2019, https://www.ncronline.org/news/people/feast-our-lady-guadalupe-approaches-virgin-mary-inspires-community.

117. Arendt, *The Human Condition*, 247.

CHAPTER 10

Recovering Woman

A Genealogy of the Feminine

MARJORIE JEFFREY

In *Familiaris Consortio*, an apostolic exhortation on the role of the family in the modern world, Pope St. John Paul II urges: "Family, become what you are."[1] Any student of Nietzsche is bound to find his famous exhortation in the mouth of a saint a strange thing, but in this case, their meanings are not entirely different. Although Nietzsche was a great blasphemer, "becoming what one is" challenges us to reach back into the origins of man's psyche in order to prepare for the most difficult task mankind has ever faced: overcoming modernity, or the reign of "the last man."[2] Nietzsche was at least right about this: the challenge for both men and women in our time is to recover our essential natures in order to overcome the spiritual dark age in which we live today.

The family, like the Church itself, must be built on the proper relationship between man and woman, and at a deeper level, between the masculine and the feminine. Men and women have their own natures. There is an interplay throughout creation of the eternal masculine and the eternal feminine. The Magisterium of the Catholic Church teaches that Christ is the bridegroom, and the Church is his bride. The Church is an essentially feminine institution. In the *Catechism*, we are reminded that "St. Paul calls the nuptial union of

1. St. Pope John Paul II, *Familiaris Consortio*, website of the Holy See, accessed November 3, 2019, vatican.va.

2. See subtitle of Friedrich Nietzsche's *Ecce Homo*: "How One Becomes What One Is."

Christ and the Church 'a great mystery.' Because she is united to Christ as to her bridegroom, she becomes a mystery in her turn."[3] The Church herself is mysterious and contains many mysteries within her, such as the sacraments. The unity of Christ and his Church—a unity of masculine and feminine—is born of polarity, not of sameness. It is a coming together of two bodies with their own natures. The *Catechism,* again, quoting St. Augustine, tells us: "They are, in fact, two different persons, yet they are one in the conjugal union . . . as head, he calls himself the bridegroom, as body, he calls himself 'bride.'"[4]

In philosophy, theology, and custom, a fundamental duality between the sexes was assumed throughout the ages. It resulted not from cultural or social construction, but from nature. Furthermore, it was understood that this duality was not merely found in the obvious physiological complementarity of the male and female sexual organs, but in the psychological and social characteristics of men and women as well. Psychologist Karl Stern writes in *The Flight from Woman* that for most of history, "[H]uman duality and human mating expressed an antithesis at the very heart of things, an antithesis striving for synthesis unceasingly, eternally—in an act of anticipation and restitution of unity."[5] Evidence of this view in traditional religions and cultures does not stop at the most obvious Western examples, such as the creation of Adam and Eve in the Garden of Eden and Aristophanes's speech in Plato's *Symposium.* Stern also gives numerous examples from ancient Chinese culture, the Kabbalah, and ancient Assyria, among others.[6] The masculine is usually expressed in the assertive and the intellectual, while the feminine is expressed in the receptive and the feeling. It is perhaps no coincidence that *logos* possesses a masculine ending and *psuche* a feminine one. The marital embrace is the only restoration possible for those who ascribe to this understanding of the dual nature of men and women. It recovers the unity broken in the Garden. The Son of God and his Church are the spiritual manifestations of that embrace in the material world.

Today we live in a world with different assumptions, which have crept from the secular realm into the Church. "Whatever the truth may be, there is no doubt that today, for the first time in history, there occurs a trend which

3. *Catechism of the Catholic Church,* 2nd ed. (New York: Doubleday, 1997), §772. Hereafter *CCC.*
4. *CCC,* §796.
5. Karl Stern, *The Flight from Woman* (New York: Noonday Press, 1969), 9.
6. See Stern, *Flight from Woman,* 10–11.

runs completely contrary to all this," writes Karl Stern in 1965. "Not only is the metaphysics of sexual polarity regarded as a residuum of prescientific superstition, but even the belief that anatomical complementariness expresses psychological complementariness is no longer taken for granted."[7] The idea that all *differences* between men and women are socially constructed was relatively new at the time of Stern's writing. Today, it is a secular sin to stray from this new understanding of the human person.[8]

The relationship of Christ, the bridegroom, to the Church, his bride, may be a mystery, but certain things can be discerned from that mysterious fact. When the sexual complementary nature of men and women becomes fractured, it is unsurprising that this disorder affects both society at large and the Church. When one dwells on this, the sexual abuse crisis afflicting and wounding the Church, even at the highest levels, is no great surprise. In this essay I argue that our modern and disordered understandings of sexual complementary, masculinity, and especially femininity are at the core of the current crisis in the Catholic Church. Part of the reason for this crisis is because femininity has all but disappeared from the modern, Western world. Using the lens of Karl Stern and investigating the work of Robert Graves, Henry Adams, and St. Theresa Benedicta of the Cross (Edith Stein), I try to flesh out masculine and feminine modes of knowing, and provide historical examples of the two modes at work in the history of the Church. I also consider some of the arguments of contemporary feminists, and show that while they are ultimately incorrect, they are right that contemporary Church leadership has failed to grasp the nature and depth of the "woman question." Ultimately, I want to try to show what we have lost and how we might get it back for the Church, and for ourselves.

The Flight from Woman

Karl Stern's seminal work, *The Flight from Woman*, illustrates one of the reasons for the decline of the feminine in the modern age. Although popular wisdom claims that women suffered in the age of tradition and are only free

7. Stern, *Flight from Woman*, 12.

8. Lawrence Summers is just one famous example. The former president of Harvard University lost his position after suggesting publicly that the reason fewer women excel at science and math might be because of differences between the two sexes.

to be themselves in the post-Enlightenment age of rationalism, Stern explains "that 'intellect' and 'heart' stand in antithesis. In this antithesis, the 'heart' is linked to the feminine."[9] In the opposition that Stern describes, there are two modes of knowledge: the rational and the intuitive.

Jose Ortega y Gasset writes of this fundamental sexual duality:

> The more of a man one is, the more he is filled to the brim with rationality. Everything he does and achieves, he does and achieves for a reason, especially for a practical reason. A women's love, that divine surrender of her ultra-inner being which the impassioned woman makes, is perhaps the only thing which is not achieved by reasoning. The core of the feminine mind, no matter how intelligent the woman may be, is occupied by an irrational power. If the male is the rational being, the woman is the irrational being.[10]

The English translation of "irrational" does not quite capture the meaning of the feminine opposition to masculine rationality. What is being described here is the transrational, that which is not necessary grasped by reason but not necessarily contradictory to reason. Nor does Gasset describe this "irrationality" as belonging to a creature lacking in intelligence. On the contrary, Gasset bemoans the fate of "any period or nation" where "intelligence remains, practically speaking, reduced to the limits of the intellectual. Intelligence asserts itself above all not in art, nor in science, but in intuition of life."[11]

The duality to which Gasset and Stern direct our attention is also taken up by the poet and novelist Robert Graves in his essay "The Case for Xanthippe."[12] In it, Graves blames the ascension of abstract rationalism for everything from the decline of poetry to the creation of a conception of politics that allows for ideological tyranny. In Graves's account, rationalism and philosophy displaced practical reason and poetry, beginning in ancient Greece. "Poets mistrust philosophy," he writes, agreeing with his nemesis, Socrates, but further adds, "[w]omen and poets are natural allies."[13] Using Xanthippe as his model, Graves proceeds to explain that with the advent of philosophy, women and poets became allies against abstract rationalism, preferring both practical

9. Stern, *Flight from Woman*, 5–6.

10. Jose Ortega y Gasset, "Landscape with a Deer in the Background," in *On Love: Aspects of a Single Theme* (New York: Meridian, 1957), 165.

11. Ortega y Gasset, "Landscape with a Deer," 161.

12. Robert Graves, "The Case for Xanthippe," *Kenyon Review*, 22, no. 4 (Autumn 1960), 597–605.

13. Graves, "Case for Xanthippe," 598–99.

reason and intuition. Xanthippe's intuitions about what her husband's activities would bring about, for her family and her city, were correct. And ever since philosophy came into being, it has gradually ascended to greater and greater power, finally conquering even the Church herself. "[A]bstract reason, formerly the servant of practical human reason, has everywhere become its master." In this brave new world, "Who cares for female intuition? . . . and who cares for poetic intuition, except perhaps women?"[14] Graves explains what he means, to some degree, by intuition:

> The word intuition must be used with extreme care. Intuition, like instinct, is a natural faculty shared by both sexes—instinct being the feeling which prompts habitual actions . . . [i]ntuition, however, has no concern with habits: it is the mind working in a trance at problems which offer only meagre data for their rational solution. Male intellectuals therefore tend to despise it as an irrational female way of thinking. Granted, fewer women than men have their intuitive powers blunted by formal schooling; yet, oddly enough, only men who have preserved them unspoilt can hope to earn the name of "genius."[15]

Graves perhaps did not foresee that the triumph of rationalism over female intuition would arrive at a point where more women receive "formal schooling" than do men. Whether or not we have reached the final stage of the defeminization of Western society is yet to be seen.

Unfortunately, much of what Sterns draws to our attention has now become normalized and mainstream. Sexual liberation is taken for granted. But Stern's description of a world without sexual difference sounds appalling and becomes even more so when one realizes that this is what has been attempted by contemporary Western political society. Stern writes:

> What began in feminism as a movement of liberation is bound to end in a slavery worse than the first. For if there really existed a world in which "sexual characteristics" are the mere "product" of "culture," in which Mark might just as well have Martha's personality, and Antigone the personality of Achilles—persons would be reduced to fleshless ciphers, to mere intersection points in the graph of a social structure. Indeed, in such a world there are no Marks or Marthas, no Antigones or Achilles. That secret of freedom

14. Graves, "Case for Xanthippe," 602.
15. Graves, "Case for Xanthippe," 602–3.

which lies at the depth of a man's or women's personality would be conjured away, and would be replaced by a vastness of social entities, faceless and manageable. There is no doubt that the original Leninist doctrine of sexual sameness . . . was not only prompted by the motive of liberating woman but contained the hidden aim of depersonalization.[16]

The slavery to which Stern alludes is apparent today. Men and women are conditioned to be treated as consumers, and the androgynous person is the best type of consumer. In order to sell the most products to the largest number of consumers, the androgynous form is the most profitable. Graves, who ultimately ties modern social maladjustment to the disjunction between rationalization and human instinct, writes: "Our civilization is geared to mass-demand, statistically determinable, for commodities which everyone should either make, market, or consume. Good citizens eat what others eat, wear what others wear, behave as others behave, read what others read, think as others think. This system has its obvious economic advantages, and supports vast populations."[17] Although economic advantages are goods, they do not constitute *the* good, particularly if they come at the expense of the breakdown of the human duality that drives social and spiritual order and cohesion.

Stern admits that once one leaves the solid ground of physiology and anatomy, it seems easy to dismiss sexual complementarity as an old-fashioned cliché. Moreover, it could appear stereotypical to assign "discursive reason" on one hand to masculinity, and "intuition," on the other, to a feminine form of knowledge. Yet a number of philosophers and psychologists have observed that these two types of knowing, or paths to knowledge, exist. Stern explicates the work of Henri Bergson, Edmund Husserl, and Karl Jaspers to demonstrate this point, and he further argues that the latter two thinkers especially are careful to show that neither of the two methods are superior. "In fact," he writes, "human knowledge seems to have the greatest chance to arrive at truth when the two methods are at a perfect balance."[18] Bertrand Russell, using different terminology, argues much the same thing, going so far as to suggest that the greatest philosophers "have felt the need of both science and of mysticism: the attempt to harmonize the two was what made their life."[19] Jacques Marit-

16. Stern, *Flight from Woman*, 15–16.
17. Graves, "Case for Xanthippe," 603–4.
18. Stern, *Flight from Woman*, 47.
19. Bertrand Russell, *Mysticism and Logic* (London: George Allen and Unwin, 1951), 1.

ain's *Science and Wisdom* presents a conflict between science and an ascending hierarchy of metaphysical wisdom, culminating in the supernatural wisdom of divine things, which can never be achieved by man alone but only received by the grace of God.[20] From Dionysus the Areopagite, Thomas Aquinas takes a similar understanding of two kinds of knowledge: knowledge of external things and knowledge of human things that we share with others because we possess a common human nature. Knowledge possessed by virtue of connaturality is a kind of human intuition: the kind that can birth poetic wisdom.

But can it be conclusively argued that these two modes of knowing are definitively masculine and feminine? One might know it intuitively. Stern suggests that "one of the reasons why we associate all praeter-rational thinking with womanhood is that the knowledge by connaturality originates in the mother-child relationship."[21] After all, a child is said to reach the age of reason sometime between the age of 7 and 12; the ages of 12 or 13 are usually when, in the Jewish tradition, a boy becomes a man, leaving childish things aside. Stern writes:

> Many contemporary rationalist philosophies (of the positivist, empiricist, naturalist variety) imply that non-scientific thinking is archaic, and is being outstripped by evolution which will lead to an ultimate triumph of discursive thought. Indeed, we are inclined to bracket different phenomena such as "poetic insight," "intuition" etc., because these forms of thinking have one thing in common: they are supposed to be close to the world of the child and the primitive while scientific thinking belongs to the world of the adult and of advanced civilization . . . [*a*]*ll knowledge by union*; all knowledge by incorporation (incorporating or being incorporated); and all knowledge through love has its natural fundament in our primary bond with the mother. The skeptic warns the believer not to "swallow" things and not "to be taken in." And from his point of view, he is right. Faith, the most sublime form of non-scientific knowledge, is (if we consider its natural history, independent of all questions of grace) a form of swallowing or of being taken in. It goes back to an infantile, oral form of union. This is also true about Wisdom. *Sapientia* is derived from *sapere*, to taste, and *Sophia* is the she-soul of Eastern Christendom.[22]

20. Jacques Maritain, *Science and Wisdom* (New York: Charles Scribner's Sons, 1940).
21. Stern, *Flight from Woman*, 53–54.
22. Stern, *Flight from Woman*, 53–54.

Unity and Multiplicity

One can see these two modes of knowing at work in the history of the Catholic Church, particularly during pivotal points in its existence. The period in the Middle Ages after the Abelardian crisis, where Christianity's theological status was in doubt, led to the brief elevation of mysticism over philosophy. It is a perfect example of the dialectic between rational and nonrational modes of knowing. Henry Adams in *Mont Saint Michel and Chartres* charts the course of the interplay between the masculine and feminine in the Middle Ages, culminating in Thomas Aquinas's attempt to synthesize the two forces in his *Summa*. Readers of Adams will recall that his articulation of the masculine and feminine forces in the world are "the Virgin" and "the Dynamo." In his more famous work, *The Education of Henry Adams*, he describes *Mont Saint Michel and Chartres* as "a Study of Thirteenth-Century Unity."[23] His intention was to find that high point of unity which he perceived might be found in the High Middle Ages, and to trace the descent of man from that unity into the endless uniform multiplicity stamped upon modern society by the rise of Enlightenment philosophy and science. His study of multiplicity in his *Education* is subtitled "A Study of Twentieth-Century Multiplicity."[24] Most interpreters see the high point of *Mont Saint Michel and Chartres* as the Virgin, whose place is in the center of the text, and not St. Thomas Aquinas, the subject of the last chapter. She is the first high point, to be sure, but this view misses the movement of Adams's work. The tripartite structure of the book is mirrored in the last three chapters. The first part of the book is about the order of the eleventh century, the masculine Archangel Michael and his cathedral at Mont-Saint-Michel, and also about the mathematic architecture of the period. The second part is about the twelfth-century cult of the Virgin, exemplified in the cathedral at Chartres, and also about the nonrational emotion exhibited by a certain type of mysticism, medieval poetry, and literature. The concluding section turns to St. Thomas Aquinas's effort to place the masculine and the feminine, the rational and the spiritual, into harmony with each other. The last three chapters mirror this structure. The antepenultimate chapter, "Abelard," is about the rupture brought about by Peter Abelard and the rise of a corrupted form of Aristotelianism, while the penultimate chap-

23. Henry Adams, *The Education of Henry Adams* (Oxford: Oxford University Press, 1999), 363.
24. Adams, *Education of Henry Adams.*

ter, "The Mystics," is primarily about St. Francis and the turning away from matter in favor of a purely spiritual understanding of man's relationship with God. The third chapter of this trio, and the last chapter of the book, "Saint Thomas Aquinas," is for Adams the pinnacle of the human attempt at unity because Thomas builds a kind of invisible theological cathedral, intuiting that the nature of man requires both sides of man's nature, attempting to intertwine Aristotelian philosophy and spiritual wisdom, and thereby putting the human being back together as a coherent whole.[25] Whereas his study of the Dynamo, *The Education of Henry Adams*, ends in disunity, his study of the Virgin ends in unity—but only with the help of St. Thomas Aquinas.

Adams's own concern, living in an age where all is being reduced slowly but surely to scientific materialism, is to show that man is neither all matter nor all spirit. Man is something more than either one, or even the sum of his parts. Abelard loses sight of the spiritual, and the Mystics ignore man's material nature. The discovery of Aristotelianism ruptured the Church's theological understanding of itself, and this rupture was left hanging, at the close of the twelfth century, with mysticism serving as the only obvious alternative to rationalism. Mysticism, however, is a way of life not possible for most believers, but only for men like St. Francis of Assisi. For Adams, Thomas Aquinas repaired this rupture in the thirteenth century, reconciling not only the spiritual and the material, but the masculine and feminine as well.

In his long descriptions of the sculptures outside of Chartres Cathedral, Adams repeatedly notes that pictured alongside the Virgin are representations of the seven liberal arts, always "testifying to the Queen's intellectual superiority."[26] Furthermore, she was the subject of equal devotion by the three alternatives Adams will present at the end: Abelard, the Mystics, and St. Thomas.

> Philosophy claimed her, and Albert the Great, the head of scholasticism, the teacher of Thomas Aquinas, decided in her favor the question: "Whether the Blessed Virgin possessed perfectly the seven liberal arts." The Church at Chartres decided it a hundred years before by putting the seven liberal arts next to her throne, with Aristotle himself to witness.[27]

25. This triangular structure is not only found in *Mont Saint Michel*; the *Education* is composed of eleven sets of three chapters, leaving only "Chaos" and "Failure" as standalone chapters in the center of the text. Adams obliquely alludes to this practice in many places, particularly in chapter 24 of the *Education*, where he says he began his "survey—a triangulation—of the twelfth century."

26. Henry Adams, *Mont-Saint-Michel and Chartres* (New York: Penguin, 1986), 72.

27. Adams, *Mont-Saint-Michel and Chartres*, 91.

Mary had mastery, it is said, of all the premodern sciences. Yet she cared little for metaphysical theology.[28] That was left to the Schools. Here, the Virgin Queen established a sovereignty that Hobbes could have only dreamed of in his *Leviathan*. Rather than all human beings being held equal before the sovereign by the passion of Fear, before her they are equal in Love. It was in the Schools that the rupture in question began with Abelard's daring and ambitious intellectual defeat of his teacher, William of Champeaux, and the Platonic undergirding of what had hitherto been the philosophic foundations of Catholic theology. Theology found itself absent philosophical support. Abelard died under censure, and his archrival, Bernard of Clairvaux, saw to it that extreme measures were taken to quash the new practice of scholasticism. Adams writes, "Unfortunately, Bernard could not put his foot down so roughly on the schools, without putting it on Aristotle as well; and, for at least sixty years after the Council of Rheims, Aristotle was either tacitly or expressly prohibited."[29] Abelard had shattered the unified foundations of the Church and had condemned the entire Church to the only readily available alternative: mystical fideism. The Augustinian underpinnings of scholasticism were undermined, and Abelard's form of Aristotelianism was incompatible with Christianity. Adams notes that "Aristotle himself would have been first to forbid the teaching of what was called by his name in the Middle Ages." This intermediate period between 1140 and 1200 is what Adams calls the "Transition." Adams writes:

> The Transition is the equilibrium between the love of God—which is faith—and the logic of God—which is reason; between the round arch and the pointed. One may not be sure which pleases most, but one need not be harsh toward people who think that the moment of balance is exquisite. The last and highest moment is seen at Chartres, where, in 1200, the charm depends on the constant doubt whether emotion or science is uppermost. At Amiens, doubt ceases; emotion is trained in school; Thomas Aquinas reigns.[30]

It was a time of profound skepticism about human reason, a period of wondering whether human reason is any good to the world at all. It was an age "of pure emotion—of poetry and art."[31] But Bernard's skeptical crusade against

28. Adams, *Mont-Saint-Michel and Chartres*, 99.
29. Adams, *Mont-Saint-Michel and Chartres*, 302.
30. Adams, *Mont-Saint-Michel and Chartres*, 302.
31. Adams, *Mont-Saint-Michel and Chartres*.

reason and scholasticism was a failure since "ascetic enthusiasm faded" and "God came no nearer."[32]

The field of philosophy was exhausted. Adams writes, "The twelfth century had already reached the point where the seventeenth century stood when Descartes renewed the attempt to give a solid, philosophical defense for deism by his celebrated 'Cogito, ergo sum.'"[33] This discovery of Descartes's maxim seemed new to his century, but "it was as old and familiar as Saint Augustine to the twelfth century, and as little conclusive as any other assumption of the Ego or the Non-Ego."[34] If Descartes is the Abelard of the seventeenth century, Adams identifies Pascal as the corresponding mystic. The whole affair was the same in the twelfth century as in the seventeenth: "They tried realism and found that it led to pantheism. They tried nominalism and found that it ended in materialism. They attempted a compromise in conceptualism which begged the whole question. Then they lay down, exhausted."[35] One can imagine that Adams himself identifies with Pascal's seventeenth-century wail of despair, which he says belongs to the twelfth century, "not to the mathematical certainties of Descartes and Leibnitz and Newton."[36] Descartes had created his own conceptual proof of God, based upon his own consciousness, but "Pascal wearily responded that it was not God he doubted, but logic. He was tortured by the impossibility of rejecting man's reason by reason; unconsciously skeptical, he forced himself to disbelieve in himself rather than admit a doubt of God."[37] To know God through speculative reasoning was not to truly know him at all. Therefore "The only way to reach God was to deny the value of reason, and to deny reason was skepticism."[38] The Virgin was a touchstone in this evacuation of reason from faith. She "made it all easy, for it was little enough she cared for reason or logic."[39] She cared for her child, simply, and as any woman would. "That, and the grace of God, made her Queen of Heaven." No reason required. She "was poetry and art. In the bankruptcy of Reason, she alone was real."[40]

32. Adams, *Mont-Saint-Michel and Chartres*, 303.
33. Adams, *Mont-Saint-Michel and Chartres*, 303-4.
34. Adams, *Mont-Saint-Michel and Chartres*, 304.
35. Adams, *Mont-Saint-Michel and Chartres*.
36. Adams, *Mont-Saint-Michel and Chartres*.
37. Adams, *Mont-Saint-Michel and Chartres*, 304.
38. Adams, *Mont-Saint-Michel and Chartres*.
39. Adams, *Mont-Saint-Michel and Chartres*, 306.
40. Adams, *Mont-Saint-Michel and Chartres*.

St. Francis of Assisi's life "precisely covered the most perfect moment in art and feeling in the thousand years of pure and confident Christianity."[41] His chief enemy was pride, and the most significant symbol of pride was the schoolmaster, "and of all schoolmasters the vainest and most pretentious was the scholastic philosopher. Satan was logic."[42] The God of St. Francis, like the God of Pascal, was one who could not be grasped, loved, or contained by the enterprise of human reason. Adams characterizes St. Francis's enterprise—in contrast to Francis Bacon's rationalist one—as an instant failure. No one, not even his own followers, could grasp what he meant. And in contrast with the Virgin, who "calmly set herself above dogma," Francis paid no attention to it but "insisted on practices and ideas that no Church could possibly admit or avow."[43] This seems to strike Adams as one of the most admirable aspects of the medieval Church: that it could tolerate the heresies of St. Francis with such grace. St. Francis was "illogical and heretical by essence," but "the charm of the twelfth-century Church was that it knew how to be illogical."[44] The duties of the schoolmen to God were different from the duty of St. Francis to God, and such is the nature of the Infinite.

What is left in this story, itself merely one striking example of the dialectical power of the masculine and the feminine—the rational and the nonrational—at work in Church history, is the person who, according to Adams, is able to achieve unity—even brief, fleeting unity—out of multiplicity. Compared with the Church of Aquinas,

> All modern systems are complex and chaotic, crowded with self-contradictions, anomalies, impracticable functions and outworn inheritances; but beyond all their practical shortcomings is their fragmentary character. An economic civilization troubles itself about the universe much as a hive of honey-bees troubles about the ocean, only as a region to be avoided. The hive of Saint Thomas sheltered God and man, mind and matter, the universe and the atom, the one and the multiple, within the walls of a harmonious home.[45]

Aquinas found a way to rescue Augustine and Aristotle, and to rest the fullness of truth upon a firm foundation that allowed both of them to bolster

41. Adams, *Mont-Saint-Michel and Chartres*, 314.
42. Adams, *Mont-Saint-Michel and Chartres*, 315.
43. Adams, *Mont-Saint-Michel and Chartres*, 320.
44. Adams, *Mont-Saint-Michel and Chartres*, 320.
45. Adams, *Mont-Saint-Michel and Chartres*, 328.

faith—the intuitive—with the fullness of human reason. And so the greatest fait accompli in Western philosophy was performed: "that celebrated fusion of the universal with the individual, of unity with multiplicity, of God and nature, which had broken the neck of every philosophy ever invented; which had ruined William of Champeaux and was to ruin Descartes; this evolution of the finite from the infinite was accomplished."[46]

The intuitive age is gone, at least for now, as is any illusion of unity between the two modes of knowing. We live in what we are told is a nearly perfectly rational age, and we are also assured that it will only get more and more rational. And according to most strains of feminist thought, women can only benefit more and more from this *novus ordo seclorum*. Yet in the decline of tradition, intuition, and the essentially poetic world, the feminine has been lost, or at least repressed and conquered. This was accomplished through the achievements of the scientific method, the industrial revolution, and the triumph of Enlightenment rationalism in politics. If this thesis is correct, the feminists have helped to bring about this triumph of the masculine and engaged in a process of attempting to erase not only what makes individual women feminine, but the feminine itself at work in the world. Stern writes of feminism that it is "an over-evaluation of masculine achievement and a debasement of values which one commonly associates with the womanly; a rejection, often unconscious, even of motherhood; an aping of man, associated with an unceasing undertone of envy and resentment . . . there is a flight from the feminine."[47]

This is not to denigrate the masculine and the rational. But one suspects that the world needs more than only one side of human nature. Moreover, the abolition of one side of human nature increases the danger that all human values are at stake, as C. S. Lewis argues in *The Abolition of Man*. The impoverishment one feels not only in Western culture at large but also in the Catholic Church might well be related to what Max Weber once described: "The fate of our times is characterized by rationalization and intellectualization and, above all, by the 'disenchantment of the world.'"[48] The societies and ages that are marked by the existence of the mysterious, the poetic, the traditional—that is

46. Adams, *Mont-Saint-Michel and Chartres*, 338.

47. Stern, *Flight from Woman*, 6.

48. Max Weber, "Science as a Vocation," accessed November 11, 2019, http://www.wisdom.weizmann.ac.il/~oded/X/WeberScienceVocation.pdf.

to say, a world where the feminine has its place, and a strong place at that—seem to have disappeared.

In the case of the Catholic Church, one sees this void in something that effects every practicing Catholic on a regular basis: the liturgy. One often hears conservative Catholics deriding the Novus Ordo Mass as something lacking in masculine authority. But if we take seriously the argument of Stern and Graves, it is in fact the feminine that has disappeared. The mysterious nature of the liturgy has been removed in an attempt to make it more "accessible" and more "rational" to the faithful. But the corruption of one side of a coin necessarily endangers the whole of it. If human beings possess this dual nature—if they are essentially "and"-creatures— then the human spirit itself is at stake. Furthermore, if sexual polarity is to be relegated to the ash heap of history, it is questionable whether the Church can survive. For "[t]he unspeakable mystery of the *and*—of God *and* His Creation, of God *and* His People, of Christ *and* the Church—would be conjured away . . . Man and Woman share that 'and.' The sexual 'and' is a reflection of the other—all being is nuptial."[49]

The Vocations of Women

For decades now, there has been an open campaign by members of the laity to admit women to the deaconate and even to the priesthood. Only relatively recently did that this campaign gain traction in the hierarchy of the Vatican. Radical feminists have even called upon the Church to abolish the "oppressive" language of gender when referring to the Trinity.[50] Feminist activists were particularly disappointed in the United States Conference of Catholic Bishops in 1995, when they finally released a document based on twenty years of study titled "Strengthening the Bonds of Peace: A Pastoral Reflection on Women in the Church and in Society."[51] The document in question affirms

49. Stern, *Flight from Woman*, 273–74.

50. The Episcopal Church is already moving in this direction; the aims of feminists in every religious denomination are similar. See the Episcopal Church's "Definition of Inclusive Language," accessed November 13, 2019, https://episcopalchurch.org/library/glossary/inclusive-language; and Julie Zauzmer, "The Episcopal Church Will Revise Its Beloved Prayer Book but Doesn't Know When," *Washington Post*, July 18, 2018, https://www.washingtonpost.com/news/acts-of-faith/wp/2018/07/18/the-episcopal-church-will-revise-its-beloved-prayer-book-but-doesnt-know-when/.

51. "Strengthening the Bonds of Peace: A Pastoral Reflection on Women in the Church and in

the equality of men and women, but not their sameness. Mary Carlson, reflecting on this document in 2016, complains that the final document relied not on "empirical" social science, but on tradition and faith.[52] While the document "denounces discrimination and espouses equality," it "more strongly emphasizes the 'diversity of gifts' offered by females and males." Calling the full document "tone-deaf,"[53] Carlson goes on to argue that women have been "hermeneutically marginalized" by the Church and that what is required is unqualified receptivity to the rights claims of all marginalized social groups. This line of argument is clearly present in the dialogue regarding the Amazon Synod in 2019.

It is likely true that the feminists are right for the wrong reasons. The Church could undoubtedly do more to cultivate the vocations of women. Restoring a clear understanding of what feminine vocations are in our world today—a world that doubts that such things exist—is one of the most important tasks we face. The first and only way of inculcating a common cultural understanding of anything is through education. At least one way the Church can begin to think again about the nature of the masculine and the feminine is with regard to female vocations, celibate and otherwise. The mass exodus of priests, monks, and nuns from the religious life, both in the immediate and long-term aftermath of the Second Vatican Council, is well documented. According to Pew Research, however, the decline of women in the religious life in the United States is far steeper than that of priests, diocesan or otherwise. Between 1965 and 2014, the number of Catholic nuns and sisters has fallen from approximately 180,000 to about 50,000—a 72 percent drop in 50 years. Comparatively, the number of priests in the United States has fallen 35 percent in the same amount of time.[54] All vocations to the religious life are in crisis, but feminine vocations have been hit the hardest.

Restoring an understanding of the feminine is the first step to restoring feminine vocations. St. Theresa Benedicta of the Cross (Edith Stein), in an extensive essay on the vocations of men and women according to their natures,

Society," United States Council of Catholic Bishops, accessed November 12, 2019, usccb.org.

52. Mary Carlson, "Can the Church Be a Virtuous Hearer of Women?," *Journal of Feminist Studies in Religion* 32, no. 1 (Spring 2016): 25.

53. Carlson, "Can the Church Be a Virtuous Hearer of Women?," 26.

54. "U.S. Nuns Face Shrinking Numbers and Tensions with the Vatican," Pew Research, accessed November 8, 2019, https://www.pewresearch.org/fact-tank/2014/08/08/u-s-nuns-face-shrinking-numbers-and-tensions-with-the-vatican/.

writes of the difference between the vocations of Adam and Eve in the Garden of Eden, and the consequences of the Fall for the vocations of men and women who possess a fallen nature. In the garden, both together are given a threefold vocation: "they are to be the image of God, to produce posterity, and to rule the earth."[55] But after the Fall, "God's call to men and men's calling appear essentially changed."[56] Both man and woman are assigned different punishments. Man has been deprived of his dominion and will have to struggle against the earth for survival and mastery. The woman will have to suffer in childbirth but receives the added punishment of subjection to man.[57] Man in his fallen nature can exploit this task, turning it into a form of tyranny. Theresa's challenge in this essay is to explain the natural vocations of man and woman in the New Covenant, after our fallen natures, while not restored, are redeemed—not least by God becoming Man through Mary, the new Eve. "According to the original order," she writes, a woman's place "is by the side of man to subdue the earth and bring up posterity." But a woman's body and soul are ill suited to the subduing part of the equation, and better suited for mothering, protecting, and preserving. She writes:

> Of the three-fold attitude to the world that consists in knowing, enjoying, and creatively shaping, the second is usually best suited to her. She seems more capable than man of reverently enjoying creatures. (We would remark in passing that *reverent enjoyment presupposes a specific knowledge of the good things that are enjoyed, which is different from rational knowledge, but is a peculiar spiritual function that is evidently a particular feminine gift.*) This is evidently connected with her function of preserving and fostering posterity. It is a sense of the importance of the organic whole, of specific values and of individuals . . . Hence, according to the original order of nature, man and woman evidently complement each other in this way: man's vocation is primarily to govern; his fatherhood is not subordinated to or co-ordinated with this, but included in it; whereas woman is primarily called to be a mother, her share in the government of the world being in some way implied in that.[58]

55. Edith Stein, *The Writings of Edith Stein*, trans. Hilda Graef (London: Peter Owen Limited, 1956), 102.

56. Stein, *Writings*, 104.

57. See Gn 3:16.

58. Stein, *Writings*, 117. Emphasis mine.

Theresa makes clear that the only path for both men and women acting in accord with their true natures is through a right relationship with God. Without this, both can become corrupt, perverted, or domineering in their distinct forms. For both men and women, she writes, all relationships become perverted when he or she says to God, "I will not serve."[59] Restoring and acting in accord with masculine and feminine natures always begins with intimate personal union with Christ and his Church. "This love," Theresa writes, "will try to know him ever more clearly; it will contemplate His life and meditate His words and want to be united to Him most intimately in the holy Eucharist. It will share His mystical life by following the Church's Year and its liturgy. This way of salvation is the same for both sexes; it redeems both, as well as their mutual salvation."[60] The relationship with Christ is much the same for men and women, though they may discover it in their lives through differing vocations—vocations anchored in a true understanding of one's body and soul, and in right relation to the divine.

As to these different vocations, owing to the differing natures of men and women, Theresa is clear that there is a masculine sphere and a feminine sphere, though individual men may possess more feminine characteristics, and vice versa. Reviewing the change brought about by the scientific revolution, she suggests that technical achievements which have eased the burden of women in the home are good in that they free up physical and creative energies for more productive tasks. But when it comes to the professions, she suggests that "[f]or the average man and woman a division between the professions will come about quite normally, since evidently, owing to their natural differences, they will be suited for different kinds of work . . . [a] sphere for genuinely feminine work exists wherever sensibility, intuition and adaptability are needed, and where the whole human being needs attention."[61] As to the religious vocation, Theresa notes that while Jesus had women among his closest friends and companions, he did not give them the priesthood—not even to his Blessed Mother. Moreover, throughout the history of the Church, God has called women to the religious life in a particular way: as spouses of Christ. Theresa writes, "[t]here is no higher vocation than to be a spouse of Christ, and a woman who sees this way open to her will desire no other."[62]

59. Stein, *Writings*, 115.
60. Stein, *Writings*, 117.
61. Stein, *Writings*, 123.
62. Stein, *Writings*, 125.

Theresa specifically searches for a clear definitional sense of the terms "masculine" and "feminine" in order to ascertain woman's nature, to determine what, according to her nature, her vocation ought to be. She investigates a variety of methods for discovering an answer to this question: psychology, abstract philosophy, phenomenological intuition, theology, and revelation, all of which offer their own share of a solution. Since it is not my purpose here to reproduce her full ontological investigation of the question, I will simply state some of her conclusions, which can serve as a guide for how women might begin to think about feminine life in our world today. First, it is clear from Scripture that the first and most obvious vocation of women is contained in two statements: "It is not good for man to be alone" and "Be fruitful and multiply." With the New Testament, however, comes the call to the ideal of virginity, which is, according to faith, a higher calling than the married state of life. Virginity as a vocation for women is present in pagan religions, but never in the Jewish tradition. Mary's dual virginity and motherhood both introduces and consecrates the celibate life. Marriage and motherhood, therefore, according to divine revelation, are not the only female vocation. Theresa concludes that "the human species develops as a double species of 'man' and 'woman,' that the human essence in which no trait should be missing shows a two-fold development, and that its whole structure has this specific character."[63] The differences are not merely bodily, but also of soul. The female "species" is "characterized by the unity and wholeness of the entire psycho-somatic personality and by the harmonious development of the faculties; the male species by the perfecting of individual capacities to obtain record achievements."[64] This philosophical account of the differences in the human species is confirmed by the theological differentiation between the sexes as shown by divine revelation, as described above. She writes:

> Both, man and woman, are meant to produce and educate posterity. Nevertheless, this is predominantly the task of woman, being physically and psychologically more closely united to the child, and through this union more restricted in her whole way of life . . . *Her particular way of knowledge corresponds to her task of being companion and mother. Her strength is the intuitive grasp of the living concrete, especially of the personal element* . . . Feeling

63. Stein, *Writings*, 142.
64. Stein, *Writings*, 142–43.

> [*Gemüt*] holds the central place in her life, enabling her to grasp and appreciate concrete being in its proper quality and specific value.[65]

Thus the woman has a natural destiny and a supernatural one. She can reach neither without the man, nor he without her. But though the feminine way of being is not solely understood through the relationship between man and woman, the whole cannot be understood without that essential striving for unity.

The natures of man and woman are tainted by the fact of original sin, but perversions are exacerbated by social conditions, culture, and education. If this was a problem in the time that Theresa Benedicta of the Cross lived, it is certainly a problem in our own. Consequently, she calls for a restoration of an education geared specifically toward the feminine, one that creates "conditions suited to counteract perversions, and to contribute to restoring nature in its integrity."[66] This is a call to action that every Catholic woman—and, frankly, every Catholic man—should embrace. The aim of Catholic education is to prepare individuals to lead a life of grace. It must do so, however, by addressing the faithful not simply as individuals, but as men and women. Our natural ends and our supernatural ends may converge, but it does not render us interchangeable cogs, regardless of sex. Theresa writes, "the education of girls should lead them to develop and affirm their proper feminine nature, and this includes the divinely willed vocation to live by the side of man, but not in his place, though neither in a humiliating position that would not be in keeping with the dignity of the human person."[67] Mary, herself virgin and mother, is the model for both feminine vocations: the married life and the celibate. Mary can be the model for all women. The imitation of Mary, herself the first imitator of Christ, must be the *telos* of feminine education. This education should also develop the individual faculties, whether they be suited to domestic work, nursing, education, art, or even the intellectual life. Theresa concludes that "every profession that satisfies the feminine soul and is capable of being performed by it is a genuine feminine profession. The inmost formative principle of the feminine soul is the love that springs from the divine Heart."[68] But the specialization must have a common foundation.

65. Stein, *Writings*, 143.
66. Stein, *Writings*, 146.
67. Stein, *Writings*, 151.
68. Stein, *Writings*, 172–73.

This kind of professional development is good not only for developing the individual human person, but also for "integrating the feminine contribution in the national and cultural life."[69]

St. Theresa Benedicta's final word on the subject should ring in our ears.

> We have to reject a social order and a form of education which completely deny the special characteristics and destiny of woman, which refuse to admit an organic co-operation of the sexes as well as organic social entities, but would treat all individuals as so many cogs in a mechanically regulated economy . . . Today there is no other bulwark against these contemporary currents than the Catholic faith and a metaphysical, social, and educational theory and practice that rest on this faith. By advocating an autonomous feminine education comprising all cultural spheres, we are defending not only the threatened position of woman in our civilization, but by doing so we are taking our place in the great struggle of the spirit against materialism and biologism, as fighters for the kingdom of Christ against all un-Christian and anti-Christian trends and movements.[70]

Conclusion

I wish to begin my conclusion by stating what I am not arguing. I hope it is clear that I do not intend to argue that women are inferior to men. To the contrary, my indictment of feminism is not that it has liberated women, but rather that the feminist movement and the cultural revolution have unwittingly participated in the conquest and attempted destruction of the feminine soul at work in the modern world.

Individual human beings have different strengths, be they men or women. Fewer women than men may want to sit around and study Plato or Nietzsche, but some do. Femininity and masculinity are expressed differently depending on the individual. Nevertheless, it is still reasonable to conclude that there are essential differences between men and women, and that the masculine and the feminine are not stereotypes but real categories with which to be reckoned. Dorothy Sayers argues this charmingly and commonsensibly in her famous address "Are Women Human?" She explains plainly why women in her day are inclined to leave the private sphere. She argues that all of the jobs that used

69. Stein, *Writings*, 159.

70. Stein, *Writings*, 159–60.

to be the work of women in their own domain—the household—have been taken by men; that is to say, they have been taken over by the public sphere. As she writes: "It is all very well to say that woman's place is the home—but modern civilisation has taken all these pleasant and profitable activities out of the home, where the women looked after them, and handed them over to big industry, to be directed and organised by men at the head of large factories."[71] At least in hindsight, however, it seems that Sayers asks the wrong question. The question that concerns us today should not be "Are women human?" but rather "Are women women?"

Alexis de Tocqueville writes in *Democracy in America* that in America, "it is woman who makes mores."[72] In democratic places and times, women shape mores, while in aristocratic ages, it is men—especially fathers—who do. "In aristocratic peoples," he says, "society knows, to tell the truth, only the father ... [t]he father therefore does not have only a natural right. He is given a political right to command."[73] What kind of social mores are shaped in a democratic age by women who are aping masculine characteristics and tendencies? At the very least, it seems like a recipe for disorder. When the natural spiritedness of women becomes warped, it can have the effect of warping the entire culture. For example, the so-called outrage culture that pervades our social space, both on and off the Internet, reeks of an application of thwarted maternal instinct. Thus many contemporary women, who do not have children to mother, seek to mother the world around them.

In the decline of religion and the ensuing revolt from traditional mores, we find ourselves unmoored. The contemporary mores shaped by women have consequences for us all. It is for that reason that the education of the Catholic woman in a democratic age is all the more important. In a democracy, every woman has to make mores for herself and her family. If enough families can share and propagate these mores, it is only then that one has the beginnings of a restoration of culture. Therefore the task for individual women in liberal democracy is more extensive and more difficult. Unless we somehow return to an age of aristocracy, every woman must choose the teaching of the Catholic Church and enforce its norms for herself and her family and community. But

71. Dorothy L. Sayers, *Are Women Human?* (Grand Rapids, MI: Eerdmans, 1971), 24.

72. Alexis de Tocqueville, *Democracy in America*, trans. Harvey C. Mansfield and Delba Winthrop (Chicago: University of Chicago Press, 2002), 279.

73. Tocqueville, *Democracy in America*, 559.

cultures do not only arise from mores: they need beauty. The restoration of beauty in the life of every individual, man and woman, is a larger task toward which every effort must be redoubled. Beauty in art, music, architecture, and throughout everyday life is one of the best paths to restoring a sense of the incarnative nature of human beings. The preceding pages are by no means exhaustive. Much fruitful work could be done in the future on the nature of postmodernity, as opposed to modernity, and whether it is a manifestation of a thwarted feminine reaction to modernity. Much could be gathered, I think, from a study of nineteenth- and twentieth-century Marian apparitions in light of the lens I have suggested here. But it is my hope that this chapter offers some fruitful basis upon which to consider not only the role of women in the Catholic Church and their formation, but also perhaps a reevaluation of Church's participation in twentieth-century rationalism itself.

CHAPTER 11

Benedict Options

JAMES KALB

A post-Christian culture hostile to the Church increasingly dominates the public order. As a result, a vision of radical human autonomy animates a progressively centralized and omnipresent state. This situation has a variety of institutional, technological, and intellectual causes. The fundamental intellectual cause is a specific and rather narrow understanding of reason that makes current tendencies difficult to oppose and seem rationally inevitable. This worldview divides reality into the deterministic world of modern physics, which is considered the real world, and the free but entirely mysterious world of subjectivity. The latter, which current thought cannot account for despite its centrality, is the origin of all moral and political evaluations. Our freedom to evaluate the world and to act upon choices as we wish is thought to make man the world's lawmaker and constitute the source of our human dignity. The choices we make inherit that dignity. All choices are viewed as equally worthy of fulfillment, subject to the consistency, reliability, and efficiency of the system as a whole. The result is an outlook that combines the modern scientific emphasis on control of the world, which is understood mechanistically, with the demand that the control be used to realize the goals of individuals as much and as equally as possible. Technocratic principles are thus viewed as the sole rational basis for social life.

In such a setting, there is no deep human interest outside the human world. Career success and individual fulfillment—participating in the system and enjoying its fruits—become the proper goals of life. Diversity, equality, inclusion, and choice become sacred principles. Every community with its particular standards, boundaries, and authorities must therefore dissolve into every other in order to protect individual choice. Even mainstream religion absorbs this outlook and adopts inclusion, encounter, accompaniment, and nonjudgmental support as its highest goals. The meaning of America, the West, and (for many people) Christianity is increasingly diluted.

This social and moral outlook pervades public discussion. It is inculcated by educators, employers, electronic media, government agencies, commercial mass culture, and religious and moral leaders. As in the case of the effort to extirpate traditional distinctions, and even natural distinctions such as sex, it is enforced by law. Opposition is seen as irrational, bigoted, and worthy of suppression rather than discussion. Religious and cultural traditions that limit choice are thought oppressive and dangerous.

The Current Situation and the Coming Crisis

Since the outlook is so radically anti-transcendental and man-centered, it is clearly at odds with Catholicism. Both faithful Catholics and secularists recognize the point, though some Catholics deny it for a variety of reasons. What, then, is the proper cultural posture of Catholics in such a setting? The question is both deep and acute. To answer it, we need to look at both basic principles and immediate practicalities.

For generations, technology and the technological ideal have swept away healthy and enduring habits. Social life is increasingly carried on through technological arrangements oriented toward economic and utilitarian ends. Work, education, entertainment, and daily practicalities, such as cooking and the care of the young, sick, aged, and unfortunate, are dealt with through commercial and bureaucratic institutions rather than traditional familial, religious, and communal arrangements. People are ever more loosely connected to each other and their traditions. Efficiency is prized more than intangible goods. The ease of travel and all-pervasive electronic communications heighten this effect, weakening our connection to specific concrete settings and bathing us constantly in propaganda and commercial pop culture. Globalism further breaks down local cultural traditions, while mass immigration leads to an open-ended increase in religious and demographic diversity.

The results are cultural incoherence, the radical weakening of specific human ties, and an ever more single-minded emphasis on individual autonomy, economic efficiency, and social management. Powerful institutional and economic forces support these tendencies because they put all social functioning and power in the hands of commercial and bureaucratic interests. Competing authorities—family, religion, local community, particular culture—are rendered nonfunctional, and the population becomes an aggregate of interchangeable human resources. Liberation turns out to be identical to the reign of billionaires and bureaucrats.

Despite the public and private miseries to which they lead, these tendencies are likely to continue until practical circumstances make them unsustainable because of the power of the ways of thinking behind them. Public thought today, for example, opposes exclusivity. That opposition is strong enough to override even the most basic concerns. Communities have boundaries, and specific culture exists through particularity. Current public thought therefore considers community and culture, at least implicitly, to be oppressive and irrational. In their place, contemporary society relies on expertise, bureaucracy, and commerce. In lieu of family life, we have fast food, day care, and therapists.

This weakening of culture, human connections, and the sense of cosmic order also disrupts identity. People rely on identity to understand themselves. As their identities become subjective, fragile, and nonfunctional, it becomes harder for them to think productively about themselves and their lives. These tendencies significantly damage private life. For example, how can children grow up when there is no idea of normal adult life? What becomes of marriage when there is no settled and realistic idea of what men, women, husbands, wives, and the marital union should be? Mutual loyalty and public spirit have no evident basis in the atomized social world now emerging. Without community and tradition, citizens have little reason to stand by each other in hard times. As the common good loses definition, public officials work increasingly for their own private interests.

What cannot go on will not go on. A society of increasingly nonfunctional people, whose motives do not transcend private interest, is not going to last. Even so, it is impossible to predict when the final crisis will come. Everyday life has enormous momentum, and the collapse of an illusion or the bursting of a financial bubble can take a long time. Although contemporary society has shown itself remarkably adaptable owing to its enormous wealth, its current tendencies are indeed unsustainable because they buy immediate power at the expense of overall rationality. The longer the delay, the more complete the wreck will be.

But what then? Fascism, the attempt to impose social unity on some crude and irrational basis through power, propaganda, and violence, is sometimes suggested as a possible outcome. It seems unlikely, however, that nonmarket and nonbureaucratic connections will be strong enough to give fascism anything with which to work. Instead, we are likely to end up with a neo-Levantine society that carries on life through networks and local communities based on primary human ties, such as the family and the tribe that reconstitute themselves when other ties fail, and perhaps to some extent through criminal mafias, as in the former Soviet Union. Unfortunately, such an outcome is likely to mean violence and a radical decline in civilization as people withdraw into insular communities that maintain a certain coherence through refusal to engage others. Already there are signs of such a development in the rise of political correctness, the growing ethnic rancor, and the great difficulty of productive public discussion among people with substantial differences of opinion.

Benedict Options

As Catholics and citizens who care about the well-being of ecclesiastical and secular communities, we need a response that offers more hope. Many Catholics emphasize that the future is unforeseeable and the gates of hell will not prevail. Creation is directed to the good, even when times seem bad, and every situation is an opportunity to live out the Gospel. Since Christ transforms culture, he can transform even a commercial, bureaucratic, and seemingly chaotic postmodern culture. He can turn the indifference and rancor of social atomization into the universal inclusiveness of love. The problem with this response is that man is a social animal who attaches himself to particulars. The vision of an absolute secular universalism redeemed by universal love is not a workable political or religious vision. The Church trusts in God, but she also believes in prudence. She does what is possible pastorally to promote favorable settings for the growth of the Catholic life among people with ordinary needs and weaknesses. To the extent that the current situation threatens our faith, we need to withdraw from it, just as we must avoid occasions of sin and pray not to be put to the test.

Our first duty is love of God. From a practical standpoint, this duty requires a focus on worship and the perfection of our own conduct. It becomes political because worship and human perfection require communities to be oriented toward these goals. If church-attending Catholics spend most of their time awash in a pop culture that trivializes religious concerns and insists on perverse conceptions of right and wrong, they are increasingly likely to lose or dilute the Faith. Those strong in the Faith will no doubt survive, but few Catholics are truly that strong. It is thus imperative for the Church to maintain herself as an overall community and to foster the communities in which Catholics can carry on Christian lives without constant calls for heroic virtue.

The "Benedict Option" is a fertile expression that refers to several ways of dealing with the problem, all worth discussing. St. Benedict's *Rule* presents one version.[1] Rod Dreher has another, and commentators have presented still more.[2] I discuss a range of them, without attending too closely to the particularities of specific thinkers.

Benedict of Nursia

Benedict himself wanted to break all worldly ties to follow Christ and grow closer to God. To that end, he went to the mountains to live away from distractions. He established a rule whereby those who wanted to do likewise could live together peacefully directed to a common good. Benedict did not originate such efforts. In the Bible, God repeatedly summoned people out of established ways of life, as when he called Abraham out of Ur and Moses out of Egypt. Similarly, Jesus called his disciples to leave home, family, and possessions to follow him. Thus the aspiration to break worldly ties is basic to Christianity. We are Christian within the Church, the Church aspires to be holy, and the Bible notes a resulting need for separation that is sometimes expressed rather sharply:

> Know you not that the friendship of this world is the enemy of God?[3]
>
> Do not love the world or the things of the world. If anyone loves the world, the love of the Father is not in him.[4]

1. Benedict of Nursia, *The Rule of St. Benedict*, trans. Anthony C. Meisel and M. L. del Mastro (Garden City, NY: Image,1975).
2. Rod Dreher, *The Benedict Option: A Strategy for Christians in a Post-Christian Nation* (New York: Sentinel, 2017).
3. Jas 4:4.
4. 1 Jn 2:15–17.

> Bear not the yoke with unbelievers . . . Go out from among them, and be ye separate, saith the Lord, and touch not the unclean thing.[5]

Experience taught Benedict to take such warnings seriously. Nor did he lack guides. Especially in the East, there was an established tradition of solitary individuals and groups pursuing a secluded life of prayer, abstinence, and penitence. Benedict wanted to follow in their footsteps, and his famous *Rule* developed a scheme of monastic life that has proved enduringly useful.

A Newer Benedict Option

Most contemporary discussions relate to a Benedict Option understood, in a figurative sense, as a way of life that maintains everyday family life, occupations, and relationships while holding mainstream secular life at a distance to protect Christian habits. Benedictine monasticism and this figurative Benedict Option are, of course, quite different. There is, however, a familial resemblance that justifies speaking of them together, especially in an age that hates the thought of separation from the social order in the way that men once hated the thought of separation from God. Both have to do with closeness to God and the fostering of a better and communal way of life that rejects the world's distractions and corruptions.

The Church has always practiced some degree of separation. In most respects, the early Christians lived in the same way as other people. They prayed for the emperor, held positions in the army and government, and accepted Roman authority within the limits of God's law. Even so, Christians acted upon a different and superior ethos. For example, they refrained from any semblance of participation in pagan worship, and they did not partake in popular festivals, which were associated with it. Serious Christians also believed that they were obligated to avoid many of the popular entertainments of the time: the theater, chariot races, and gladiatorial contests. Yet the Roman culture was less intrusive than today. For most it was a world of peasants, artisans, small shopkeepers, and face-to-face relationships. Education occurred mainly at home, privately, or locally. The Roman games and temple prostitutes were not livestreamed everywhere. The religious unity of the ancient city had long been lost. Life, then, centered much more on the household and in-

5. 2 Cor 6:14–17.

formal local communities, where Catholic understandings could carry weight even when there were few Catholics.

Today, most practical activities are carried on through large formal institutions committed to anti-Catholic understandings. Powerful organizations, businesses, and educational institutions insist on the celebration of every religion, way of life, and purported family form. Electronic media disintegrate close social connections and pervert relationships. If we are immersed in those settings, most of us will go wherever the current carries us. Consequently, faithful Catholics must establish what amounts to a parallel society with its own system of education, sources of livelihood, and informal social life.

There is evidently a need for something of the sort. Without tradition and culture, life loses form and becomes stupid, brutal, and aimless. Tradition and culture are always particular. They are tied to a particular community and dependent on boundaries that define and guard them. To carry on a Christian life in an anti-Christian society, Christians must therefore form their own communities with a certain degree of separation from the world. The future of the Church thus seems certain to include an emphasis on some form of the Benedict Option.

Separation

Monastic life and a degree of social separation seem to be part of all higher religions. An ideal of life based on a direct relationship to ultimate reality always sits awkwardly with the actual system of life that grows up in everyday society. Cities are notoriously full of distractions, and we cannot expect Alexandria, Ashtabula, New York, or Rome to be Christian in more than a faltering way. Many people despair of making spiritual progress in such settings, so they separate themselves—leaving home, property, and human connections—to focus on the one necessary thing. Others withdraw in a more limited way, holding themselves and their families aloof from aspects of the world around them. The effort has sometimes succeeded and sometimes failed, but overall it has been enormously fruitful, often in unexpected ways.

Our habits develop out of what we believe to be important. We naturally try to promote cooperation and reduce misunderstandings and disputes by associating with people who have similar habits, attitudes, and beliefs. People with similar interests form clubs. Scholars join together in colleges and universities. In large cities, like-minded people gravitate to specific neighborhoods. The British and American press ran a number of sympathetic pieces a few years ago on the plight of people who found they had neighbors who voted for Brexit or Trump.[6] Some were thinking of moving elsewhere. How could intelligent and sensitive human beings, they wondered, feel at home in such a setting?

It is therefore natural for religious groups to distance themselves from secular society without special effort or intention. People naturally link up with like-minded people who make similar choices. If they do not like the spectacles in the Colosseum or on television, they go square dancing together. If they think the schools are bad, they set up their own. As common practices develop, separate communities form. These communities become aware of themselves and develop ways of discussing common concerns and pursuing common interests. Others come to view them as separate groups, and they acquire a certain position in the world, especially in a somewhat fluid society like our own. In a similar way, monastic communities developed historically out of collections of individuals who independently decided to abandon worldly ties and pursue a more holy life.

Others usually let them do so because they want to avoid the conflict and unpleasantness that arise from interfering with their neighbors' preferences. Thus secularists should not oppose separation. If they celebrate diversity, as they claim, they should celebrate when some go off to follow their bliss in company with others. Other Catholics should support them as well. Even apart from specifically religious considerations, Catholic social teaching views such communities as a realization of subsidiarity, the principle of making life more participatory by carrying it on as locally as possible.

Addressing Christian Objections

Even so, people object to the Benedict Option. In part, they do not like to have their way of life questioned. Moreover, many Christians are inclined to

6. Karl Whitney, "Why Andy Martin, Documenter of a Changing Sunderland, Has Left His City," *The Guardian,* December 21, 2016, https://www.theguardian.com/cities/2016/dec/21/sunderland-stranger-home-town-brexit-andymartin-3077; Michael Kruse, "What Do You Do if a Red State Moves to You?," *Politico Magazine* (January/February 2017): https://www.politico.com/magazine/story/2017/01/blue-red-state-democrats-trump-country-214647/.

view withdrawing from the world as self-centered and even self-contradictory. They would rather emphasize serving the poor, fighting for peace, and other social projects. But such an outlook is too narrowly utilitarian. It is even somewhat reminiscent of Judas's protest against wasting on a religious observance what could be given to the poor.

The Goodness of Monasticism

The objections of the Benedict Option ignore the ways in which all lives are intertwined. God sometimes puts aside everyday utility, and he often acts through remote causes. Human life is complex, and we affect each other in a variety of ways. Jesus and the early Christians did not try to reform the Academy, run the synagogues, lobby the emperor for social reform, or engage culturally with the shows at the Theater of Marcellus. Nor did St. Francis run for the governing board of the local cloth merchants' guild or try to get a position at the University of Bologna. They concentrated on God, lived their lives accordingly, founded brotherhoods, and presented their views and way of life when the opportunity arose. They offered their contemporaries an alternative that attracted people because of its grandeur. And that changed the world.

Benedict's project benefited the world immensely even by the most narrowly practical standards. It made monasteries more stable and functional. It improved the lives of monks and provided examples of an ordered and productive community in a chaotic world. Over the centuries, his movement helped to civilize all of Europe. It preserved classical learning, extended charity and hospitality, developed better agricultural, industrial, and organizational techniques, and ensured a nucleus of civilized learning in a time of forgetfulness and barbarism. All things considered, no man of action ever did more to improve the world than Benedict and his successors.

Man is called to love God first, and we cannot live other people's lives for them. People must choose their own way. They often learn from seeing the lives of others, so few things can be more helpful to them than showing them a better way of life. This experience can even help those who do not or cannot completely follow it, by changing their worldview in subtle but powerful ways.

Something like monasticism is necessary to Christianity, just as pure science concerned only with truth is necessary to applied science and technology. The need for its guidance is especially great when life is either too hard or too soft. When worldly life is brutal and disordered, the Church needs a place where she can withdraw, contemplate, and act upon her ultimate goal. When worldly life is easy, lax, and prosperous, believers grow worldly and mediocre. The Church becomes too easily compromised and needs to have examples of heroic dedication to her fundamental vision.

Today, the West faces both problems simultaneously. Society is increasingly disordered, inhuman, and anti-Christian. It is physically soft for most people and offers endless opportunity for distraction. Powerful forces within the Church support assimilation to secular society. Consequently, there is reason to expect—to the extent that such things can be predicted—a revival of monasticism. There is a need for the serenity and focus it can provide, and at some point Christians must hear and answer the call. Some see signs of such a development already, though many remain skeptical about its value and the proper way to proceed. Such considerations, of course, leave out the benefits to the world of prayer and contemplation. Catholics have traditionally taken such things seriously; the more Christians value prayer and contemplation, the more they will appreciate the full vision of Benedict's way of life.

The False Charge of Escapism

There are many other objections to a generalized Benedict Option. Some are mostly cosmetic. "Benedict" sounds antiquarian, while "Option" sounds optional. Its most vocal advocate, Rod Dreher, is also known for "crunchy conservatism," which sounds like a post-hippy lifestyle choice for high-flown conservatives who think they are too good for a mass consumer society. Similarly, the Benedict Option sounds to some like a self-indulgent escapist fantasy for bored middle-class people. It is thus viewed as a rejection of the Great Commission, a refusal to engage the world, and in effect a call for retreat, indifference, and self-involvement.

There is also a tendency among many Catholics, in line with the anti-transcendental trend of modern life, to treat the secular world as the real world. That is why, for example, many Catholics believe (apparently falsely) that St. John XXIII said he wanted the Second Vatican Council to "open the windows"[7] of the Church and let in fresh air, and it is why St. Paul VI noted that the Council had "felt the need . . . almost to run after [the society in

7. "Vatican II: 'Open the Windows'—? Not Exactly," *Casa Santa Lidia* (blog), December 30, 2010, https://casasantalidia.blogspot.com/2010/12/vatican-ii-open-windows-not-exactly.html.

which the Church lives] in its rapid and continuous change."[8] Finally, it is worth noting that the Benedict Option of any sort is not for everyone. Missionaries like St. Paul do not live it, although the communities they establish may.

Still, the Benedict Option is not a complete disengagement from the world. Everyone involved in the discussion recognizes that we are called to love our neighbor. Love, however, is willing our neighbor's good, not agreeing with him or joining in everything he does. Current tendencies are making it harder for Catholics to participate in general social institutions and practices. Catholic physicians cannot in good conscience participate in abortion. Increasingly, electoral politics is being inundated with views on sex and gender identity that are contrary to Catholic teaching. Catholics cannot conform to the secularism that undergirds projects like modern social democracy, which aims to serve man by integrating all social life into a system that refers to nothing beyond man himself. As a result, we need to put most of our social efforts into proposing alternatives and educating and evangelizing the public, while continuing to provide services directly and often informally.

In educating the world, we would continue political engagement in a way that carries forward the mission of the Church. The political goal would be to change the common understanding of the good life and society. The most debilitating feature of public discussion today is its extreme narrowness. Only a small range of views are allowed to play a political role. Basic human realities are left out of consideration. The silencing of views has allowed transgenderism to become mainstream very quickly. It has also caused people to lose their jobs for supporting the traditional and natural definition of marriage.[9] The range of acceptable discussion badly needs expansion and shifting. Catholics will not move that process along by always emphasizing "what brings us together" and showing the dominant powers they can work with us on their own terms. If the only intransigents are progressives, then giving way to them will always be the fast and easy way to social harmony.

The technocratic conception of life that dominates public thought today makes it difficult for people to understand the Catholic view. The health

8. Paul VI, "Conclusion of the II Vatican Council: Speech at the Last Public Session," website of the Holy See, accessed August 21, 2019, https://w2.vatican.va/content/paul-vi/en/speeches/1965/documents/hf_p-vi_spe_19651207_epilogo-concilio.html.

9. *United States v. Windsor*, 570 U.S. 744 (2013).

care system, for example, is becoming a means for maintaining and managing human resources for the sake of the economic system, and for providing biotechnological consumer goods like babies for people who want them and abortions for people who do not. Economic rationality and consumer choice make that tendency seem unquestionable, and people even dress it up in the language of rights.

Under such circumstances, the most important thing in public life is to demonstrate the Catholic view in practice, so people can see what it is and explain it in general, accessible terms. Anything else would corrupt our efforts and make it impossible to get our point across. To that end, Catholic scholars, clergy, and bishops need to place far more emphasis on ways of communicating unchanging Catholic understandings to the laity and to an uncomprehending world that no longer recognizes natural law. The laity then needs to provide a public witness. The defense of marriage and family, for example, should involve the laity structuring their lives in accordance with the natural order, with the support of a genuinely pastoral clergy, while clergy and scholars explain and argue in favor of Church teaching.

The General Objection of Exclusion

The most basic objection to the Benedict Option is that it views contemporary Western life as fundamentally misdirected, and Western ideals as degraded and increasingly nonfunctional. This view, of course, is not welcome. Our elites believe that mankind has begun only recently to break free from the horrors of the past. They point to the current emphasis on equality and human rights, often novel ones. They are naturally appalled by the fundamental rejection of that and other current tendencies in the name of traditional religion. Many within the Church share such views. In the wake of the call by the Second Vatican Council for greater openness to the modern world, many influential clerics see a large overlap between the demands of the Faith and those of secular political progressivism.[10]

Much of the worry has to do with exclusivity. The Benedict Option wants strong local communities that are somewhat separated from the world around them. It desires boundaries, which liberal elites now consider socially and morally dubious. It also wants to be traditionally Christian and rooted in the

10. Second Vatican Council, *Vatican Council II Church in the Modern World: Gaudium et Spes* (San Francisco: Ignatius Press, 2004).

natural law teachings regarding the family. By current standards, those goals appear sexist, patriarchal, homophobic, and transphobic. Communities based on commitments and personal connections restrict freedom and incur accusations of racism.

Many have said that the most segregated hour of Christian America is eleven o'clock on Sunday morning. This is a stubborn tendency in even the most liberal denominations; some mainstream commentators have begun to think it is connected to positive things about congregational life.[11] In theory, cohesive local communities that are fundamental to the lives of their members might be held together simply by a common faith that is equally available to all. This principle held the earliest Christians together in a sort of primitive communism, as described in Acts 2. Ideally, Benedict Option communities would possess a degree of holiness that would make something similarly possible. As a practical matter, however, such a situation would not last long, any more than it did for the early Christians. Consequently, these communities would need to be rooted in specific common traditions not everyone would share, as well as in the common aspiration to sanctity.

At the very beginning of his *Politics*, Aristotle teaches that human communities arise naturally out of the primordial community of the family.[12] Communities are thus based on familial ties and related connections such as blood and marital relationships, ties of friendship, and common history and culture. Hence renewed local communities would not be altogether inclusive and multicultural. They might even drift toward what progressives would see as a more or less Christianized tribalism. For an extreme example, consider the Middle East, where there are long-established local religious communities that are fundamental to the lives of their members, but the tribal aspects seem to dominate the religious ones.

The comparison is not pleasing, but utopia is not available to us. Every possible society has features that can lead to serious problems, and that is why prudence is necessary in political matters. A movement toward particularity is now inevitable. The abstract simplicity of basic liberal principles makes liberal society prone to extremes and unable to distinguish progress from degenera-

11. Martin Marty, "Taking the Unitarian Universalist Diversity Crisis Seriously," University of Chicago Divinity School, May 15, 2017, https://divinity.uchicago.edu/sightings/taking-unitarian-universalist-diversity-crisis-seriously.

12. Aristotle, *Politics*, 2nd ed., trans. Carnes Lord (Chicago: University of Chicago Press, 2013).

tion. Its continuing development breaks down the connections and excludes from public life the goods by which people live. It denies that man is a social and religious animal and so perpetuates a false view of relationships. Thus it is not surprising that many people, including devout Catholics, are weakening in their loyalty toward an ever hollower public order and turning toward something more particular.

If we do not have the Benedict Option, we will have political fanatics, gated communities, and ethnic separatism instead of a Christian particularity that accepts ultimate loyalty toward something substantive and universal. These scenarios would leave little hope for a peaceful and humane world.

Challenges to the Benedict Option

Legal Challenges

There are bound to be legal problems with any sort of Benedict Option. A genuine Catholic hospital cannot perform any form of euthanasia. A Catholic school cannot teach the equivalence of all religions and ways of life. It seems likely that the Church's chief practical political efforts in the foreseeable future will involve a defense of her own freedom against claims that her practices and doctrines have the effect of oppressing people, including her own members. The Church's defense will need to include the freedom of Catholics to speak freely and live their faith while running their affairs, educating their children, and providing charitable services.

The First Amendment provides some protection for the freedom of the Church, but contemporary interpretations make it unreliable. Since the Constitution is interpreted against the intellectual background of the times, First Amendment jurisprudence often changes. Influential thinkers are increasingly losing their commitment to special protection for speech and religion. They note that speech can cause injury and see nothing special about religion other than what they consider its irrationality.[13] It seems likely that such protections will tend more and more to be interpreted in a minimalist way.

The changing constitutional regime means Catholics will have to engage in constant political action to prevent the straightforward application of prin-

13. Christopher Shea, "Beyond Belief," *Chronicle of Higher Education*, June 9, 2014, https://www.chronicle.com/article/The-Limits-of-Religious/146971.

ciples like inclusiveness that are now considered utterly compelling.[14] It will not be easy. It will be necessary for Catholics to know core Church convictions and their consequences because they must be ready to stand up and defend them steadily and articulately in the face of opprobrium. Under such circumstances, the Church needs to take special care to avoid undercutting the efforts of her advocates by blurring the clarity of her doctrine.

Social Challenges

It is hard to break with the customary ways of doing things. Benedict Option communities would most easily arise gradually, through abandonment of some connections and practices and emphasis on others, and through the development of new habits among networks and circles of friends. But the contemporary world is intrusive, so community members will need conviction and endurance, and there is likely a need for definite rules. Although some communities may remain a bit vague in their outline and demands by relying solely on the active commitment of their members, most would eventually desire specific standards and boundaries to protect and support their way of life. This transition may be bumpy.

Among other things, Catholics would need to find ways to counter the world's intrusiveness. We assimilate to our environment, and as St. Paul notes, "evil communications corrupt good manners."[15] Catholics would need to limit, for example, their use of electronic media. The Church accepted the Greek and Roman classics because of what is good in them. HBO is not Homer, however, and the Church rejected a great deal of Roman popular culture. Of course, the communities will have to make their own internal life attractive, in the ways communities have always found to make community life attractive. Once texting and online videos are mostly off the table, it should not be difficult for them to find their way to something more engaging. Festivity and friendship spring eternal in the human heart.

14. Consider, e.g., the proposed Equality Act and the US bishops' response to it. "US Bishops: Equality Act Will Hurt More Than Help," *Catholic World Report,* March 20, 2019, https://www.catholicworldreport.com/2019/03/20/us-bishops-equality-act-will-hurt-more-than-help.

15. 1 Cor 15:33.

Economic Challenges

It is likely to be a struggle finding ways to make a living without offering a pinch of incense to Caesar. Paul could make his living as a tentmaker without hiding his beliefs. Employees of large companies and other institutions are becoming less able to profess and hold Catholic views publicly. The problem becomes acute because of the scale and ambition of the modern state. The Roman state was tiny by modern standards. Christians did not pose an immediate practical problem, at least until they became numerous and influential enough to be a threat to Diocletian's vision of a glorious, restored empire. Despite sporadic persecution, they were mostly left alone to live as they chose and persuade others to their way of life.

Our modern Caesars have far more resources and their ambition extends to all aspects of life. Anti-discrimination laws make it impossible to give a business organization of any size a specifically Catholic identity. They limit the extent to which Catholic organizations can prefer employees who are committed to Catholic principles, or even prefer natural law understandings of human relations in providing employee benefits. Indeed, they are forcing large organizations to adopt implicitly anti-Catholic identities.

Catholic business will therefore have to be small and mostly informal, perhaps taking the form of networks of independent contractors. This arrangement fits the emphasis on local and community life, but it will have a financial cost. Possibly Christians will concentrate on the trades, becoming plumbers, electricians, and auto mechanics, and so on. The pay is generally good, there is always a demand, and there seems to be less spiritual slavishness than in white-collar occupations. The heresy hunters will still be with us and may eventually feel called upon to do something about the ability of "extremists" to find refuge in such occupations, but we can only do our best to adapt to the times.

We will also need to reduce our wants and restore as much as we can of the practical functions of the home. It will reduce our need for money, and it can be educational as well as liberating. Wealth allows those who have it to be stupid. It takes thought and skill, in contrast, to make a little go a long way. Functional households have other benefits as well. Specialization, the industrial system, and the cult of the expert are destroying the competence and self-government of individuals, families, and local communities. Home and family are the school of such things. Homeschooling makes the household and local networks far more serious enterprises. Gardening, do-it-yourself projects, home-based business, the arts of homemaking, and all the other ways people provide for their needs by engaging directly and practically with the world around them all help create a healthy culture.

Intellectual Challenges

If sink-or-swim is bad for ordinary Catholics, it is a thousand times worse for their children. It is imperative to have schools that are authentically Catholic. More generally, the Church must sponsor intellectual interest on the part of ordinary Catholics. The current situation has deep intellectual roots. Catholics must be able to respond effectively at that level. We cannot rely exclusively on other people's thoughts. A Catholicism that becomes too cozy with the modern outlook will simply fail to remain Catholic. Therefore we also need more universities, publications, and other cultural institutions.

In recent decades, Catholic institutions have tended to assimilate to the world around them. Many Catholic schools are not authentically Catholic. This tendency needs to reverse, and it is likely to do so in the coming years. The reasons are intellectual, cultural, educational, and specifically religious. Before the Second Vatican Council, many people complained about the narrowness of the Catholic ghetto. They claimed that the Church was not integrated with the world and should throw open her doors and windows and go where the action is. This strategy injured Catholic intellectual and cultural life, which declined through its ties to a secular culture whose rejection of natural law, adoption of pragmatism, and aggrandizement of choice as the highest good shuts out the richness of truth. The conversion of St. Augustine came at a time when the exhaustion of classical culture had made the Church the natural home for intellectual life. If we are right that the Church has a better grip on reality than today's secular culture, the same seems likely to happen again.

Spiritual Challenges

A Church largely made up of Benedict Option communities will be like the early Church, unable to rely on wealth, power, prestige, or social position. It will have benefits since it will increase the commitment involved in membership and focus attention on the Church's essential nature. Members will be faithful and loyal because they want what only the Church can provide: God incarnate and eternal life.

A more devoted Church will require overcoming stubborn ecclesiastical vices. She will, of course, have to reject the world as a standard. She will have to overcome the tendency in her members to treat themselves as the standard. Pompous self-will is hard to root out of any organization, and cultishness is hard to avoid in small, self-selected ecclesial communities with an outlook radically at odds with the rest of society. The Church will need to overcome these faults through what she always needs: sanctity. Sanctity requires the selflessness that sets the faithful free and allows them to see reality, but it cannot be attained without daily self-denial. All this sounds difficult, a job for saints and those who seriously aspire to become saints. Yet that is what is needed now. The Church depends on her saints. As the ark of salvation in a less and less livable world, she will more than compensate for the effort and sacrifice. May many of us be ready to do what the times require![16]

Conclusion

In spite of its triumphalism, liberal modernity is neither eternal nor invincible. The attempt to transcend nature, history, and tradition through technology cannot succeed because those things remain basic to human life. But they are not self-sufficient any more than the human will and modern natural science are. To accept nature, history, and tradition as legitimate authorities, they need to be seen not as brute facts that are thrust on us, but as part of something larger and friendlier to human concerns. In the long run, that requires supernatural faith, together with a community that bears and defends it. Without such a community, there can be no escape from the black hole of modernity. This is one reason among many that *extra ecclesiam nulla salus.*

Beyond the mediocrity and corruption of the day, there are countermovements and signs of new life. Some aspects of this resurgence are evident, and some are invisible to people who spend too much time reading weblogs and Twitter. No doubt there are others that are hidden from almost everyone.

16. This discussion of spiritual issues in the future Church draws on then-Father Joseph Ratzinger's 1969 address "What Will the Church Look Like in 2000," printed in Joseph Cardinal Ratzinger, *Faith and the Future* (San Francisco: Ignatius Press, 2009).

"The kingdom of God," we are told, "cometh not with observation."[17] As always, the Church remains an oasis of life in a desert.

The Church needs reform at all levels, but she and the faithful will eventually do what they need to maintain the integrity of the Faith in adverse times. Groups as different as the Amish and Latter-Day Saints have been able to thrive in America while maintaining their distinctiveness. What works for us will no doubt evolve through trial and error, with different people finding different solutions. St. Benedict presents one form of the Christian life, St. Paul another, the congregations to which Paul ministered yet another, and the groups Rod Dreher describes in his book still more.

Although current trends are alarming, it is necessary to remember that evils often conflict with each other and cannot all coexist. Future developments and even evils may help maintain the freedom of Catholics. The demographic diversity that seems almost certain to continue increasing in a globalist age involves the growing presence throughout the West of people who are neither Western liberals nor beholden to Western liberalism.[18] The inefficiency, irrationality, and corruption produced by an ever more incoherent culture are likely to make enforcement of official principles like transgenderism hit-or-miss. And they are likely to generate a demand among ordinary people for something better.

From a natural standpoint, what works wins, and what cannot remain will not remain. From this perspective, the Church and her vision are likely to prevail over her modern opponents. Insanity can be enormously destructive before it destroys itself. There are going to be storms and losses on the way. Thus the Barque of Peter needs to prepare for them, and some form of the Benedict Option seems a necessity for keeping her seaworthy.

17. Lk 17:20.

18. Consider, e.g., the use of "white left" as a Chinese Internet insult. Chenchen Zhang, "The Curious Rise of the 'White Left' as a Chinese Internet Insult," *Hong Kong Free Press*, May 20, 2017, https://www.hongkongfp.com/2017/05/20/curious-rise-white-left-chinese-internet-insult/.

CONTRIBUTORS

RYAN J. BARILLEAUX is a professor of political science at Miami University (Ohio). He is the author or editor of ten books on the presidency and American politics.

GERARD V. BRADLEY is a professor of law at University of Notre Dame Law School and senior fellow of the Witherspoon Institute. He is the author of numerous books and scholarly articles on constitutional law, law and religion, and other topics.

STEVEN J. BRUST is an associate professor of political science at Eastern New Mexico University. He is the coeditor of *Natural Law Today: The Present State of Perennial Philosophy.*

GARY GLENN is distinguished teaching professor emeritus of political science at Northern Illinois University. He is a student of the history of political philosophy, American political thought, and the relation of religion to both. In recent years, his scholarship has focused primarily on the relation of Catholicism to American democracy.

KENNETH L. GRASSO is a professor of political science at Texas State University. He has edited or coedited several books, including *Theology and Public Philosophy; Rethinking Rights: Historical, Political, and Philosophical Perspectives;* and *Catholicism and Religious Freedom: Contemporary Reflections on Vatican II's Declaration on Religious Liberty.*

ROBERT P. HUNT is a professor of political science at Kean University. He has coedited several books, including *Catholicism and Religious Freedom: Contemporary Reflections on Vatican II's Declaration on Religious Freedom*, and written numerous articles and reviews. He received his PhD from Fordham University.

MARJORIE JEFFREY is an independent scholar.

JAMES KALB is a lawyer and an independent scholar. He is the author of *The Tyranny of Liberalism: Understanding and Overcoming Administered Freedom, Inquisitorial Tolerance, and Equity by Command.*

ASHLEEN MENCHACA-BAGNULO is an associate professor of political science at Texas State University. She is coeditor of *Augustine in a Time of Crisis: Politics and Religion Contested.*

JAMES R. STONER JR. is the Hermann Moyse Jr. Professor and director of the Eric Voegelin Institute in the Department of Political Science at Louisiana State University. He is the author of *Common-Law Liberty: Rethinking American Constitutionalism* and *Common Law and Liberal Theory: Coke, Hobbes, and the Origins of American Constitutionalism.*

Thomas F. X. Varacalli is an assistant professor of Great Books at Belmont Abbey College. He is coauthor of *An Invitation to Political Science.*

INDEX